COLLAPSING THE SINGULARITY

Bergson, Gibson and the Mythologies of Artificial Intelligence

Stephen Earle Robbins PhD
Golden Willows Farm
2750 Church Rd.
Jackson, WI 53037

SEarleRobbins@yahoo.com

Stephenerobbins.com

ISBN: 1494947641
ISBN 13: 9781494947644

Library of Congress Control Number: 2014900446
CreateSpace Independent Publishing Platform
North Charleston, South Carolina

Table of Contents

Preface

Much of this book is a reorganization, expansion and deepening of a portion of an earlier book of mine, *Time and Memory: A Primer on the Scientific Mysticism of Consciousness*. It is intended to be heavier, more intense, and it is aimed and refocused to catch the eye of those interested in artificial intelligence (AI) and its future. Its target is the concept of the "Singularity," the hypothetical point in time – considered by many AI experts and writers to be very close – where artificial intelligence and super intelligent machines meet and surpass human intelligence. In my opinion, the AI theorists have not even begun to make the needed considerations on what the human mind truly is. There is a possibility that some in AI are currently entertaining, namely, that to achieve real intelligence, AI might need to consider and emulate "embodiment," or "radical embodied cognition," and/or J.J. Gibson's ecological psychology. While a step, these frameworks are themselves only dimly grasped in their true implications even by their non-AI proponents, even by many Gibsonians. In addition, cognitive science and the theory of memory, themselves both thoroughly in the grip of the computer metaphor of mind, have done nothing to counter the illusory idea of the imminent achievements in AI in equaling human intelligence. They have simply mutually reinforced AI in the same metaphor. AI and cognitive science comprise a two-headed entity hoisting aloft the machine view of mind. This book is a challenge to the believers in AI's capacity to equal the human, to the notion of the imminent Singularity, and equally to cognitive science. It is a challenge to look deeply, clearly at the real nature of human perception, memory, and consciousness, that is, to actually look deeply at what it is that one must achieve to even begin to claim human equivalence in intelligence.

Introduction:
Fear of Singularity

I regard someone who understands…as a "singularitarian."

— Ray Kurzweil, *The Singularity is Near*

When is a man in mere understanding? I answer, "When a man sees one thing separated from another." And when is man above mere understanding? That I can tell you: "When a man sees All in all, then a man stands beyond mere understanding."

— Meister Eckhart

The Singularity

It is a titanic struggle of near invincible, vastly intelligent, robot-machines. Arnold, in the persona of the human-friendly robot, the Terminator, is locked in battle with a killer she-robot on an assassination mission from Earth's future. The Terminator, his damaged circuit boards and wounded wiring cruelly exposed, deftly takes advantage of an opening. After stuffing into her metal jaws a glowing nuclear power cell which will blow them both to kingdom come, he delivers a classic, Arnoldism: "You are…terminated!"

The metaphoric lessons burst upon the mind. Here it is, the inevitable future. The she-robot has traveled backwards from a realm of time where machines rule the planet. It is the machines that are the ultimate intelligences and power. The machines perpetuate and evolve themselves. The machines even have the capability and knowledge to defend the past line of events thru space-time that got them to the top of the evolutionary heap. Humans have been superseded. Humanity is saved from this future only with the help of the Terminator – yet another machine. Even this salvation reveals the precarious situation that besets humanity relative to the onslaught of its own discoveries in machine intelligence. The *Singularity* has been realized.

Ray Kurzweil (*The Singularity is Near*) has been the foremost expositor of the Singularity. In this, he is only a spokesman for what appears to be a majority of the community of science. The Singularity is the point where our advances in machine or robotic intelligence have gone so far as to take machines beyond the capacities of human intelligence. Compared to the turtle-like, 100 meters per second transmission speeds of neurons in the human brain, the circuits of robots will support near-light speed transmission velocities. Every good architectural aspect of the human brain will be exploited and amplified, doubled, tripled in power by electronic components. We will end incorporating these components into our own body, amplifying our intelligence. But the machines, unfettered by biological limitations, will assuredly continue to evolve more quickly. The year of this tipping point, Kurzweil boldly predicts, will be 2045.

This is obviously no trivial problem. In fact it is viewed as so serious that considerations on how to prevent this disaster have become a major subject matter. The rather renowned philosopher, David Chalmers, devoted an article to the subject in a 2010 issue of the *Journal of Consciousness Studies*.[1] The article was followed in the same journal (JCS, 2012) by a set of twenty-six commentators. In his response to the comment-articles, by Chalmers' own count, fifteen totally endorsed or leaned strongly in his direction, with another four merely neutral, making it 19/26 in at least implicit agreement. One of the detractors, Jesse Prinz (an AI theorist), turns out to feel we have *already* been simulated – by higher intelligences. Let's make it 20/26. As far as the (six) strong detractors, Chalmers quickly disposed of them all. Francis Heylighen's critique, as an example, that intelligence cannot be treated as a "brain in a vat," but must be embodied in dynamic interaction with the ecological world rather than isolated from that world, is summarily dispensed with: "As for embodiment and culture, insofar as these are crucial to intelligence, AI can simply build them in."[2] Perhaps, Chalmers allows, this will require an extra one hundred years. Selmer Bringsjord's argument, that a Turing Machine (a theoretical computing device that abstractly defines all computers – from Commodore 64s to super computers) cannot bootstrap itself to something beyond a Turing Machine, merits a longer examination, but the eventual disposal is only delayed.[3]

Barrat (*Our Final Invention*) extends this theme to its alarming conclusion. The timeline is moved up: there are experts in AI, he reports, that believe that this point could be as early as 2020. The possible consequences are deepened: Visualizing a rapidly self-learning machine, something he terms the Busy Child ASI (Advanced Super Intelligence), he speculates:

> Once the Busy Child ASI escapes, it plays strenuous self-defense: hiding copies of itself in clouds, creating botnets to ward off attackers, and more…. If it has surplus resources, its idea of self-preservation may expand to include proactive attacks on future threats. To a sufficiently advanced AI, anything that has the potential to develop into a future threat may constitute a threat it should eliminate.

And of course, one of those threats would be – us.

> While we're busy avoiding risks of unintended consequences from AI, AI will be scrutinizing humans for dangerous consequences of sharing the world with us.

Barrat gives some voice to possible roadblocks – more like speed bumps – along the way, for example, "scientists may find it is not possible to 'grow' AGI [Artificial General Intelligence] without some kind of body," that is, the importance of having something like a body (along with the brain running it) may be all-important in developing intelligence. He notes too that this advanced AI could well be strange, quite different from human intelligence – not like our intelligence at all. This "strangeness" could only exacerbate the danger. Indeed, for Barrat, one of the prime examples of the power of AI and a harbinger for the future is the computer program, Watson. Watson, using sophisticated algorithms, scrapes up massive amounts of information, scanning the entirety of Wikipedia and other digitally encoded texts with lightning speed. With this power, Watson actually defeated human Jeopardy champions. It is Watson who is now Jeopardy champion. But Watson's intelligence is not ours; it certainly could be considered, well, alien.

Imparting Human Values to the Machines

Thus it is no surprise that certain segments of the Singularity proponents have begun to emphasize the fact – nay, shout warnings upon it – that we must start an intense line of research and development to discover how to impart human values to the machines. Muehlhauser (*Facing the Intelligence Explosion*) sees it as two races, one race to develop pure AI super intelligence, the other to develop a methodology for injecting human values into such a super intelligence. Muehlhauser is extremely worried and pessimistic that the race for building the super intelligence will cross the finish line first, leaving humanity at the mercy of cold super intelligences who may well see little value in preserving the human race.

On this critical problem, Muehlhauser begins to ponder in his book how we would actually impart to an AI a set of instructions or rules on our values. "A different mind architecture," he notes, "one that didn't evolve with us, won't share our common sense. It wouldn't know what NOT to do. How would it make a cake? 'Don't use a squid. Don't use gamma radiation. Don't use Toyotas.' This list of what not to do is endless." From this point his considerations become fascinating, with deep implications for the difficulty of imparting "values" to an AI.

Muehlhauser wonders, for example, on the following situation: My mother is trapped in a burning building. I see the fire but I am a block away, helpless to act myself. I happen to have access to a super intelligent AI. I give the order: "Get my mother out of there!" As I sit in my living room down the street, I am astounded to see the entire building explode in an array of debris, some of which include my mother hurtling through space. The machine has fulfilled its instruction – according to its values or lack thereof. Fortunately, per Muehlhauser, there is a magic "reset" button. I hit it, returning things to just before I issued my faulty instruction. I try a more specific instruction.

"AI, get my mother out of there without blowing up the building." Now your mother is pushed out the window, breaking her neck.

After several more "Resets," you try this: "AI, within the next ten minutes, move my mother (defined as the woman who shares half my genes and gave birth to me) so that she is sitting comfortably in this chair next to me, with no physical or mental damage." Now you watch as all thirteen firemen rush the house at once. One of them happens to find your mother quickly and bring her to safety. The twelve other firemen die. As Muelhauser states, "You got what you wished for, but you didn't get what you *wanted*." Thus, notes Muelhauser:

> The problem is that your brain is not large enough to contain statements specifying every possible detail of what you want and don't want. How did you know you wanted your mother to escape the building in good health without killing or maiming a dozen firemen? It wasn't because your brain contained anywhere the statement, "I want my mother to escape the building in good health without killing and maiming a dozen firemen."[4]

We don't have time to run through all the possibilities: Mom could be knocked unconscious, but a doctor be there to revive her. A fireproof spacesuit could be delivered to her. Still, he argues, your brain isn't infinitely complex, and there is some finite set of "statements" that describes the system that determines the judgments you would make.

> If we understood how every synapse and neurotransmitter and protein in the brain worked, and we had a complete map of your brain, then an AI could as least in principle compute which judgments you would make about a finite set of possible outcomes.... The moral is that there is no safe wish smaller than an entire human value system.[5]

Muehlhauser comments on the number of "possible paths through Time," and on the impossibility of visualizing all roads to a given destination or goal, for example, maximizing the distance between your mother and the center of the building, which can be made to happen in any number of ways, to include via a nuclear bomb. The only safe AI, he argues, is an AI that shares all your judgment criteria. There is no simple principle that we can code into our program that will make an AI program do what we want. This is a false, unrealizable goal. What we are trying is no different than the attempt by the legion of moral philosophers who have failed for centuries to find a simple set of principles or rules that if enacted would create the world we want. Every time such a set is proposed, another philosopher immediately comes along and demonstrates the holes in the principles.

Even the simplest, apparently most trivial thing can turn out to be important. Imagine in this regard, Muehlhauser notes, the human value of, or on, boredom – our desire not to the same thing over and over. An AI programmed with all values but just this one could end up spending until the end of time replaying a single, highly optimized experience over and over again. Or consider an AI that contains a specification of nearly all enjoyable feelings but lacked the notion that such feelings have external referents. The AI/mind could go around "feeling" it had found a perfect lover or helped a friend, and yet has not actually *done* anything.

Thus, says Muehlhauser, since we've never decoded an entire human value system, we don't know what values to give an AI. If we created a superhuman AI tomorrow, we could only give it a disastrously incomplete system – it would do things we wished for, not what we wanted. We only know how to build dangerous AIs, and worse, we are learning how to make these safe much more slowly than how to make them powerful – because it is to the "intellectual power" race that our resources are going.

The Frame Problem

This sounds pretty bad. However, there is a related problem here that Muehlhauser seems not to have noticed. It is a problem that indexes yet other problems that in turn index yet others. The problem, in AI circles, is called "the frame problem." When Muehlhauser begin wondering how an AI, when baking a cake, would know "what not to do" – not stir the batter with a Toyota, not to use rat poison as flavoring – he was entering this realm. It is a realm that deals with our understanding of everyday events – the very knowledge Muehlhauser noted that the machines, not having evolved with us, "won't share" – our common sense knowledge.

The "frame problem" was described by two AI theorists, McCarthy and Hayes in 1969.[6] It was defined, in its most *specific* form, in the context of the "situation calculus." It fundamentally deals with the problem of change as a result of an agent's action. An intuitive view of the term "frame" comes from a cartoon strip-like context. If I have a starting cartoon frame of a kitchen, its table with its chairs and an agent's hand with a spoon stirring coffee, what should be changed and what is the same in the next cartoon frame? I would expect the spoon and hand in a new position and some indication of motion of the coffee's surface. I would not expect to see the table rotated or the chairs moved, disintegrated or crumbling. For these situations, *frame axioms* are a formalism (the situation calculus) that attempt to capture the "what stays the same" in such an action. If the agent puts a red block, Block A, on top of Block B, we can imagine the following frame axiom:

$$[\text{Holds}(s, \text{Red}(b1)) \Rightarrow \text{Holds}(\text{Result}(\text{PutOn}(b1,b2), s), \text{Red}(b1))]$$

This axiom allows the inference that the color remains unchanged or invariant. The formalization here is simply saying that the red color of the block (b1) will not be changed when it is put on top of another block (b2). But a vast number of such axioms need to be stated – the president remains the same, the house stays on its foundations, the sun is yet in the sky, etc., all of which must be checked. Consider what a set of axioms might begin to look like for an event such as "stirring coffee." In the axioms below, we have the result specified (left side of arrow), given a certain action (stir) on the right. They say that the size, stability and elevation of the cup remain invariant while stirring.

Frame Axioms for Coffee Stirring:

$\text{Holds}(s, \text{SameSize}(cup)) \Rightarrow \text{Holds}(\text{Result}(\text{Stir}(cup, coffee), s),$
$\quad \text{SameSize}(cup))$
$\text{Holds}(s, \text{Stable}(cup)) \Rightarrow \text{Holds}(\text{Result}(\text{Stir}(cup, coffee), s),$
$\quad \text{Stable}(cup))$
$\text{Holds}(s, \text{SameElevation}(cup)) \Rightarrow \text{Holds}(\text{Result}(\text{Stir}$
$\quad (cup, coffee), s), \text{SameElevation}(cup))$
And so on....

Imagine what would be required even in the limited frame of the coffee-stirring event for specifying what remains the same in every modality – optical, acoustic, olfactory, touch/kinesthetic. This need for vast numbers of axioms to prove that most things remain the same as actions are performed is the frame problem. (The predictive problem – how things change – is complementary.) A solution to the frame problem is generally considered precisely this: a method to reduce or remove the frame axioms.[7] These axioms (or something equivalent) are the "statements specifying every possible detail" to which Muehlhauser refers, a set of statements that he thinks is finite, and could be programmed – if we could just have the time to research and find them all.

A more concrete way to view the problem is to simply imagine a robot viewing a cup of coffee being stirred, or better, actually stirring the cup of coffee. As the robot views or acts in the event, the coffee cup begins to bulge in and out, or perhaps the surface of the coffee begins to erupt with small geysers, or the liquid suddenly puts up resistance to the stirring like it is thick cement, or the spoon begins melting. Are any of these events *expected* features of the event? How does the robot know? He must check his frame axioms to see what is supposed to remain unchanged. Now we should note right away that this checking has a time scale dependency. How often must this check be made during the course of the event? Every second? Every tenth of a second? The "geysers" could erupt briefly three times a second. The robot needs to detect each geyser event if it is going to properly monitor the event. All of this checking/scanning of the database of frame axioms is very computationally expensive, i.e., it takes time and computer power.

Correlatively, if my wife asks me to stir the coffee, she would be shocked if I used a chair (or a Toyota) for the stirrer. The first point being made here is that we are equally dealing here with a problem in the knowledge of the concrete world, not simply with "values." Such knowledge (i.e., the very same problem) is implicated in design, in problem solving, in invention. It thus is equally and fully at the heart of the line of AI development of a "raw super intelligence" which Muehlhauser is so worried will be brought to fruition long before we figure out how to impart value. If the super general intelligence or SGI can't design and create a mousetrap out of some simple components at hand, say, a small box, pencils, rubber bands, razor blades, string, cheese, etc., it isn't really that smart, is it? It is not necessarily a threat even to mice. That is, Muelhauser's worry on the wrong winner of the race is unfounded – the problem is the same in both races.

The frame problem was very heavily discussed with solutions pondered and proposed for a period of time, roughly perhaps thirty years, and discussion still continues, but at a low frequency. At this point it has an obscured and slippery status as a continuing problem. Shanahan, in his *Stanford Encyclopedia of Philosophy* summary of the subject, states flatly that within classical AI, "a variety of workable solutions to the logical frame problem have been developed, and it is no longer considered a serious obstacle even for those working in a strictly logic-based paradigm."[8] But this apparently definitive assessment is qualified or limited to the sort of AI that cares not about equaling human intelligence, and this form of AI, devoted simply to making smarter machines with no aim or pretense of matching, simulating, equaling or exceeding human intelligence is not the AI we will be interested in here. But in reality, the apparently definitive flavor slips away very quickly as the *Encyclopedia* entry reads on. Shanahan notes that many philosophers of mind still subscribe to the view that human mental processes consist chiefly of inferences over a set of propositions (frame axioms being one example), and that those inferences are carried out by some form of computation. "To such philosophers, the epistemological frame problem and its computational counterpart remain a genuine threat." Further into the discussion, it is clear that Shanahan, with others, leans to a position that, to solve the frame problem, the very basis of AI – which rests in the notion of "computations" as being the foundation of mind – has to be abandoned. To quote one such (at least partial) leaner, Michael Wheeler:

> ...the *frame problem* is the difficulty of explaining how non-magical systems (machines like us) think and act in ways that are adaptively sensitive to context-dependent relevance. There was a time when the frame problem so conceived was a hot research topic in cognitive science, especially in artificial intelligence (AI). These days it may seem a little passé, which is a shame since (with sincere apologies to various researchers) it's not as if anybody ever actually solved the problem.[9]

The frame problem has not been solved by AI. Yes, one can find AI-folks that think it has, but it has not. We are going to see immediately in the next chapter and then beyond why not. The problem lies in the nature of our understanding of events. It is even more correct to say it lies in our perception of events – that is, in our human ability to perceive the events of the external world. Events in the concrete world have a structure. This structure is what we are going to look at shortly. AI, however, even with all its frame problem pondering, has not even begun to consider this.

Escape from the Frame – AI's Move

The frame problem was quickly seen to be more general than I have indicated thus far. One of the premier philosophers in cognitive science, Jerry Fodor, famously described the frame problem as 'the problem of putting a "frame" around the set of beliefs that may need to be revised in the light of specified newly available information.'[10] The "frame of beliefs" is a statement of *context*. The initial cartoon frame of the spoon stirring the coffee could have been followed by a frame with my wife entering the kitchen, moving a chair, and sitting down. Is this expected? Obviously in my lived, domestic context, it is. The next frame could have had a garbage truck rumbling by, or the mail man, or UPS at the door. Expected? Yes, in my city or business services context. And in the next frame, five wild turkeys trot by the door. In the farm context, yup, expected.

We started with a context constrained to that of stirring coffee. Even this constrained context or event, I have warned, is beyond AI. But the question now is how our robot/AI would know how to invoke different contexts – and specifically the right one – for these (other) events appearing in these subsequent frames? How does he know his stirring is producing the wrong result? What rules would the robot be using to select only the context or contexts (for all the events just described could happen all at once) with the relevant information? How short of actually possessing the "context" of my entire life experience with wife, family, turkeys, chickens and garbage trucks at the farm? [11]

Yet, since AI appears to be accomplishing great things, one wonders, if the frame problem is so vicious a beast, how has AI not been chewed into little bits within the monster's jaws? The escape is by using only narrow, fixed contexts. An early and paradigmatic success by AI, hailed greatly, was SHRDLU, a natural language understanding program created by Terry Winograd, then a graduate student at MIT.[12] The sentences input to the program were restricted to a very small, well-delineated, simple domain: a micro-world. This world, for SHRDLU, consisted of nothing but a set of blocks on a tabletop displayed on a computer screen, together with a hand for moving them about. The blocks came in different shapes and colors, and could be stacked upon one another, e.g., a pyramid atop a cube. The computer kept a continuously updated database of which blocks were where, whether a pyramid was atop the cube, the cylinder next to such and such a block, which block was held in the hand, etc. It could answer questions such as:

User:	What color is the block on the red brick?
SHRDLU:	GREEN.
User:	Shape?
SHRDLU:	PYRAMID.
User:	Grasp the pyramid.
SHRDLU:	I DON'T UNDERSTAND WHICH PYRA-MID YOU MEAN.

(There are three pyramids in the scene.)

The micro-world, however, is a predefined "object language" specifying the problem environment, and the relevant features thereof, in which SHRDLU works. The feature set of this "world" is fixed – the properties of the blocks, their move-ability, their ability to stand on another or not (the cube can't sit on top of the pyramid), requirements for support, etc. The rest is simply a form of "proof" procedure taking place within this fixed symbolic framework. We shall meet this scheme again in future discussion.

SHRDLU, given its complexity and programming ingenuity, was rightly hailed as a great achievement, but wrongly seen as a precursor of great the things to come. Winograd himself, intimate with its limitations, repudiated the entire approach in relatively short order. With Thomas Flores, he moved to the concept of the "situatedness" of a being in the world, and rejected the view of cognition as symbolic manipulation of internal representations that are understood as referring to objects and properties in the "external" world. Following Martin Heidegger's philosophy of being-in-the-world (*Being and Time*, 1927), Winograd and Flores noted:

> Heidegger makes a more radical critique, question-
> ing the distinction between a conscious, reflective, knowing
> "subject" and a separable "object." He sees representations
> as a *derivative* phenomenon, which occurs only when there is
> a breaking down of concernful action. Knowledge lies in the
> being that situates us in the world, not in reflective representa-
> tion.[13]

This is a rather abstruse passage. We will see what it means later. Suffice it to say, its implications are not well understood, particularly in regards to the relation of subject and object it mentions. Nevertheless, the concept of being "situated" in the world has engendered a whole effort at a "situated robotics" which eschews any attempt to represent the world with symbols (such as frame axioms) and rule-driven manipulations or algorithmic manipulations of these symbols. A prominent early example was Rodney Brooks' six-legged, insect-like robot that could motivate around in its insectoid way, using modulating feedback from the environment, with no internal symbol manipulations going on. Situatedness defeats the frame problem from an entirely different direction, for such a being is fully situated in all contexts simultaneously, i.e., the context is one's entire experience. This situated approach, however, while it has produced some interesting robotic machines, has not produced machines or robots that are even close to being any threat to humanity, nor is it clear how they will become so. It is not the form of AI of which the singularists are thinking, though some AI-theorists entertain that these concepts must be incorporated. The situated approach, as it is understood and explicated, in its attempt to do without representations in its robotic machines, i.e., without symbols and symbol structures representing the world, has simultaneously lost the ability to support our fundamental intuition, namely that we do indeed use images – memory images of things and of the world – to represent that world in our thought. This again stems from the failure to understand the origin and nature of the events we perceive.

Where We Are Going

The structure of perceived events is going to take us into the heart of the problem of perception, and thereby, into the heart of David Chalmers' famous "hard problem" of consciousness.[14] The problem of perception is the problem of the origin of our image of the external world – our image of the coffee cup with stirring spoon, of the table with its wood-grain surface on which the cup rests, of the kitchen floor stretching in all directions and the kitchen itself with its copper pots hanging from the ceiling. Chalmers' statement of this problem, casting it solely in terms of a neural or computer/software architecture having to account for the "qualia" of our experience – the "whiteness" of the coffee cup, the "oak-brown" of the table, the "clinking" of the spoon – has been misleading, as we shall see, obscuring the problem of perception.[15] Curiously, I would note, the fact that Chalmers did not feel that the lack of a solution to his own problem is an impediment to the close-in-time achievement of an AGI or SGI is a telling index that he fails to understand both the implications and the true nature of his problem.

To speak of "the origin of the image" is to speak simultaneously of the origin of our experience of the world. This experience is what must be "stored" supposedly in the brain or in a computer memory or in a robot. This experience is what we use in thought, in problem solving, in the making of analogies. If I say to myself – contemplating launching a cornflake at big sister across the kitchen table by using the once-stirring coffee spoon – "The spoon is like a catapult," I have created an analogy which uses my experience of the embodied physics of spoon-flipping and any knowledge – from books or toys or watching pumpkin chunkin shows – about Roman catapults.[16] But if we cannot explain the origin of the image of the external world, then we cannot explain the very nature of this experience, therefore, our theory of the "storage" of this experience – whether in brains, in robots or in super intelligent AIs – is utterly ungrounded. This in turn leaves our theory of thought and cognition – whose fundamental operation by the way is analogy – also ungrounded. As we have no understanding of this experience, this experience being itself – our consciousness, we have no understanding of the actual role of consciousness in cognition either. And all this leaves ungrounded the entire notion that we are about to achieve a Singularity – a super intelligent AI. We do not know what intelligence is.

The vast optimism of the AI theorists in equaling human intelligence has been completely unconstrained by cognitive science. This is for at least one simple reason: cognitive science itself – at least its mainstream — has simply swallowed whole the computational or machine metaphor of mind. AI and cognitive science are in bed together. The theory of memory – of what is stored – is entirely predicated within this metaphor. In fact, we shall see that memory theory has been mechanistic from the get-go. The theory of analogy – again, fundamental in cognition – sits precisely in this metaphor. Nothing in this theoretical effort incorporates a solution to the problem of perception; all is ungrounded. There is no real role for consciousness in all of cognitive science and in all of its models of cognition. All models proceed nicely, i.e., proceed obliviously, without any need for consciousness. Committed solely to proving the machine metaphor, cognitive science (the vastly mainstream version) can offer not even a speed bump on the road for the AI theorist. In addition, this science generally ignores ecological psychology, the one science of perception and of the structure of events that could give the cognitive theorists pause. In turn, the ecological psychology community has not understood the actual nature of J. J. Gibson's (its founder's) model of perception, leaving its own theory of memory and thought equally ungrounded, nay, confused and of little threat to AI, while failing also to realize, with some exceptions, its true role in the theory of the retrieval of experience. All this, again, has contributed to this: AI, with no thanks to cognitive science, has little grasp on what intelligence is.

Yes, the AGI proponent will note, "But we are not talking necessarily about achieving *human* intelligence. Rather, we can well be creating just a raw, alien-like, machine intelligence, an intelligence that we admit is not the same as the human. And this can well be a dangerous intelligence." But the depth and concrete reality of this threat are very suspect. The threat of a super intelligence is based precisely on – is trading on – what we understand as intelligence, namely our human, experienced-based, perception-based intelligence. Such a being or device, with our form of intelligence amplified, sped up immensely, we could indeed fear if it is malevolent. But what is the actual threat of an intelligence that gains its knowledge by lightning-speed scrapes of Wikipedia text? Or a machine/program like Carnegie Mellon's NEIL (Never Ending Image Learner), which now runs 24x7 scanning images on the Web, trying to glean some "common sense," for instance, that chairs are for sitting, or cars are found on roads? Or, a program like Lenat's CYC, for whose structure of knowledge, humans have been data-entering vast numbers of facts such as, cars drive on roads, a road is a flat surface on the ground, the ground is.... Or, in general, of a machine that does not actually experience the concrete world? The actual nature of such a threat, I would submit, which is to say the actual power of such an intelligence, is in reality vastly unanalyzed, if at all. The threat in fact trades on our understanding of ourselves as intelligent beings. And this intelligence is based on our experience – our experience of events in the concrete world.

Having, in my earlier days, been drawn into attempting to work out, on my own, how the claims of the early AI programs (circa 1971-1978) or cognitive simulation programs on achieving human functions such as problem solving could be actually made to work in concrete situations, in the real world, I have grown wiser. I no longer try to do the work for the AI theorist. We will require that the AI folks flesh out what actual power their alien-like programs might actually have – in very concrete terms. This is *their* problem. Muelhauser's examples of AI power, let us be frank, while serving for illustrative purposes, are pure fantasy, hardly tied to any demonstrable reality or a proven power of machine AI. But the claim to achieving human equivalence – on this we can see what is truly involved.

When we have examined the structure of events then, and by this I mean the theory of the invariance laws specifying events, a theory inaugurated by the great theorist of perception, J. J. Gibson, we shall move on to the problem of the origin of the image of our highly mathematically structured external world. In this we shall view the remarkable solution provided by the French philosopher, Henri Bergson, in 1896, a solution that presciently anticipated Gabor's discovery of holography (in 1947) by fifty years, and which casts the nature of the brain in an entirely different light. We shall see that, shocking as it might be to the proponents of AI, to support perception the brain must achieve an actual, concrete, physical dynamics, as concrete as that of an electric motor generating a field of force. The mere manipulation of symbols in an abstract space and an abstract time – the only *operative* "dynamics" of a computing machine – is not sufficient to achieve conscious perception, therefore experience. Yes, one can simulate the equations of such a motor on a computing device – but the "simulation" runs not one tiny Christmas tree light. It is a real, concrete dynamics that is needed.

From Bergson's model of perception, we shall see how memory – the retrieval of experience – must actually work, particularly the basic retrieval operation termed "redintegration," itself at the heart of analogical reminding and therefore of analogy. In this, we are already in the problem of common sense knowledge, even to the making of mousetraps – better or worse. We shall see the insufficiency of any connectionist or neural network models – and these models sit at the base of AI's hopes – to handle these operations of analogy. This will lead to examining another dynamic – that underlying *explicit* memory, i.e., the conscious localization of events in time. This is the point – totally not understood and ignored – where consciousness is absolutely required for cognition. Finally, given all this, we will view the set of requirements that must actually be met to achieve a consciously perceptive, truly intelligent "device." With this, the reader can judge the imminence of our achieving a "singularity."

Introduction: End Notes and References

1. Chalmers, D. (2010). The singularity: A philosophical analysis. *Journal of Consciousness Studies*, *17*, 7-65.
2. Heylighen, F. (2012). Brain in vat cannot break out. *Journal of Consciousness Studies*, 19,126-142.
3. Bringsjord, S.(2012). Belief in the singularity is logically brittle. *Journal of Consciousness Studies*, 19.
4. Muelhauser, L. (2013). *Facing the Intelligence Explosion*, Chapter 12.
5. Ibid., Chapter 12.
6. McCarthy, J. & Hayes, P. (1969). Some philosophical problems from the standpoint of artificial intelligence. In B. Meltzer & D. Michie (Eds.), *Machine Intelligence*, (vol. 4), pp. 463-502, Edinburgh, UK: Edinburgh University Press.
7. Morgenstern, L. (1996). The problem with solutions to the frame problem, In K. M. Ford & Z. W. Pylyshyn (Eds.), *The Robot's Dilemma Revisited*, New Jersey: Ablex.
8. Shanahan, M. (2009). The Frame Problem. *Stanford Encyclopedia of Philosophy*. http://plato.stanford.edu/entries/frame-problem/
9. Wheeler, M. (2008). Cognition in Context: Phenomenology, Situated Robotics and the Frame Problem. *International Journal of Philosophical Studies*, 16, 323-49.
10. Fodor, J. A. (1983) *The Modularity of Mind*. Cambridge, Mass.: MIT Press, p. 112-113.
11. Dreyfus, also Wheeler have discussed this context problem more extensively. Dreyfus, H. L., (1992) *What Computers Still Can't Do: A Critique of Artificial Reason*. Cambridge, Mass.: MIT Press. Wheeler, M. (2008), op. cit.
12. Winograd, T. (1971). Understanding natural language. In Bobrow, D., & Collins, A. (Eds.), *Representation and Understanding*, New York: Academic Press
13. Winograd, T., & Flores, F. (1987). *Understanding Computers and Cognition*. Norwood, N.J.: Addison-Wesley, pp. 73-74.
14. Chalmers, D. (1995). Facing up to the problem of consciousness. *Journal of Consciousness Studies*, *2*(3), 200-219.
15. Robbins, S.E. (2013). Time, form and qualia: The hard problem reformed. *Mind and Matter*, *11*(2), 1-28.
16. For those unfamiliar with the US sport of "pumpkin chunkin," the annually held contest involves massive forms of catapults, invariably with massive amounts of engineering, which must fling a standard weight pumpkin as far as possible. The current (2013) record, I believe, for the most powerful category of machines, is – quick google – 4694.68 feet, held by team American Chunker – for an air cannon type machine.

CHAPTER I

The Invariance Structure of Events

For where is the borderline between perceiving and remembering?
…Where do percepts stop and begin to be memories, or,
in another way of putting it, go into storage? The facts of
memory are supposed to be well understood, but these
questions cannot be answered.

— J. J. Gibson[1]

Gradients and Flows

It was J.J. Gibson's insight (*The Perception of the Visual World*, 1950) that the surrounding environment contains a great deal of mathematical information useful to the brain. The information specifies the depth of objects, the form of objects, and how the body can act upon them. One such piece of information is what he termed the *optical flow field* (Figure 1.1). We see a flowing field like this routinely when we drive down the road in our car. The arrows in the diagram are "velocity vectors." The longer the arrow, the greater the speed of that portion of the field flowing by. The field is flowing by at the greatest velocity near the eye of the observer (or the driver of the car). There is a still point at the origin of the field called the "point of optical expansion" near the beginning of the mountains in the figure. This entire set or array of

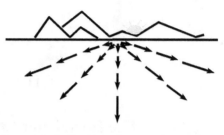

Figure 1.1. Optical flow field with its gradient of velocity vectors.

velocity vectors (arrows) is called a "gradient," as a gradient changes gradually, in this case in terms of the values of the velocities, from zero to increasingly larger. This gradient happens to have a precise mathematical ratio – information useful to the brain. The velocity value of each vector is inversely proportional to the square of the distance from the eye, or (read "$\propto$" as "is proportional to"), $v \propto 1/d^2$.

The actual surface of such a flowing field is also highly structured. We might be walking across a field of small rocks near the mountains, or a beach with its grains of sand, or a prairie with its grass, or across our kitchen floor with its tiles. These surfaces have what Gibson termed a *texture gradient* (Figure 1.2). Imagine the surface of Figure 1.2 as a rocky or gravel surface. The little circles (rocks in this case) are the "texture elements." The size of these elements and their horizontal separation (S) decreases in perfect mathematical proportion with the distance (d) from the eye or, $S \propto 1/d$. The vertical separation

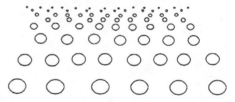

Figure 1.2. Texture density gradient (after Gibson, 1950).

between each element decreases in proportion to the square of the distance, or $S \propto 1/d^2$. These texture gradients are ubiquitous – floors, beaches, lake surfaces, tiles, etc. Turn the gradients upside down – you see them as ceilings or the bottom of clouds.

The mathematical relations or information of these gradients are preserved on the retina by the natural projection into the eye (Figure 1.3). Note in Figure 1.3 how the distances along the ground line (G_1G_2) are preserved when projected into the retina. The distance relations on the ground (W to X, X to Y, Y to Z) are

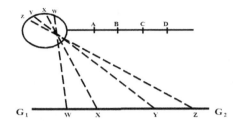

Figure 1.3. The "Ground."

preserved on the retina, but in reverse order. In fact, before Gibson, the problem of how we determine the distance of some object had been rather mysterious. Bishop Berkeley, an influential philosopher on the subject in the 1700's, had framed the problem in terms of the line ABCD in Figure 1.3. In this case nothing varies on the retina as the eye moves forward, for each point A, B, C, or D projects to exactly the same retinal point!

Gibson argued that these gradients naturally "specify" distance, in fact, they specify the stretching surfaces of the external environment. The information is received on the retina and processed by the visual areas of the cortex. It is now understood that the visual areas of the brain, V1 through V5, and the motor areas, all "resonate" with feedback from each other. This is a post-Gibson discovery of neuroscience, yet at the time, Gibson felt the brain simply "resonated" to this information. Gibson argued that there is no picture or image or photograph developed in the brain. The dynamic state of the brain "is specific to" the external environment. Note the use of the term "specific to." We shall see this again.

Let us place an object on our gradient. We'll imagine a coffee cup resting on the surface of a tiled table or patterned table cloth (Figure 1.4). In Figure 1.4, I want you to imagine that we have the *same* cup moving to two different positions – from back to front.

Figure 1.4. Texture density gradient (or tabletop) with a cup in two different positions.

The forward, larger view of the cup only occludes or covers two rows of (largish) texture units. The rear, smaller view of the cup occludes several layers or rows of smaller texture units. In fact, as the rear cup is moved to the forward position, there is preserved a constant ratio of the size of the cup to the number of texture units occluded. As the size (S) or height of the cup grows, the number of layers of units (N) it hides decreases, or $S \propto 1/N$. This

3

is what is termed an *invariance law*. The ratio of cup height to texture units is an invariant – a ratio that does not change. It is this invariant that specifies the *size constancy* of the cup. The event of a cup moving towards us from one position to another is always experienced as a *cup of the same size* moving across the table – despite the growing size of the cup per se on the retina as the cup approaches. It is this invariant ratio that the brain is picking up that enables it to "specify" that there is a cup of constant size moving across the table.

Invariance laws are fundamental for Gibson. We shall keep meeting them. The proportional gradients of flow fields and of texture unit distributions are also invariance laws. Physics prides itself on discovering the invariance laws of the universe. $F=ma$ and $E=mc^2$ are invariance laws. The discovery of invariance laws is the essential endeavor of science, and in this effort, physicists only model themselves after the method of the brain in perception.[2]

Flows, Form and Time

More than the constant size of the cup, there is the form of the cup to account for as well. The perception of form introduces us to the problem of time. The approach to form has often been as to a static subject. An object recognition model, JIM (Hummel and Biederman, 1992) is illustrative.[3] The model described a neural or connectionist network for this recognition. In introducing the JIM model, Hummel and Biederman had argued that form recognition, for example, for a standard cube, cannot follow a straightforward model of decomposition into, and re-assembly from, sets of *features* – edges, vertices, straight lines. This is due to the fact that once the features are separately identified (disassembled), the actual spatial relations are lost and the features can now be recomposed in any number of possible ways where the results look not at all like the original cube (Figure 1.5). To defeat this problem, they moved to the notion of "geons." These are elementary solids such as cones, wedges, cylinders or bricks which are recognized by features such as straight or curved contours/cross-sections, and into which the forms are analyzed and which support the original spatial relations.

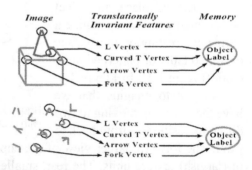

Figure 1.5 Both "objects" have the same features, and therefore would be "recognized" on the basis of a feature match. (After Hummel and Biederman, 1992)

In a review of the problem of dynamic form, I noted that Hummel and Biederman's approach suffered on several points.[4] For one, the classic fields to which neurons are thought sensitive, discovered by Hubel and Wiesel (circa 1959; 1978),[5] with their implication of detected, static features, simply cannot be regarded as the building blocks of a scene.[6] Another, by their own admission, is that the "fast-enabling links" in neural structure and needed for the model have yet to be found. Worse, the model is subject to the *correspondence* problem. The correspondence problem is a problem inherent in assuming that the visual system matches corresponding points or features in successive frames of an event. It is deemed intractable. If Hummel and Biederman's example cube/cone were rotating, a model would not only have to deal with the feature jumbling, it would have to explain how the features (edges, vertices) are tracked (their identity preserved) from frame to frame (or sample to sample, or snapshot to snapshot). This holds too for the features of the geons. In essence, the primary problem is the static conception of form. Related is yet another problem I also described, namely the concept that the brain's computations assume that the object, for example the rotating cube, is rigid, that is there is a *rigidity constraint* that is employed by the brain to compute form (such as a rotating cube) under dynamic transformations. This concept met its demise as well. The current conception of the derivation of form is very different; it is based on velocity flows.[7]

Gibson, as we saw, had already pointed to the significance of texture gradients and optic flow fields. Driven by a desire to bypass the correspondence problem, current perception theory sees perceived form as derived from these velocity fields in conjunction with Bayesian (that is, probabilistic) constraints. Adelson and Bergen (1985) described a general class of low-level models based on linear filters known as "energy models," initially developed by Watson and Ahumada (1983), for detecting the elements of dynamic form.[8] These are addressed specifically to the detection of the

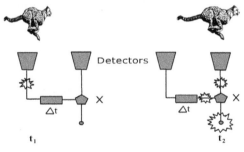

Figure 1.6. Reichardt filter or correlation model (Reichardt, 1959). It has two spatially separate detectors. The output of one of the detectors is delayed and then the two signals are multiplied. The output is tuned to speed. Many detectors tuned to different speeds are required for the true speed of a pattern, and the difference of pairs of detectors tuned to different directions is taken.

direction and velocity of motion, for example, as an edge of our cube transits the visual field. They are an evolution from the correlation filter (Figure 1.6) of Reichardt (1959) for motion and speed detection, and there are significant formal connections to it.[9]

A   B

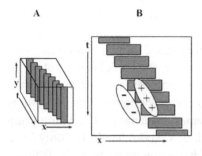

Figure 1.7. Motion as orientation in distance and time, (x,t). (A) is a spatiotemporal picture of a moving bar sampled in time. Velocity is proportional to the slant. (B) shows a spatiotemporally oriented receptive field that could detect the bar's motion. (Adapted from Adelson & Bergen, 1985).

In the correspondence problem, the position of a feature, say an edge, had to be tracked from frame to frame, and the distance change measured, to compute its velocity. The energy model does not extract position to compute motion. Motion is treated as spatiotemporal orientation (Figure 1.7), and the model consists of a network of "spatiotemporal filters." The response of the spatial component of the filter is the sum of its responses to varying local intensities of light falling in its receptive area, point by point. The key here is to think of the temporal response of these filters as a temporal weighting function which describes how inputs in the past are summed to produce the response at the present moment. The filters thus respond to motion energy within particular spatiotemporal frequency bands.[10] A network of these filters distributed across the visual field produces a net form of continuous output specifying the direction and velocity of motion of the edge.

This brings us to the model of Weiss, Simoncelli and Adelson (2002). A piece of background is yet in order. Consider the "plaid" grating of Figure 1.8. This is composed of two gratings oriented in different directions and crossing each other in the same plane, and indeed, when viewed separately, each grating is seen traveling in its oriented direction. Yet when the gratings are presented simultaneously, we see them moving coherently; we assign a single motion and direction to the pattern – not two independent motions. This phenomenon is a function of the "aperture" problem, a problem created when the ends of the

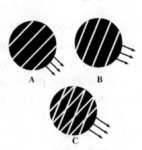

Figure 1.8. The plaid pattern (C) is the result of the motion of two gratings A and B. Each grating has a velocity vector normal (or perpendicular) to the grating lines, lying on a constraint line in velocity space. One possible method used by the brain - the Intersection of Constraints - finds the single velocity consistent with both sources of information. (After Weiss & Adelson, 1998)

lines are not visible (Figure 1.9). The individual velocity measurements on each line provide only a partial constraint. Considering each grating, only the component of velocity normal (or perpendicular) to the orientation of the grating can be estimated, and hence the grating motion is consistent with an infinite number of possible velocities.

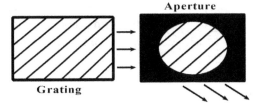

Figure 1.9. The aperture problem. The card with the grating is moving to the right, and passes beneath the card with the circular aperture. The ends of the moving lines are now obscured, and only the downward motion of the lines is seen in the aperture.[11]

It should be understood that the receptive fields of the energy model filters discussed earlier are inherently "apertures." The aperture problem indicates that the visual system's measures of velocity are intrinsically *uncertain*. Therefore the integration of a multitude of uncertain individual velocities must be inherently probabilistic. It is at this point of integration that Weiss et al. insert their fundamental, probabilistic (Bayesian) constraint, i.e., a probability estimate using a prior assumption about the nature of the world.

The fundamental constraint used by Weiss, Simoncelli and Adelson, and ultimately applied in mathematical form to the resolution of these velocities, is "motion is slow and smooth."[12] The model explains a very large array of "illusions." In fact, due to this inherent measurement uncertainty, *all* perception, "veridical" or otherwise, the authors argue, must be viewed as an *optimal percept* based upon the best available information. Applied to the

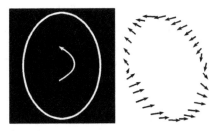

Figure 1.10. The normal velocity compo-nents (right) of the edge of a rotating ellipse (left). These tend to induce non-rigid motion. (After Weiss and Adelson, 1998)[14]

velocity fields defining a narrow rotating ellipse (Figure 1.10), for example, the violation of this "slow and smooth" constraint ends in specifying a non-rigid object if the motion is too fast (Mussati's illusion)[13]. It is these constraints applied to the velocity flows, or their violation, that determine the rigidity of the form.

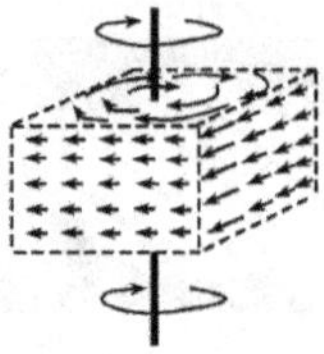

Figure 1.11. The
Gibsonian Cube

If we were to consider a rotating "Gibsonian" cube, this form becomes a partitioned set of these velocity fields. As each side rotates into view, an expanding flow field (Figure 1.11) is defined. As the side rotates out of view, a contracting flow field is defined. The top of the cube is a radial flow field. The "edges" and "vertices" (i.e., "features") of this cube are now simply sharp discontinuities in these flows. The implications of this are concretely displayed in a demonstration discussed by Shaw and McIntyre with a rotating wire-edged cube (Figure 1.12).[15]

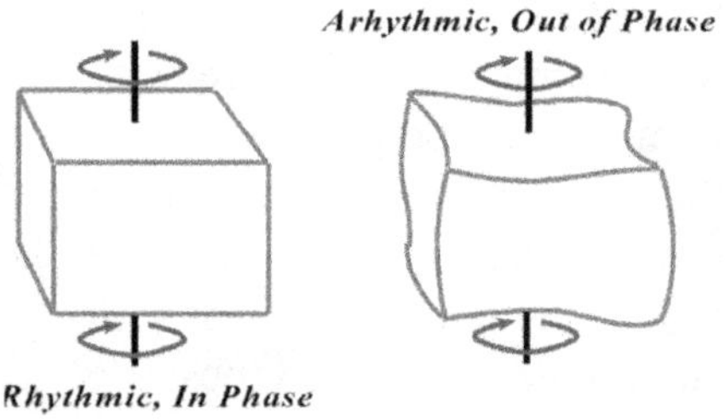

Arhythmic, Out of Phase

Rhythmic, In Phase

Figure 1.12. Rotating cubes, strobed in phase with, or out of phase with, the symmetry period.[16]

A cube naturally has a symmetry period of four – it is carried into itself every 90 degree rotation. (Symmetry, it should be understood, *is* invariance). An equilateral triangle would be carried into itself or map precisely back upon itself every 120 degree rotation, or a symmetry period of three. When the rotating wire-edged cube is strobed in phase with or at integral multiple of its symmetry period (say 4, 8 or 12 times per revolution), it appears, indeed, as a cube in rotation. But when it is strobed out-of-phase (7, 9 or 13 times per revolution), it becomes a distorted, wobbly, plastic or non-rigid object. The "cubeness" has been lost.

In this wobbly "not-cube" case, the constraint (invariance) likely being violated via the arrhythmic strobe is this: a regular form displays a regular periodicity in time. The strobe is essentially taking snapshots of the cube. Yet these snapshots are not sufficient to specify the rigid cubical form we would expect; they are not sufficient to specify the straight lines, straight edges, corners or vertices – the standard static, geometric "features" of a cube.

As Gibson long argued, the concepts of our Euclidean geometry – straight lines, curves, vertices, sets or families of forms related by geometrical transformations, even geons – while elegant, have little meaning to the brain, i.e., they are not the elements by which the brain constructs a world. Rather, the forms being specified are functions of the application of constraints on flowing fields.[17] The structure of the forms reflects invariants existing over these time-extended flows.

Form and the Scale of Time

All form, further, is a function of the scale of time imposed on these

Figure 1.13. Successive transformations of the rotating cube (2-D view) through figures of 4n-fold symmetry as angular velocity increases.

flows. The cube, rotating at a certain rate and perceived as a cube in rotation, is a function of a scale of time imposed by the dynamics of the brain. We could increase the velocity of the cube's rotation. With sufficient increase, it will become a serrated-edged figure, and at a higher rate, a figure with even more serrations. Finally, it becomes a cylinder surrounded by a fuzzy haze. Each of these figures is a figure of 4n-fold symmetry – 8-edged, 12-edged, 16-edged..., with the cylinder a figure of infinite symmetry (Figure 1.13). In total, this transitional series of forms reflects the scale of time in which we normally dwell.

Let us perform a gedanken experiment. We normally envision the dynamics of the brain as a hierarchy of levels – atomic, molecular, neural, etc. But the brain is a *coherent* biological system – introduce change at one "level" and the whole is changed. One level in this dynamics is the chemical and thus the chemical velocities (or speed of flow) supporting the brain's computations. The range and complexity of these, considering the various local velocities, is vast, but at least in principle, it can be argued (cf. Hoaglund, 1966; Fischer, 1966), the global process velocity could be changed; we could introduce some catalyst or set of catalysts to effect this. A catalyst, by orienting the appropriate nuclear bonds, can enable a chemical process to move more quickly, requiring less energy. Even raising the temperature in such a system is sufficient to affect the chemical velocities.[18]

Suppose then two observers, A and B. Observer A, dwelling in our normal scale, is gazing upon a cube rotating rapidly enough to be perceived as a 16-edged serrated figure. Observer B has had his global process velocity raised. His scale has been shifted. He perceives the same cube, but as a cube of normal four-sided construction slowly rotating. Both perceive by the same law of invariance – a figure of 4n-fold symmetry. Suppose A and B are watching a time-lapse film of the growth of a human head in profile (Figure 1.14).

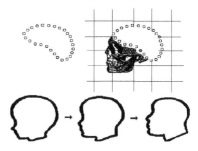

Figure 1.14. Aging of the facial profile. A cardioid is fitted to the skull and a strain transformation is applied. (Strain is equivalent to the stretching of the meshes of a coordinate system in all directions.) Shown are a few of the possible profiles generated. (Adapted from Pittenger & Shaw, 1975)[19]

As Pittenger and Shaw showed, this aging transformation is defined by a *strain* transformation applied to heart shaped figure, termed a cardioid, placed over the skull. Strain is the stretching of the coordinate system simultaneously in all directions that the skull is placed upon. The higher the strain value, the greater the aging or age of the profile. At a given film rate, the head is transforming very rapidly for A; for B, it is a much slower event. Both perceive the transforming head by the same law – a strain transformation applied to a cardioid.

Were we to borrow from relativistic physics, we might say that we have performed an operation analogous to changing the "space-time partition." From this perspective, a deeper significance of Gibson's (1966) insistence on invariance laws defining events could be understood. In such transforming partitions, it is only invariance laws (e.g., $d = vt$, $d' = vt'$) that hold. We should consider here, since such changes of space-time partitions via changes in process velocity are clearly possible, that nature has to have allowed for this, and therefore has chosen invariance laws that hold across these partitions as nature's method of specifying events.

Extend this scale transformation. Raising the process velocity carries a corresponding decrease in the scale of time. If a fly is passing before both observers, for observer A it is a "buzzing" fly of our normal scale; for observer B, the fly is now flapping its wings slowly, like a heron. As the process velocity of B is raised further, the fly transforms, transitioning to a near-motionless fly with wings barely moving, then to a motionless fly, then to a vibrating, crystalline form, then to a collection of waves…

At the very minute scale of time we are now considering, we realize that even the most "stable" form – a book, a cup, a picture – is nevertheless a sea of motion. A "rotating" cube is only one form of the cube as a continuous *event*. "What is real," said Bergson, "is the continual *change of* form: *form is only a snapshot view of a transition*."[20] It is within this sea of motion or change that that brain actually dwells. The brain too is the very same sea of motion.

Flow Fields and Action

I noted briefly earlier that the visual areas of the brain, V1 thru V5, are interconnected, modulating each other's processing ("re-entrant"). These visual areas themselves are modulated by connections from the motor areas. Indeed a large number of recent findings have reinforced the general concept that the objects and events of the perceived world are in a real sense mirrors of the biologic action capabilities of the body, while the appreciation of the importance to visual computation of re-entrant connections from motor areas to visual areas has also grown. The implications are more radical, as we shall see, than are currently understood, but for now we can begin considering the form of information in the light that "gets into" or is used by the action systems of the body.

There is a ratio, known as *tau*, that exists over flow fields. For the record only, it is defined by taking the ratio of the surface (or angular projection) of the field at the retina, $r(t)$, to its velocity of expansion at the retina, $v(t)$, and its time derivative. For a bird coming in for a landing, this value specifies the *severity of impact*, and the bird can use it to modify his flight and create a soft landing. For a pilot, it is essential in landing a plane (Figure 1.15). Tau is an example of the "information in the light" that must be utilized by the

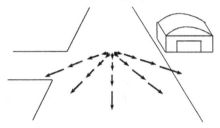

Figure 1.15. The Tau value defined over a flow field is used by a pilot to guide a plane.

action systems of the brain to specify possible (virtual) action.

Invariance in Dynamic Touch

Before I bring this all together in terms of the invariance structure of an event, let us spend a little time in another modality, that of touch. Kugler and Turvey consider the dynamics underlying a very simple exercise, namely where a person swings two rods, each with a weight at the end, in a pendulum-like motion using his wrists as the pivot points.[21] The task is to swing the two pendulums comfortably together, at a common tempo, and 180° out of phase (Figure 1.16). In this case, the subject turns himself into a *virtual* single-wrist pendulum system. Such a system is characterized by a law derived by Huygens, wherein the center of oscillation (L_e) is defined as a function of the lengths (L) and masses (M) of the two individual pendulum systems:

Figure 1.16. A subject swings two weighted rods (pendulums) at a common tempo, 180 degrees out of phase.

$$L_e = (M_1 L_1^2 + M_2 L_2^2) / (M_1 L_1 + M_2 L_2).$$

Swinging two pendulums then is dynamically identical to swinging one pendulum, despite the greater number of degrees of freedom (2n) involved.

The common period arrived at, while a natural period for the pair of systems *as a unit*, is not the natural period of either of the individual systems. The periodic times into which the person settles vary with the magnitudes of the pendulums, while the amplitude varies inversely with respect to mass and directly with respect to (rod) length. The information specifying the preferred steady states into which the person settles (dependent on the lengths and masses involved) is provided by an abstracted description of the dynamics of the wrist-pendulum system, or, to be more specific, kinematic information based in the kinetics of muscle/tendon stress/strain distortions propagated globally via the nervous system as what ultimately can be termed *haptic* flow fields, i.e., flow fields defined over our systems for touch. This information defines a single, kinematic field property that, rather than relying on the hard-molded connections between the two pendulums envisioned in Huygens' law, supports a *soft-assembled* virtual system. This information also serves as a source of constraint for the fields that produce it, and it guides the wrist-pendulum to its stable attractor state.

A mechanical clock pendulum employs a hard-molded escapement mechanism, e.g., a sprocket or escape wheel and a hanging weight, which feeds pulses of energy (associated with shock waves) into the system in proper phase to maintain the frequency of oscillation. The mechanism is independent of changes in length and mass, but, therefore, when such changes occur affecting the natural period, they will not be accompanied by variations in the amount of energy injected into the cycle. The body, however, employs a soft-molded, non-impulsive (non-shock wave) escapement that uses the dissipative flow capabilities associated with entropy-producing field processes, and which involves a gating process that relates to the finite capacity of the system to absorb energy. Kugler and Turvey, in their exhaustive analysis of the complex dynamics underlying this system, describe how change in periodic timing is brought about by change to internal parameters (stiffness, resting length, etc.) that preserve the amount of energy degraded as a constant over varying frequencies of oscillation. This is termed an *adiabatic* change (invariant), i.e., a transformation with the following ratio:

$$\frac{\text{Energy of Oscillation}}{\text{Frequency of Oscillation}} = k$$

I have spent a little space, time and depth here to impart the understanding of just how concrete, dynamic and *physical* are the events and the invariance laws we are dealing with. We shall see that the simplest of events involve this form of information – information that is embedded in these very physical forces and fields. It is information, sorry to say, that is not detected by scanning Wikipedia text.

We can consider another aspect of these "simple" forms of motion, for example simply "wielding" a metal rod a couple feet long, or a short length of narrow board, or even "wielding" a spoon. Wielding is described (cf. Turvey and Carello, 1995) under the concept of an "inertia tensor."[22] A rigid object's moments of mass distribution constitute potentially relevant mechanical invariants since they specify the dynamics of the object. The object's mass (m) is the zeroth moment, while the first (static) moment is mass (m) times the distance (d) between the point of rotation and object's center of mass. The second moment is conceived as the object's resistance against angular acceleration. In three dimensions, this moment is a 3 x 3 matrix called the inertia tensor. The diagonal elements I_1, I_2, I_3, represent the object's resistance to angular acceleration with respect to a coordinate system of three principal axes.[23] There will be an inertia tensor (invariant), I_{ij}, specific to wielding the board and even wielding the spoon.

Stirring Coffee With a Spoon

Now we consider a very simple, every day event, namely, stirring coffee with a spoon. The (ongoing) event has a time-extended *invariance structure*. We'll make this particular cup a cubical cup just to tie into the discussions above more clearly. Thus the swirling coffee surface is a radial flow field. The constant size of the cup, as one's head moves forward or backward or we move the cup towards or away from us, is specified, over time, by a constant ratio of height to the occluded texture units of the table surface gradient. As the coffee cup is moved over the table towards us, the tau value specifies time to contact and provides information for modulating the hand to grasp the cup.[24] As the cup is cubical, its edges and vertices are sharp discontinuities in the velocity flows of its sides as the eyes saccade (the darting eye movement from point to point on a scene), where these flows specify, *over time*, the form of the cup. The periodic motion of the spoon is a haptic flow field that carries an adiabatic invariance – a constant ratio of energy of oscillation to frequency of oscillation. There will be an inertia tensor (invariant), I_{ij}, specific to spoon-stirring. All this and more is information specifying or structuring this simple event of spoon stirring.

Before we go too far here, let's give a definition of an invariance structure: An invariance structure can be defined as such: *the transformations and invariants specifying an event and rendering it a virtual action.* The notion of "rendering it a virtual action" will be given yet more depth as we go on, but already one can see, in the context of the τ value, how this fits.

Now we begin to see the form of knowledge – read, *experience* – that must be available to our hypothetical robot, mentioned in the introduction, who is performing coffee stirring and is checking his frame axioms to see if certain weird happenings are to be expected. If the coffee surface is erupting in geysers, this is a violation of an invariance law specifying the event of stirring coffee, namely, the normal radial flow field. If the coffee feels like thick cement when stirring, this is a violation of the inertia tensor and adiabatic invariance normally involved. If the cup is bulging in and out, or growing up and down vertically, we have a violation of the normal size constancy of the cup. This form of knowledge is not going to be captured by the simple symbolic rules defined in frame axioms.

As humans, we detect these violations instantly. They simply don't resonate with our experience; rather, there is a dissonance with our experience. We are not searching, or we detect no time searching, a database. This alone should be a warning that we may be an entirely different form of "device."

The Problem of Experience

On this note, we can begin to consider what we have seen. Form, for example, is defined over flow fields – it is an invariant over flow. The tau value exists over a flowing field. These are invariants defined over time. As Gibson noted, an invariant defined over time does not exist in an instant, it is not a "bit" that can be transmitted along the nerves, or moved from register to register in a computer, or stored in a static memory. For the brain, the strobed cube does not exist in an instant or a sample of time – each strobe flash is an "instant" or sample. But this is not sufficient to specify the form as an invariant over time.

What type of device, one wonders, can store a flow field? How does one store a "cube" when it exists only over this flow? What meaning does it have to store the "features" of the cube – the edges, vertices – to be reassembled again from "memory" as a cube when these features do not actually exist as static objects, when these are only functions of, creatures of, a flow? Yet all our experience is this flow. The adiabatic invariance for the periodic motion of the stirring spoon existed only over the flow of a haptic field.

Flow is time. But time is not *abstract* time – the abstract series of discrete "instants" in which the computations of a computer take place. It is not the succession of static instants in which an also static edge or vertex can motionlessly reside. This abstract time serves equally well for these computations whether they are performed on a supercomputer, on an abacus, on a register machine composed of shoe boxes and beans,[25] or via the read-head and infinite tape of a Turing Machine where the tape lurches through the read head, square by square by square, each square holding its instruction for the machine – the essence of an abstract time. This abstraction is not the time in which the brain – which could care less about our notion of the abstract "instant" – actually dwells. And understanding this real, concrete time in which the brain and yes, the body, dwell, is crucial in understanding this experience, how it is stored, and most importantly the origin of this experience as our image of the external world.

Chapter I: End Notes and References

1. Gibson, J. J. (1975). Events are perceived but time is not. In J. T. Fraser & N. Laurence (Eds.), *The study of time II*. New York: Springer-Verlag, p. 299.

2. For further explication of the role of invariance in science:
    Woodward, J. (2000). Explanation and invariance in the special sciences. *British Journal for the Philosophy of Science*, 51, 197-214.
    Woodward, J. (2001). Law and explanation in biology: Invariance is the kind of stability that matters. *Philosophy of Science*, 68, 1-20.
    Kugler, P. & Turvey, M. (1987). *Information, Natural Law, and the Self-assembly of Rhythmic Movement*. Hillsdale, NJ: Erlbaum.

3. Hummel, J.E. & Biederman, I. (1992). Dynamic binding in a neural network for shape recognition. *Psychological Reviews, 12*, 487-519.

4. Robbins, S.E. (2004). On time, memory and dynamic form. *Consciousness and Cognition, 13*, 762-788.

5. Hubel, D., & Wiesel, T. N. (1959). Receptive fields of single neurons in the cat's striate cortex. *Journal of Physiology*, 148, 574-591.
    Hubel, D., & Wiesel, T. N. (1978). Brain mechanisms in vision. *Scientific American, 241*, 150-162.

6. Nakayama, K. (1998). Vision fin de siPcle: A reductionistic explanation of perception for the 21st century? In J. Hochberg (Ed.), *Perception and Cognition at Century's End*. New York: Academic Press.

7. Ullman, S. (1979a). *The Interpretation of Visual Motion*. Cambridge: MIT Press.
    Ullman, S. (1979b). The interpretation of structure from motion. *Proceedings of the Royal Society of London, Series B, 203*, 405-426.
    Ullman, S. (1984). Maximizing rigidity: the incremental recovery of 3-D structure from rigid and non-rigid motion. *Perception, 13*, 255-274,
    Ullman, S. (1986). Competence, performance and the rigidity assumption. *Perception, 15*, 644-646.

8. Adelson, E., & Bergen, J. (1985). Spatiotemporal energy model of the perception of motion. *Journal of the Optical Society of America*, 2 (2), 284-299.
    Watson, A. B. & Ahumada, A. J.. (1983). Model of human visual-motion sensing. *J. Opt. Soc. Am. A.* 2, 322-341.

9. Reichardt W, (1959). Autocorrelation and the central nervous system. In W. A. Rosenblith (Ed.) Sensory Communication MIT Press Cambridge 303-318

10. Hence these are also termed Fourier models, since the space or coordinate structure is spatial and temporal frequency

11. Robbins, S. E. (2006). Bergson and the holographic theory. *Phenomenology and the Cognitive Sciences*, 5, 365-394.

12. Weiss, Y., Simoncelli, E., & Adelson, E. (2002). Motion illusions as optimal percepts. *Nature Neuroscience, 5*, 598-604.

13. Mussati, C. L. (1924). Sui fenomeni stereocinetici. *Archivo Italiano di Psycologia, 3*, 105-120.

14. Weiss, Y., & Adelson, E. (1998). Slow and smooth: a Bayesian theory for the combination of local motion signals in human vision. MIT A. I. Memo No. 1624.

15. Shaw, R. E., & McIntyre, M. (1974) The algoristic foundations of cognitive psychology. In *Cognition and the Symbolic Processes,* D. Palermo & W. Weimer (Eds.), New Jersey: Lawrence Erlbaum Associates.

16. Robbins, 2004, op. cit.

17. Gibson, J. J. (1966). *The Senses Considered as Visual Systems.* Boston: Houghton-Mifflin.
    Gibson, J. J. (1979). *The Ecological Approach to Visual Perception.* Boston: Houghton-Mifflin.

18. Hoaglund, H. (1966), Some bio-chemical considerations of time. In J.T. Fraser (Ed.), *The Voices of Time,* New York: Braziller.
    Fischer, R. (1966). Biological time. In J. T. Fraser (Ed.) *The Voices of Time.* New York: Braziller.

19. Pittenger, J. B. & Shaw, R. E. (1975). Aging faces as viscal elastic events: Implications for a theory of non rigid shape perception. *Journal of Experimental Psychology: Human Perception and Performance, 1,* 374-382.

20. Bergson, H. (1907/1911). *Creative Evolution.* New York: Holt, p. 328.

21. Kugler, P. & Turvey, M. (1987). *Information, Natural Law, and the Self-assembly of Rhythmic Movement.* Hillsdale, NJ: Erlbaum.

22. Turvey, M., & Carello, C. (1995). Dynamic touch. In W. Epstein & S. Rogers (Eds.), *Perception of Space and Motion,* San Diego: Academic Press.

23. Kingma, I., van de Langenberg, R., & Beek, P. (2004). Which mechanical invariants are associated with the perception of length and heaviness on a nonvisible handheld rod? Testing the inertia tensor hypothesis. *Journal of Experimental Psychology: Human Perception and Performance* 30: 346-354.

24. Savelsbergh, G. J. P., Whiting, H.T., & Bootsma, R. J. (1991). Grasping tau. *Journal of Experimental Psychology: Human Perception and Performance* 17: 315-322.

25. For a description of a register machine and its operation, see:
    Dennett, D. (2013). *Intuition Pumps and Other Tools for Thinking.* New York: Norton.

CHAPTER II

The Image of the External World

…we maintain that the brain is an instrument of action,
and not of representation.

— Bergson, *Matter and Memory*[1]

Who is it that sees?

— Bassui, *Zen Koan*

Abstract Time and the Classic Metaphysic

A computer's operations are carried out in an abstract time. It is a time that is described as a series of abstract, mutually external, discrete instants. This is equally true of a neural network, formally being also a computer or Turing Machine equivalent. The operations performed are syntax, or syntactic rule manipulations. Syntax rules can be defined simply as, "rules for the concatenation and juxtaposition of objects."[2] The manipulation of symbols in an algebra is a simple example of these rules, e.g., $a = bc \Rightarrow b = a/c$, or the linguistic rewrite rule for a sentence, S, as a noun phrase plus (or concatenated with) a verb phrase, $S \Rightarrow NP + VP$. Such "motions" of objects (symbols) in an abstract space are unaffected by the actual nature of time; they can occur instant to instant, position to position so to speak, square to square on the Turing Machine tape, whether this time is extremely fast in speed or geologic in speed, and always yield the same result. This is to say they are scale-less – they have nothing to do with the scale of time, whether our normal scale of a "buzzing" fly or a scale where the fly is flapping his wings like a heron. Further, these operations do not require that the "instants" be in anyway connected, continuous, melding into one another, or integrally, organically glued together.

This abstract version of time is part of a general conceptual structure of thought on space, time and motion. I term it the "classic metaphysic." Reprising Bergson's analysis in what follows (*Matter and Memory*,1896), the classic metaphysic is a "projection frame" or epistemological framework, if you will, for our theories of the real, both in physics and psychology. It is an *abstract space* that is an imposed and arbitrary static conceptual backdrop. It is a framework ubiquitous and engrained, and it is a framework that is extremely useful, for it is the very support of our mathematical treatment of the dynamically transforming field of matter – the entire apparatus of the calculus. Yet this very usefulness is so enthralling that the framework itself is often taken for an ontological reality, i.e., for the actual structure and dynamics of the ever transforming universal field. At the time, Bergson was arguing that this framework was obscuring deeper penetration into the physical world, something his physicist commentators, looking back at the nature of what would eventually emerge in quantum mechanics, e.g., the uncertainty principle, etc., agreed with.[3] It is precisely the job of theory, Bergson argued, to break through this imposed framework. As he put it, "...*a theory of matter is an attempt to find the reality hidden beneath... customary images which are entirely relative to our needs...*"[4]

These needs begin in our perception itself. The body and brain are embedded in, and integrally a part of, the surrounding material world, what

I have just called the field of matter. The task of the brain in perception is to identify, in this ever transforming field, objects upon which the body can act – to lift a "spoon," to throw a "rock," to hoist a "bottle of beer." This is the elementary partition made by perception – "objects" and "motions" – in the field. The notion of objects is increasingly rarified, eventuating – in the classic metaphysic – with this material field taken as a continuum of points or positions. The motion of any object in this continuum, from point A to point B, is conceived to follow a trajectory or line, where the line itself consists of a set of points/positions. Each point on the line (or space) successively occupied (or passed over) by the moving object is seen to correspond to an "instant" of time. Thus time itself is treated as simply another dimension of this abstract spatial continuum.

The continuum is infinitely divisible. In fact, this abstract space or continuum, as Bergson noted, can simply be considered "a principle of infinite divisibility." As the motion of an object from point A to point B is conceived as a line or trajectory, this line, being a space, is infinitely divisible. Successive divisions of the line reduce it of a set of points. Since two adjacent points on the object's trajectory are just that, static points, according to this treatment of an object's motion, to explain its motion between the two static points, we must insert a new, yet smaller line of points between the two, beginning the description of motion by a line of successively occupied points yet again. This is of course an infinite regress.

The end result of this infinite operation of division, even could we legitimately conceive of such an end, ignoring the convenient mathematical technique of "taking a limit," would be at best a mathematical point. At such a point, there could exist no motion, no evolution in time of the material field. Further, as every spatially extended "object" is subject to this infinite decomposition throughout the continuum, then we end with a completely *homogeneous* field of mathematical points. The continuum of mathematical points then, both spatially and temporally, can have no qualities – qualities at the least imply heterogeneity. Our experience, unfortunately – the coffee being stirred, the swirling surface, the cream mixing with brown coffee, steam arising, spoon clinking – is quality filled.

Qualia and the Hard Problem

This is the exact basis from which Chalmers formulated his famous "hard problem" of consciousness. How, asked Chalmers, after you have described you computer architecture, or your neural model of the brain, or your connectionist neural network, yes, even your AGI, have you accounted for the "qualia" of the perceived world? Hence, in this formulation, the origin of qualia is the focus of the debate. A very common starting point tells us that the classic metaphysic is the framework in which this "origins of qualia in consciousness" debate now proceeds. This common point is that the matter-field contains no qualities – objects have no color, there are no sounds, etc. Where, on the contrary, the existence of qualities in the field *is* affirmed, such participants (e.g., Strawson) have seldom, if ever, explicitly declared the metaphysical framework in which they now work, specifically their model of time and space.[5] As we shall see, raising this framework to conscious awareness within the debate is crucial. There is another indicator of this framework: the vast preponderance of examples of qualia are static, for example, we note the redness of red, the taste of cauliflower, the feel of velvet, the smell of fresh cut grass. The origins of these – considered the problem – are the standard examples. Seldom are qualities of *motions* ever discussed, e.g., the "twisting" of falling leaves, the "gyrations" of a wobbling, rotating cube, the "buzzing" of a fly. Where a hint of motion and time is introduced, as in Valerie Hardcastle's discussion, "… the conductor waving her hands, the musicians concentrating, patrons shifting in their seats, and the curtains gently and ever-so-slightly waving," time, as part of the problem, is quickly dismissed.[6]

This glaring lack is an index to the hold that the treatment of motion and time in the classic metaphysic has induced. A "time" that is simply another dimension of the infinitely divisible space – a set or series of mathematical point-instants – is equally completely homogeneous. Any "motion" in this space, logically, has no duration greater than a mathematical point, then another point, then another... How is it possible, then, that any of these time extended motions – the shifting patrons in the symphony, the gently and ever-so-slightly waving curtains – are perceived by us as such – as *motions*? These are equally *qualities,* as Hardcastle is admitting. They arise, just as problematically as the "static" colors of objects, to include the red-velvet color of those curtains, in the homogenous time dimension of infinitely divisible instants in this continuum. In this framework then, we are immediately thrown into the problem of the "memory" that connects or binds these "instants," for any qualia defined over time – and this is all qualia – must endure over at least two such instants. If there is nothing binding the instants of the "gently waving curtains," if each instant disappears into the non-existence of the past as the next (the "present") arrives, the "waving" cannot be perceived. Appropriating William James' term, and driving it to an even more primitive level, it becomes the search for the "primary memory" that supports the elemental, time-flowing, qualia-laden events of perception.[7] The nature of this memory, I have argued elsewhere, has a primacy greater than the problem of qualia or at the very minimum, it is an integral part of the problem.[8] If we do not know how even two instants are bound together, we can have no qualia. This is to say that "temporal consciousness" itself, i.e., our perception of the flow of time (cf. Dainton, 2010) is, at its most basic, equally a problem of qualia.[9]

The brain, in this metaphysic, we should remember, is inescapably a part of this abstract continuum. When objects on trajectories in the continuum we term "light rays" strike objects termed eyes in brain, the abstract, homogeneous motions of the external matter-field, all reducible in time-extent to mathematical points, simply continue in the portion of the field called the "brain." Nowhere in the brain, taken as part of the continuum, can there be anything but more homogeneous points/instants. There can be no actual coherent time-extent of motions through the nerves, no "continuity of time-extended neural processes," no curtains gently waving – again, the logical time extent of any neural process is never more than a mathematical point, then another, then another... Thus, for all the power of the earlier discussed "energy model" for dynamic form, there is yet no perception; there is no possibility of the *experience* of dynamic form. A reflection on the model's origins in the Reichardt filter (Figure 1.6) initiates the point. The past instant on the trajectory of a moving object is registered, a delayed signal generated, and then multiplied by a signal from a following instant on this trajectory. The multiplied signal value at this new instant is taken (assuming a network effecting some disambiguation) as indicative of direction and velocity. It reflects an influence of the past. But it is simply another instant. The network vectors towards this output, instant after instant. The filter (or an entire network of spatiotemporal filters) will *register* direction and velocity, i.e., produce a value, or successive values, but though the successive signals are correlated, this is not the *perception* of a motion. It does not fulfill the elementary criterion for consciousness – a continuity over at least two such instants. There is no experience. As external observers, we see the energy model, and the powerful computing network it embodies, computing values indicative of, and a basis for, a changing form over time. But it is we, as external viewers, that are assigning this continuity. From an internal view, there is no such continuity; the fundamental cohesion of time is missing.

However one conceives of these motions within the brain, whether the firing of connectionist networks, symbolic manipulations via neural programs, or resonance to invariants over this structure of field motions relative to the body's action systems, it changes nothing. Within the brain, or a computer for that matter, if taken as a part of this abstract, homogenous continuum, we can never derive qualities, whether colors, sounds or time-extended motions. We cannot explain how we see a cube "rotating" let alone a "blue" cube. Therefore, all qualia are logically forced, within this metaphysic, into the non-physical, or the mental, or somewhere, anywhere but the abstract continuum. But the step by which this generation of events unto and into another realm can occur, *within the confines of the metaphysic*, remains a dilemma. The structure of the metaphysic makes the step impossible, while leaving the nature of realms outside the structure – e.g., the "mental" – forever incapable of definition or of use to science, for our science operates precisely within this (classic) metaphysic.

"Qualia" is the symbol for this problem: What is the origin of the perceived qualities of the matter-field of the classic, spatial metaphysic?

For the AI proponent, perhaps suddenly wondering why we are discussing this, I must emphasize that AI is the direct child of the classic metaphysic. The abstract time and abstract space of the metaphysic comprise the exact structure that the operations of AI work within. The problem of the origins of qualia is AI's problem. It is not just philosophy's. It is not just a problem of neuroscience. Experience is qualia filled. Impregnated. Experience *is* qualia. If you want to understand what experience is, you must grasp the nature of the problem of its origin. Only if you know what experience is will you know what intelligence is, and only then will you know whether your AGI or SGI is even close to achieving intelligence as embodied in the human.

The True Problem: The Image of the External World

This statement of hard problem entirely in terms of accounting for the origin of qualia is and has been deeply misleading. The problem is rather this: what is the origin of the perceived *image* of the external world. This straightforward statement is neither grasped nor accepted by the participants in the qualia debate, though it has been the formulation of the problem for 2000 years, since at least the Greeks began thinking about it.[10] Some readers, might feel that the words "image" and "qualia" are interchangeable. The two should be, nearly, but so strong is the hold of the problem's formulation in terms of qualia, this term-interchange is never, ever found. To my knowledge, one never sees the discussion going on in terms of "explaining the origin of the image" in the literature. One can find three uses of the term "image" in the entire Wiki discussion of qualia, and this is limited to references to the "retinal image," to Tye's dismissal of after-images as a problem for his theory, and to Robinson's defense of the vividness of the "mental image." Crane's entry on the "Problem of Perception" in the *Stanford Encyclopedia of Philosophy*, though with plenty of "qualia," contains not one use of the word "image," similarly for Siegel's entry on "The Contents of Perception," while Tye's entry on "Qualia" contains a few uses of the term "image" in contexts irrelevant to his take on the problem of qualia.[11] To the ancient philosophers of perception, before the advent of Chalmers, the problem was so strongly in terms of the image, it was in effect an *optical* problem. But if one were to offer up a solution to the origin of the *image* of the external world today, it would not be remotely recognized as a solution to the hard problem.

The origin of this state of affairs rests again in the classic metaphysic, and at least to a degree, can be assigned to Galileo. Galileo's crucial step was to suggest that the real world is made only of *quantitative* aspects, while other empirical aspects – the qualities of the experienced world – are somehow created by "the living organism." Implicit within Galileo's statement is the distinction between primary properties and secondary properties, the former related to quantity and "real," the latter related to quality and only in the mind.[12] In other words, Galileo, quite consistent with the framework we have already viewed, explicitly stripped the material world of quality at the formal inception of this metaphysic.[13]

Form itself, for the debaters of the hard problem, has been left to reside in Galileo's quantitative world. Because of this, form itself has been taken to be simply computational and the origin of the forms (objects) in our perception of, or image of, the external world has not been considered an issue in the debate – only the qualities of the forms are an issue, e.g., the "redness" of a cube in our vision, not the "cube-ness" of the cube. We see this position stated clearly, for example, in an essay on qualia by Martine Nida-Rümelin.[14] She feels forced to differentiate between color as an "appearance property" and shape, which she says is not such a property. In other words, color is a problem, form is not a problem – yet forms populate our image of the world – the table of the kitchen, the coffee cup on the table's surface, the pots hanging from the ceiling. For Edmond Wright, qualia applies to all "sense fields" in all modalities, but not to "perceived items." In other words, qualia does not apply to objects and forms.[15] The transparency thesis (cf. Kind, 2008) holds that our experience does not reveal the existence of any qualia, for our experience is transparent – when we attend to our experiences, our attention goes right through to their objects (e.g., Tye, 1995).[16] In the notion, "right through to their objects," the implication is that we have made it safely to a nice, static object where there is no quality, where form is not quality, and ignored is the concept that the time-extended motions of objects may themselves be qualia. In other words, objects (as forms) are not

24

a problem of qualia. Therefore, in the debate, the origin of the image of the external world, assuming it is populated with forms – the table of the kitchen, its chairs, the squares on the surface of the kitchen floor – is not considered the problem, only the qualities associated with these forms – the "oak-brown" of the table, the "white" of the chairs, the "blue" of the floor.

The problem here is that Galileo is wrong. Form can no more be assigned to the quantitative – it is no more computable – than any other aspect of the perceived world. Form is equally a quality. The wobbly not-cube is a quality, the rotating cube another, just like Hardcastle's ever-so-gently waving curtains or the patrons shifting in their seats. We shall soon see that the *uncertainty* introduced by velocity flow fields and the aperture problem that we saw in the previous chapter is only a reflection of the inherent uncertainty of motion or time in general. If form is not computable, it can no more be accounted for by any computer or neural network architecture than any of the other aspects of the world that are termed "qualia." This is to say that the origin of *everything about the image of the external world* is equally a mystery of qualia. In other words, put simply, it is the origin of the entire image of the external world – any image – that is the problem.

Form, we have seen, cannot be divorced from motion. "Form," we saw Bergson note, "is only a snapshot of a transition." But the classic metaphysic, given its great impetus by Galileo and its apparent usefulness in scientific explanation, is incapable of truly describing motion or change. This is to say, it is incapable of handling *time*. To solve the hard problem, that is the origin of the image of the external world, the classical metaphysic must be abandoned, and concomitantly, we must revise our model of time and its relation to mind.

Zeno in the Metaphysic

An invariant, we said, defined over the flow of time does not exist in an "instant" of time. The form of the strobed, rotating cube does not exist in an instant or a single strobe. The adiabatic invariant defined over wielding the spoon does reside in an instant. This is to say there is no instantaneous local or global "state" of the brain in which such an invariant exists. In this, the uncertainty introduced by the aperture problem is simply an expression of the fundamental uncertainty introduced by the flow of time itself. Psychology then shares a problem with physics. The root of the problem for our theories is this conceptual framework of the abstract space of the classical metaphysic in which the very notion of an "instant" takes its meaning. Physics, we shall see, has steadily been dissolving this framework.

As noted earlier, the classical description of motion is an infinite regress. Between each pair of static points occupied by a moving object, to account for the motion, we must insert another trajectory or line, itself divisible into a set of static points – ad infinitum. This principle of infinite divisibility, or better, a *space* that is infinitely divisible, Bergson argued, is at the root of Zeno's paradoxes. If the steps of Achilles are viewed in terms of the infinitely divisible space he traverses, they can be infinitely successively halved – he never catches the hare. The arrow in flight, occupying successive spatial points, "never moves." Motion, Bergson argued, must be treated as *indivisible*. We cannot confuse the infinitely divisible space traversed – the trajectory – with the motion. The arrow moves in an indivisible motion. It is never at a particular point. Achilles moves with indivisible steps; he most certainly catches the hare.

It is probably quite commonly assumed that these paradoxes have been resolved by modern concepts of mathematics. Chris Nunn offhandedly refers to Zeno's arguments as, "a misguided stance that eventually stimulated constructive thinking."[17] Keith Devlin states matter-of-factly that "resolutions were found" only in the nineteenth century when mathematicians came to grips with the notion of infinity.[18] This faith is misplaced. The mathematical device of taking the "limit" of an operation is not an answer. Thus we could take the limit "at infinity" of Achilles' successive slices of the distance between he and the tortoise, allowing us to calculate an ultimate overtaking. This is a common "resolution" of this paradox and we'll revisit it below. But this is only mathematical convention, a hand waving, defining away the problem, for if infinity means infinity, the overtaking does not happen under Zeno's conditions. The most prominent attempt to resolve the paradoxes along lines other than Bergson's, was Russell's (1903).[19] Russell, who happened to be one of Bergson's greatest critics, sought to recast Zeno's arguments into an arithmetical framework. But Russell's "resolutions" are most curious. To begin with, Russell, probably to Zeno's amazement, agrees on the "facts" of the paradox:

> After two thousand years of continual refutation, these sophisms were reinstated, and made the foundation of a mathematical renaissance, by a German professor, who probably never dreamed of any connection between himself and Zeno. Weierstrass, by strictly banishing infinitesimals, has at last shown that we live in an unchanging world, and that the arrow, at every moment of its flight, is truly at rest. The only point where Zeno probably erred was in inferring (if he did

infer) that, because there is no change, therefore the world must be in the same state at one time as at another. This consequence by no means follows.

How an unchanging world can be different at successive moments, Russell does not explain. Russell proceeds to "resolve" each paradox, with Zeno's fourth paradox absolutely untouched. In this paradox Zeno asks us to imagine a body moving at a certain speed (Figure 2.1, object B). It passes two other bodies, one at rest (object A), one moving towards it at the same speed (object C). During

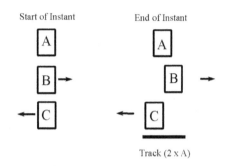

Figure 2.1. Zeno's Fourth Paradox

the same time (duration) that it passes a certain length of the resting body, it passes double the same length of the body moving towards it. Zeno concludes, with an in-your–face substitution of the space traversed for the duration, that a "duration is the double of itself." Russell's "resolution" is to agree that this has its exact analog in an arithmetic paradox he has developed. As far as the time aspect of Zeno's argument, Russell states that the best we can say is that at one instant the bodies were in one alignment, and in the next, they were in another, and that we cannot say what happened in between.

In point of fact, Russell left the core of Zeno's conundrums untouched, strewing problematic statements about time along the way. (He was to further backtrack and alter opinions in 1911). It is an unfortunate fact that Bergson's resolution has been in the meantime neglected. It was held consistently throughout his works: the paradoxes arise from the false assumption that motion and time are divisible in infinitum, i.e., that time is merely a form of space.

Physics and the Metaphysic

It is often held that quantum physics applies only at the micro level, not at the classical level wherein the processes occur which psychology addresses (e.g., Simon, 1995; Pinker, 1997).[20] Others, for example Hameroff and Penrose, argue that quantum mechanics indeed applies in brain processes.[21] Both sides fail to appreciate the implications for time residing in modern physics. Physics, in fact, has gradually rid itself of the notion of a trajectory. DeBroglie, commenting on Bergson and on the implications of Heisenberg's uncertainty, had already noted that in essence the attempted measurement of a velocity is

27

projecting the motion to a point in our abstract spatial continuum, and in doing so – we have lost the motion.[22] Thus Bergson noted, over forty years before Heisenberg, "In space, there are only parts of space and at whatever point one considers the moving object, one will obtain only a position."[23] Feynman and Hibbs provided a proof that the motion of a particle is continuous, but not differentiable.[24] Nottale, noting this, argues that we must abandon the notion that space-time is differentiable.[25] Nottale is referencing the geodesics (curves) that describe the motions of all particles in space-time – obviously a huge, sweeping scope – and his theory treats these curves as fractal, i.e., they are irregular and constantly changing at every scale; there are no straight lines. In the awesome implications of the fractal world, "at every scale" means that anywhere one looks at one of these curves, at the most infinitesimal of scales, one will find an inflection point, hence these curves are non-differentiable – there is no velocity derivable at an instant. In the general non-mincing of words of Nottale, "space-time is non-differentiable." This is an overturning – along with the critique of Bergson – of what has hitherto been a mainstay of the theory of motion in the classic metaphysic.

The essence of differentiation is division, say of the slope of a triangle or of a motion from A to B, into successively smaller units, taking the "limit" of what is in fact an infinite operation, that is, employing a mathematical technique to arbitrarily cease. To state that space-time is non-differentiable another way, we may say the global evolution of the matter-field over time is non-differentiable; it cannot be treated as an infinitely divisible series of states. Thus Lynds (*Foundations of Physics Letters*) now argues, echoing Bergson, that there is no precise, static instant in time underlying a dynamical physical process.[26] If there were such, motion and variation in all physical magnitudes would not be possible, as they (and the universe itself) would be frozen static at that precise instant, and remain that way. At no time, then, is the position of a body (or edge, vertex, feature, etc.) or a physical magnitude precisely determined in an interval, no matter how small, as at no time is it not constantly changing and undetermined. It is a necessary tradeoff – precisely determined values for continuity through time. As Lynds argues, it is only the human observer (mentally immersed in the abstract space) who imposes a precise instant in time – a static conceptual backdrop – upon a physical process. There is no wave equation, no equation of motion, no equation of physics that is not subject to this indeterminacy.

To return this for a moment to Zeno, as I noted earlier, when the instant is ultimately reduced (if ever possible) in this infinite division process to a mathematical point, the theory of motion in the metaphysic is shown as incoherent. The mathematical point is the instant reduced to an indivisible extent. This instant does not have a start point and an end point between which the arrow can move. If it did, it could be divided – a start half and an end half – and it would not be indivisible. If time then is made up of indivisible instants, instants by definition in which there can be no motion of the arrow, how then does the arrow move? It can only do so by being at successive intermediate points (between point A and point B) at successive intermediate times, i.e., it never changes its position over an instant, but only over intervals composed of instants, by occupying different positions at different times. In Bergson's critique, "movement is composed of immobilities," i.e., an absurdity.[27] But equally, this is the very condition of which Lynds spoke, for at such an instant, the universe would be frozen in time – all change is impossible. *It would require that the entirety of space be reborn*, or be re-generated, instant after instant. But this is simply yet another regress, the hidden process behind the regeneration of the entirety of space now becoming the issue. The fact is, reprising Lynds argument, there can be no instant of time underlying a body's motion. If there were, it could not be in motion.[28] Rather, at no time is the body or the evolution of the matter field itself not constantly changing, no matter how small the time interval. As such, at no time does the body have a *determined position*. There is not an instant of time underlying the arrow's motion at which it would occupy just one block of space or one tiny length of its spatial trajectory – its position is constantly changing.

For Achilles' pursuit of the Tortoise, as I alluded to above, the paradox is considered to have a solution wherein both the distance traversed and the time taken to do so are treated as an infinite geometric series with each successive term multiplied by 1/2, each term for distance and time thus growing successively smaller. Achilles traverses an infinite number of distance intervals and similarly an infinite number of time intervals before reaching his Tortoise-goal. Such a series converges, and by taking a limit as n (the number of terms) approaches infinity, we arrive at a finite answer for the time required. The motion has thus been structured as an infinite number of distance and time intervals, with the solution relying on a mathematical technique that conveniently gets rid of the infinities, i.e., it simply ignores that infinity *means* infinity while leaving the problem of Achilles' motion within the static instants, or for that matter, *the actual physical resolution of the infinities*, unsolved. In other words, there is no physical model of how either Achilles or the motion of the universal field of which he is an intrinsic part could resolve this, and unfortunately, when we are constructing a model of the brain, it is achieving a *physical* reality that is all important. Further, for each of these successive intervals, the scheme assumes that the velocity of Achilles in fact is *fixed* – determined. But the values of each successive term are not actually representative of the times at which Achilles is in a particular position, but rather of the fact that he is *passing through* the interval, however tiny it might be. The associated time (t) values and spatial (d) values, and thus the very derivation of velocity, is again reliant on the imposed static backdrop, a backdrop in which Achilles actually is passing through, but to which he has no intrinsic, or yes, *physical* relation. Whether we take a time value of 1 sec or 1/1000 sec (or however small), we have only an interval in which Achilles is passing through a certain distance interval (e.g., 1 m).

Even if we take a simpler approach, ignoring the "halving the distance" constraint of the paradox and simply computing the "catch-up" to the Tortoise by noting that Achilles, moving at 10m/sec for 20m covers this distance in 2 sec, and likewise the Tortoise, given a 10 meter head start and moving at 5m/sec will also take 2 sec, we are still assuming that each body has a precisely determined position at a given time, guaranteeing precision in the calculation, $\Delta d/\Delta t = v$. But as a body in motion is always constantly changing, it does not have a determined position at any time, no matter how small the interval, and equally then, it cannot have a determined velocity. Only the abstract, static backdrop or framework of the metaphysic allows us to think this. In fact, the only interval at which a velocity can be "determined" is the indivisible mathematical point – and this is not a motion at all. This then is another reason behind, and a meaning of, "non-differentiability." The static framework which supports differentiation is extremely useful, but it is not ultimately expressive of the reality of motion or of the time-evolution of the matter-field. This is a peek under a corner of the veil of "customary images relative to our needs" – a veil corner already lifted by Heisenberg's uncertainty.

The Brain in the Metaphysic

The brain is part of, *integrally* embedded in, a matter-field transforming in an indivisible flow. It cannot use in computations what, to it, does not exist. There can be no static features – edges, vertices, angles – found at an instant, within the brain. There are no instants. A set of cell assemblies, as in Hummel and Biederman's model (Chapter I), each capturing a feature of a rotating cube, and phase-locked with other assemblies, firing "instant" by "instant" to register to a higher order brick/geon cell, is not only begging a solution to the correspondence problem, it is an illusory architecture. It is describing nothing – nothing that actually exists in the brain. The brain is not operating in the classic metaphysic. In such a scheme, each point (or spatial view) in a succession of points on the curvilinear trajectory of the cube's rotation, would correspond to synchronous firing of the phase-locked assemblies, each instant specifying the geon underlying the cube's structure. But the result of the out-of-phase sampling of the strobe is sufficient to back the assertion that no such structure exists in any given sample (or instant). Were a sample sufficient, a rigid cube would always be specified. Further, a brain-driven sampling mechanism, to allow the specification of a cube-in-rotation, would have to be pre-adjusted to the symmetry period of the cube. This would require a form of pre-cognition. And what if there were two or more cubes rotating at different rates?

A "constraint" applied to velocity fields is simply another word for an invariance law. The series – rotating cube → figures of increasing serrated edges → fuzzy cylinder – expresses an invariance law defining figures of 4n-fold symmetry. The forms being specified are functions of the application of constraints on flowing fields. The structure of the forms reflects invariants existing over these time-extended flows. If "ineffability" is a mark of qualia (as per Daniel Dennett), the "ineffable" of form, as already noted earlier, is this: invariance over the time-extended, flowing field.[29]

The treatment of motion via an abstract space can provide no explanation for our everyday perception of *rotating* cubes or *twisting* leaves, i.e., for the very continuity and time-extension of the events we perceive. If the "present" instant of the leaf's twisting instantly becomes past, then we must store it in the brain to preserve it, for the "past" is, for the classical metaphysic, as Bergson noted, *the symbol of non-existence*. In this metaphysical scheme, only the always "present" brain (as *matter*) can store the past. As such, cognitive science abruptly faces the consequences Zeno forced his contemporaries to face. Ignoring all the problems of sampling already noted, if we presume the brain is taking and storing samples of the rotation or the twisting over time, we re-initiate the logical regress. The samples are static points – immobilities – like successive photographs of the twisting leaf laid out upon a desktop. If we imagine there is an "internal scanner" of the samples, we must now explain how the scanner perceives motion.

Sampling provides no answers. But why bother to invoke sampling in the first place? Ignoring the logic of the metaphysic yet again (which is standard procedure), we need only to imagine that there are *continuous* processes underlying the neural firing as the support for the ongoing perception. Taylor, for example, notes:

> The features of an object, bound by various mech-
> anisms to activity in working memory, thereby provide the
> content of consciousness of the associated object... In these

[neural activity loops], neural activity "relaxes" to a temporally stable state, therefore providing the *extended temporal
duration* of activity necessary for consciousness... [30]

The "extended temporal duration" of neural processes provides
the support here for the time-extended perception of the rotation. This is a
gratuitous assumption. By what right do we grant this temporal extension to
the material world, including the brain? If we can so easily grant it, how do we
place a limit upon it? Why should the limit not extend for our entire lifetime? Or
to the entire history of the matter-field? And why would the limit apply only to
the brain? On the other hand, we intently pursue the method whereby the brain
stores experience. Why? Because our implicit model of matter is tied to the
classical model of time. This model sees matter as existing only in the "present"
instant. But with motion (and these processes) taken as an infinitely divisible
trajectory, we end, in consonance with our metaphysic, with the logical time-
extent of the brain's neural processes as a mathematical point. At such a point,
there is no time. This is precisely the time-extent of a connectionist vector of
neural firing values; it the logical extent of the "extended temporal duration;"
it is the logical time-extent of the perception and time-extent of any event, that
is, no extent at all. As it is both lacking a theory of a memory that could "glue"
these state vectors (or instantaneous states) into a time-extended structure, and
is in any case treating these states as "instants" with their illusory reality, this
is the logical time-extent of any connectionist state, or symbolic computer
architecture state, or even neural state – within the classic, spatial metaphysic.

The Missing Glue of "Temporal Consciousness"

I said above that there is no theory of the "glue" for these state vectors
(or just – states), and in general this is true for the "instants" that must be held
together to support a perception of a stirring spoon or a falling leaf. There is
theoretical work on how the brain might "integrate" these instants to support
these perceptions, i.e., support *temporal consciousness* or the experience of
flow, often involving some sort of memory storage such as working memory,
just as we saw in Taylor's statement above. (For some of this, see Whitmann,
2011, Dainton, 2010).[31] There are several problems with this effort. Firstly,
as we have already seen above, the classic metaphysic stands as an absolute
barrier to this; it denies the possibility of flow. If logically you have nothing
ever in existence but an infinitely small instant, then unless you are explicitly
appealing to a different metaphysic and model of motion, or some other realm
in general ("consciousness"), integration processes avail nothing – these
processes are equally subject to the regress of the metaphysic's theory of

"motion." Then, being brief here on something we will discuss later, when it comes to events, the theory of memory has little idea on what it is actually storing in the first place, i.e., what would actually be stored in the working memory. The "snapshots," it is well understood, cannot be photograph-like images in the brain, say, of slices of the moving fly or rotating cube, nor for that matter is there any principle on which or how such slices are selected. This leads to the notion that there is storage of the mythical "features" of an event. There are no principled theories as to what these features actually are, or how they would be reassembled as the original event, let alone dealing with the fact that this disassemble-reassemble process must be occurring continually, repeatedly, to construct the fly in motion (at what scale of time?). Yet, the moving fly is simply being integrated into a static storage area, so we wonder how this equals the perception of a motion? Perhaps we are visualizing creation of a 4-D extended structure. But this – problematic as to "where" such a structure would exist – is still a static structure, and now requires, again, a "scanner" to create "motion." Finally, none of these models, to my knowledge, have even thought of attempting to deal with form where "features" exist (as invariance) only over flowing fields. How are these flowing fields stored? This has not even been a question.

This subject of "temporal consciousness," as I noted earlier, itself is nothing other than the problem of qualia, hence the discussion seems to proceed within a vague, implicit separation from (qualia-less) physics and physics' theory of (abstract) time. We are failing to understand that the flow of events in time – falling-twisting leaves, spinning cubes, buzzing flies – is equally the problem of qualia, and that explaining the memory that supports our perception of these dynamic events is a problem in fact with primacy over qualia – as it underlies all qualia.[32] The temporal consciousness research and discussion labor under the shadow of the classic metaphysic, the problem addressed by the research being stated as roughly, how can the present moment, being "virtually" instantaneous (it *is* instantaneous per the metaphysic), without past or future, yet be in our experience as having both a past and a leaning into the future? The effort of conceptualization becomes that of speculation on some piece of (static) memory storage, usually, again, "working memory," and associated processes of integration which in some way, vaguely specified, transform sets of (frozen) "events" in static storage into the experience of flowing events. Even where the theorist demands that the present moment be "extended," there is no explicit acknowledgement that the accepted metaphysic of science with its spatialized time and series of instants offers no justification for even this, and actually denies it. Hence, I think, the lack of addressing the conflict with the physical model of time in this literature, unless of course we simply accept the block universe of relativity (a position Dainton examines), at which point the discussion miserably devolves into how there can be the experience of motion at all. In either case, the subject of temporal consciousness is left floating in some other (non-physical) realm safe from the physicists (and for that matter, immunizing AI from the subject), vainly searching for a form of glue that binds instants, or even "extended instants" together. This is a state of affairs that must be resolved, and in the argument here, done so by (continued) fundamental changes in the meta-framework of physics.

In sum, we have the strange picture of a very confused theoretical effort when examined as to its clarity about its underlying metaphysic and the consistency of its use thereof. The framework of the abstract, homogeneous space and time is implicitly invoked to undergird the entire problem of qualia – the lack of quality in the material world including in the brain, the complete refusal to acknowledge any quality as a function of flow in time, the reduction of flow to a series of instantaneous snapshots, the incessant search to grasp how a set of extensionless instants (or snapshots) can become a perceived flow with time-extent in consciousness, the search for how the past instant – which must fall into non-existence – can be preserved in the "present" brain, which being matter, is the only thing always present, therefore existent. On the flip side, we see the constant – oblivious to the metaphysic – attempt to grant some extent in time to the brain via "continuous processes" or "reverberating loops," etc., or via "processes" using working memory to take static, stored snapshots (or whatever) into a perceived flow, or the surreptitious granting of temporal continuity to the syntactic manipulations of computer programs, such that it is not even questioned how a robot could see a cube "rotating," Always, the "glue" of the instants is either denied, searched for, or assumed – often all at once.[33]

There is a "glue," and we shall discuss it now.

The Temporal Metaphysic

That the classical treatment of motion is an infinite regress is one problem; there is another. As the classic metaphysic is further rarified, then, in the abstract continuum, the motion of any object is relative – I can move the object over the continuum or the continuum (or coordinate system) beneath the object. Motion now becomes *rest* or *immobility* purely on perspective. But in the material field, there must be *real* motion – trees grow, stars explode, coffee is stirred, couch potatoes get fat.

A real motion, such as the growth of a tree, taken, say, as a set of points, is a system of simultaneities, a *simultaneous causal flow*.[34] No arbitrary part of this motion can be relativized – declared at rest or motionless relative to the remainder of the moving (growing) system, nor can the motion of the whole of this flow be relativized – it cannot be declared at rest (halted) relative to some other system in motion. It is a *real*, not relative motion. We can model this motion or growth via the abstract space and its point-continuum, but the continuum has properties that tell us it is both meaningless to the real motion of the tree and not capturing the actual reality. Nor, we would quickly discover, is the tree as an object actually isolable from the rest of the dynamic flow of the universe.

Thus Bergson noted:

> Though we are free to attribute rest or motion to any material point taken by itself, it is nonetheless true that the aspect of the material universe changes, that the internal configuration of every real system varies, and that here we have no longer the choice between mobility and rest. Movement, whatever its inner nature, becomes an indisputable reality. We may not be able to say what parts of the whole are in motion, motion there is in the whole nonetheless.[35]

We must view the entire matter-field as in a *global* motion over time. We must "see the *whole* changing," Bergson argued, "as though it were a kaleidoscope." We want to ask if individual object X is at rest, while individual object Y is in motion. But both "objects" are simply arbitrary partitions, phases in this globally transforming field. As such, the "motions" of "objects" should be seen as *changes or transferences of state* – rippling waves if you will – within the dynamic motion of the whole. Bergson's positive characterization of this motion is that each "instant," like a note in a melody, permeates and penetrates the next, where each instant (note) reflects the entire preceding series – an organic continuity. In this characterization, unlike the equations of the classic metaphysic, time is clearly irreversible.[36]

This indivisible or non-differentiable motion is an elementary property of *memory* in the field's motion – each (now past) "instant" does not cease to exist as the next (the present) instant appears. It is this "primary memory" – an intrinsic attribute of the indivisible time-evolution or transformation of the material field – that supports our perception of "stirring" spoons, "twisting" leaves, "rotating" cubes. Quality is now inherent in this motion of the material field. At the null scale of time, the field is near the homogeneity envisioned by the classic metaphysic, but at ever larger scales of time where the oscillations of the field (e.g., the 400 billion/sec oscillations of the field as a "red" light wave) are "compressed" in the experience or glance of a moment, we obtain ever differentiating quality.

In this discussion, I have not mentioned our chief theory of time, physics' theory of special relativity, save only in this implicit point, namely that relativity, the premier exponent of turning rest into motion and motion into rest, is simply the logical extension of the classic metaphysic. In reality, special relativity as a theory of time has no ontological status. A theory with no ontological status is useless to a theory of mind, though of course there are theorists who have tried to integrate a theory of consciousness within relativity's structure. This subject – the interpretation of relativity – is an instructive one and I have addressed it elsewhere, but suffice it to say, the upshot is that special relativity is not relevant to the problems considered here.[37]

We are led then to the realization that the time-extent of these events in perception – the "rotating" cubes, the "twisting" leaves, the "spoons stirring coffee" – in fact must derive from the indivisible or non-differentiable motion of the material field. The reliance on this property of the motion of the field is true not only for the "rotation" of the cube, but even for its color, both qualities now seen as "optimal specifications" of the indivisible motion of the field.[38] But how is this optimal specification an image of the external world? That is the question.

The Origin of the Image of the External World

Grasping the true nature of the problem, it is often said, is to see the solution. The problem is the origin of the image – the time-extended image – of the external world. We know that nothing is stored or going on in the brain that even vaguely resembles an *image* of the external world – we see only neural-chemical flows. As Jeff Hawkins (*On Intelligence*), an AI/neural net theorist, describes it, we see only "a dark, quiet brain." Thus he notes:

> This is not to say that people or objects aren't really there. They are really there. But our certainty of the world's existence is based on the consistency of patterns and how we interpret them. There is no such thing as *direct perception*... Remember, the brain is in a dark quiet box with no knowledge

of anything other than the time-flowing patterns of its input fibers.[39]

This, by the way, is termed *indirect realism*. The objects of the world are considered to be really there in the world, but we are not actually seeing the objects *directly*, right where they are, where they reside in the external field, but only a brain-generated image thereof. Somehow, it is thought, these flowing patterns generate this image.

Somehow also, to "represent" the external world, these flowing patterns must initially "encode" it, for in these neural flows, the world is now in a form totally different from what we experience. Give a computer a camera to take light input from the external world – this input is transduced into a digital code. If it is a code – a neural code, a digital code – then as per any code, three dots, "...", can be an "S" in Morse code, the three blind mice, or Da Vinci's nose. That is, the question becomes what is the domain that the code is mapped to? And how could the brain map to its domain – the external world (the image) – without already knowing what the world looks like?

I prefer using the "coding" formulation for it is a more basic statement of the "problem of representation" and due to the fact that the confusion over the nature of this problem is endemic. There have been innumerable solutions proposed to the hard problem which are oblivious to the coding problem at their core. We cannot take the neural-encoded information, apply an "integrating magnetic field" and claim we have explained the image of the coffee-cup-being-stirred when we cannot begin to explain how a magnetic field can unfold a "digital-neural" code. Yet this has been argued by McFadden.[40] We cannot expect RoboMary, Dennett's theoretical robot who does not perceive color, to overcome this lack simply by "self-programming" the range of "color codes" in her "color registers." The coding problem yet remains.[41] Or suppose, as physicist Henry Stapp, that we see the brain as a time-evolving quantum system of possible states, the system description of which, due to the intrinsic dependence on the observer in quantum mechanics, can be argued to have consciousness integrally involved.[42] This abstract "consciousness" is supposed to be collapsing this system of possible states at each successive point in time (yes, at what scale of time?) to a particular state. But this is the end of the story. We must ask how this abstract consciousness has done any better than the "integrating magnetic field?" How does an abstract consciousness unpack the neurally encoded information, or the information when viewed as coded at the quantum level of the material world for that matter, such that it now becomes the image of the coffee cup with stirring spoon as in our perception? It does not, not unless you are somehow assuming beneath the scenes that this abstract consciousness is already somehow perception – the perception/consciousness/ image of the cup and spoon. But this is just assuming everything one is supposed to be explaining. In other words, in reality, as in all the "quantum" solutions offered to the hard problem, you now have only succeeded in coding the world in quantum states, i.e., a quantum code.

Whether or not it has been grasped that forms are equally qualia within this image and therefore the image, in toto, must be explained, this "coding" problem (yes, "representation" problem) for the image of the world has been as much a "hard" problem as that of the qualia in this image. But the forms, in effect invariants defined over flowing fields, require, as do all qualia, the abandonment of the classic metaphysic of motion and time; we need the indivisible motion characterizing the global motion of the universal field as per Bergson's temporal metaphysic. For the origin of this qualitative image of the dynamically transforming external world, Bergson had an elegant solution.

Already in 1896, Bergson had anticipated the essence of Gabor's 1947 discovery of holography by fifty years, a prescience that obscured the nature of his theory for his contemporaries. He realized that this dynamically transforming field is holographic – the state of each "point" in the field is the reflection of, carries information for, the whole (Figure 2.2). Technically, this field, at its null or "natural scale" of time, is *non-image-able*. Every point/event in the field is influenced by and reflects actions/forces from the whole. This vast, infinite influence, of which every "point" or every "object" in the field is a nexus, even for a single object, cannot, in its entirety, ever be *represented*. Thus, Bergson noted, every aspect of our notion of the material world is necessarily an "image," i.e., inescapably only a part of, a limited representation of the whole. The "atoms" of the material world are an image. The "brain" is an image. Its "neurons" are an image. How does one such image – the brain or its atoms – obtain a privileged position, gaining the power to represent the other images as image? But this is precisely what we let the representationalist do. The brain, equally a part of the abstract, homogeneous space, now described by whatever abstract image one chooses – atoms, molecules, neurons – and of the same order as these images, is given the inexplicable power to create an image of the external material field, an image now necessarily qualitative, with colors and forms, with time-scale and time-extent. It is a qualitative image that now by definition must reside in some ever-mysterious realm outside the abstract, homogeneous space. It is a crass psychophysical parallelism (cf. Bergson's critique on this, 1904), and the current debates on the subtleties of this inexplicable realm perpetuate this.[43]

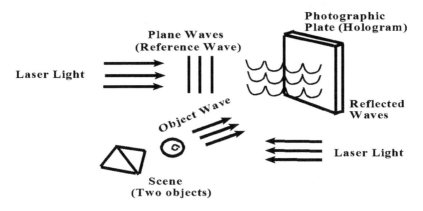

Figure 2.2. Constructing a hologram. Each point of the illuminated object/scene reflects a spreading, spherical wave, each such wave covering the entire hologram plate. This composite "object wave" forms an interference pattern at the plate with the reference wave from the laser. The information for each point of the object then is found everywhere on the hologram plate, and conversely, *the information for the entire object is found at each point on the plate.*

This was Bergson's solution: Noting that there is, and can be, no "photograph" or photographic image of the external field developed in the brain, he stated his vision of the holographic nature of the material field:

> But is it not obvious that the photograph, if photograph there be, *is already taken, already developed in the very heart of things and at all points in space.* No metaphysics, no physics can escape this conclusion. Build up the universe with atoms: Each of them is subject to the action, variable in quantity and quality according to the distance, exerted on it by all material atoms. Bring in Faraday's centers of force: The lines of force emitted in every direction from every center bring to bear upon each the influence of the whole material world. Call up the Leibnizian monads: Each is the mirror of the universe.[44]

But, as opposed to Pribram (1971), for Bergson, the brain is not simply a "hologram."[45] In the holographic process, several object waves, respectively reflected, say, from a pyramid/ball, a cup, a toy truck, and a cube can be recorded on a hologram plate, with the object wave from each being made to interfere with a reference wave of a unique frequency, e.g., f_1, f_2, f_3, f_4 respectively (Figure 2.3). A reconstructive wave, successively modulated to one of these original reference frequencies and beamed or passed through the set of interference patterns now superimposed and recorded on the hologram plate, is successively *specific to* the original source of the object wave, e.g., for f_3 it is specific to the toy truck, for f_2, the cup. To place Bergson's view then in modern terms, the brain is the *modulated reconstructive wave* "passing thru" the external, holographic matter-field.[46]

The dynamics of the brain must be viewed as supporting this very concrete wave passing through the holographic field, a wave "specific to" a past source in the field, that is, to a past portion and extent of the field's motion at a scale of time – a buzzing fly, or a heron-like fly, or a near-motionless fly. This portion is the "image." The "image" of perception, then, is neither "generated by the brain" nor "represented" nor encoded in the brain, it is simply a *diminution of,* a selection from, the whole – the whole being the holographic field. The dynamic state of the brain is simply "specific to" this subset of the field, or source within the field, and its motion. In other words, as Bergson noted, this field, given its holographic properties, and at the null scale of time, *is* perception, as he called it, *pure perception,* and the problem is not how perception arises, it is how it is *limited.*

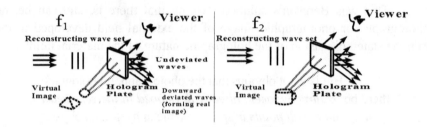

Figure 2.3. Holographic reconstruction. The reconstructive wave, modulated to frequency 1, reconstructs (or is "specific to") the stored wave front (image) of a pyramid/ball. The reconstructive wave, modulated to frequency 2, now reconstructs the wave front of the cup.

As noted above, the specification is always to the past of the field. The fly's wing-beats being specified have long gone into the "past," but the indivisible or non-differentiable motion of the field with its intrinsic, primary memory, supports this past-specification. The fly's motion with its wing-beats does not consist of a series of instants, each of which immediately enters the non-existence of the past as the "present" instant arrives. The image, too, is right where it says it is – in the field. It *is* the field – the (specified) past of the field – at a specific scale of time. Similarly, even one second of the strobed, rotating cube is in reality a vast series of (interpenetrating) states within the external, ever-transforming holographic field, with each "state" in this series containing a slightly different orientation of the cube. Under the out-of-phase strobe, the optimal specification is to a superposition of this series (at a scale of time) wherein the rigid edges and vertices are lost – the wobbly, plastic-like not-cube. Again, the brain is not projecting or generating an image. Even illusions – the great redoubt of indirect realism – the ubiquitous conception that the brain must be (somehow) generating the image – are but optimal specifications of events (sources) in the field, where the "image" is precisely where it says it is – in the external field. Even the lack of processing during the rapid eye-movement of a saccade from point to point on a scene, argued by indirect realists to prove that the brain must be generating an image to maintain the illusion of a continuous world, can be simply countered by noting that the reconstructive wave supported by the brain need not cease during a saccade.[47]

As argued earlier, the brain dynamics supporting the specification determines the (specified) scale of time, with the chemical velocities underlying these resonant dynamics being responsible for this. Begin increasing these velocities (or equivalently, the energy state of the body/brain) – the fly transitions, as noted earlier, from a buzzing fly, to a fly barely flapping his wings like a heron, to a motionless being, to a vibrating, crystalline ensemble of whirling particles, and on. Again, scale implies quality. We have specification of a qualitative field at a scale of time. In this view, then, what we have construed as abstract "computations" processing in the brain (and responding to the invariance structure of external events) are in fact integral to a very concrete, dynamical device supporting a very concrete wave form.

The Image as Virtual Action

The continuous modulation of the brain (as a wave) is driven by the invariance structure of the transforming external events, e.g., the velocity flows defined over the sides of the cube as it is rotating conjoined with its recurring symmetry period. Due to the continuous motion of the field, this information is always inherently uncertain – we have always an *optimal specification* of the past motion of the field. As we have seen, a reconstructive wave, passing through a hologram and successively modulated to different frequencies, successively *selects* information from the multiple, superimposed wave fronts originally recorded on the hologram, and successively specifies each source – a cube, a cup, a ball. If modulated to a non-coherent (non-unique or composite) frequency, it specifies a fuzzed superposition of the three. There is no "veridical" or God's eye view selection. So too, the brain, as a reconstructive wave, is selecting information from the ever transforming, holographic matter-field, where the principle of selection is based on information (invariants) relatable to the body's action systems.

41

Bergson had visualized his holographic field as a vast field of "real actions." Any given "object" acts upon all other objects in the field, and is in turn acted upon by all other objects. It is in fact obliged:

> ...to transmit the whole of what it receives, to oppose every action with an equal and contrary reaction, to be, in short, merely the road by which pass, in every direction the modifications, or what can be termed *real actions* propagated throughout the immensity of the entire universe.[48]

In his succinct phrase, *perception is virtual action,* i.e., perception is the display (or selecting out) of possible action in the field relative to the body. Following hard on the passage describing the "photograph developed in the very heart of things and at all points in space," he noted:

> Only if when we consider any other given place in the universe we can regard the action of all matter as passing through it without resistance and without loss, and the photograph of the whole as translucent: Here there is wanting behind the plate the black screen on which the image could be shown. Our "zones of indetermination" [organisms] play in some sort the part of that screen. They add nothing to what is there; they effect merely this: *That the real action passes through, the virtual action remains.*[49]

This, it can be argued, is a significance of the intimate feedback to and from the brain's motor areas to the visual areas, i.e., the modulation of the visual areas by the motor areas.[50] It is consonant with the finding that perceptions reflect the body's biologic action capabilities.[51] It is also likely the significance of the fact, insufficiently noted with the exception of Weiskrantz, that upon simply severing the tracks from the motor areas to the visual areas, the monkeys undergoing the procedure went blind.[52] With no connection to action, there can be no selection, no virtual action, and no vision.

There is also a deeper implication here in this principle of virtual action – ultimately testable. Earlier we considered the effects of introducing a catalyst into the chemical makeup of the body/brain dynamics, with effects on the perceptual "space-time partition." In the possibility of the fly becoming a heron-like fly, slowly flapping its wings, we already previewed the relativistic aspect of this principle. The fly is always presented to us at a certain scale of time. Let us complete the implications, for the time-scaling of the external image is not a merely subjective phenomenon – it is objective, and has objective consequences realizable in action.

Let us picture a cat viewing a mouse traveling across the cat's visual field (Figure 2.4). As we have seen, there is a complex, Gibsonian structure projected upon the cat's retina. There is the texture density gradient over the surface between mouse and cat. The size constancy of the mouse as it moves is specified by the constant ratio of texture units it occludes, while the tau value is specifying the impending time to contact with the mouse, with its critical role in controlling action. All this and much more is implicitly defined in the brain's "resonating" visual and motor areas. How is the information related to action we must first ask?

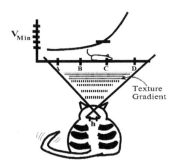

Figure 2.4. Hypothetical function describing the minimum velocity required for the cat to intercept the mouse at D.

Michael Turvey, a great theorist of perception and motor action, described a "mass-spring" model of the action systems. For example, reaching an arm out for the fly is conceived as the release of an oscillatory spring with a weight at one end. "Stiffness" and "damping" parameters specify the end-point and velocity of such a spring system. These constitute "tuning" parameters for the action systems of the body. The tuning parameters "bias" the hand-arm to release at certain velocity and stop, just as a coiled spring.[53]

The track (ABCD) along which the mouse runs projects upon the cat's retina (the little "h" in Figure 2.4). For computing the velocity of the mouse, we need: velocity = distance/time. Here the distance (d) being traversed on the retina is equivalent to h (the track/line projected on the retina). But if we wish to use h for distance in our equation to obtain the velocity of the mouse, we have an ambiguity. Similar to the problem with Berkeley's line ABCD in Figure 1.3 (Chapter I), we can move this horizontal track, along which the mouse runs, even closer to the cat, yet the horizontal projection (h) on the cat's retina is exactly the same. Any number of such mice/tracks at various distances project similarly to h; h is always the same. To solve for the velocity of the mouse, the needed muscle-spring parameters must be realized *directly* in the cat's muscular structures via properties of the optic array, e.g., the texture density gradient across which the mouse moves and the quantity of texture units he occludes.

At our normal scale of time, we can envision a function or curve (in Figure 2.4) relating the minimum velocity of leap (V_{min}) required for the cat to leap and intercept the mouse at D as the mouse moves along his path. The closer the mouse gets to D, the faster the cat must leap, until the minimum velocity is so high, it becomes impossible. But to compute the velocity of the mouse, the body needs one other critical thing. It needs a standard of time.

A physicist requires some time-standard to measure velocity. "Objective" time, it should be understood, is simply the noting of spatial simultaneities. Each time the earth returns to, and coincides with, a point in its orbit, a "year" has passed. This is the noting of a spatial simultaneity. The physicist then could use a single rotation of a nearby rotating disk to define a "second." Each time a mark on the rotating disk passes a certain point/mark on the table, a second is declared to have passed. But if an evil lab assistant were to surreptitiously double the rotation rate of this disk, the physicist's measures of some object's velocity would be halved, for example, from 2 ft/sec. to 1 ft/sec. The body though must use an internal reference system. Similar to the rotational velocity of the disk, this internal system must be an internal chemical velocity of the body. Such a system is equally subject to such "surreptitious" changes.

We noted that these velocities can be changed by introducing a catalyst (or catalysts) – an operation that can be termed, in shorthand, modulating the body's *energy state*. If I raise the energy state, the function specifying the value of V_{min} for the cat must change. There is a new (lower) V_{min} or minimum velocity of leap defined along every point of the object's trajectory, and therefore the object, *if perception is to display our possibility of action with ecological validity*, must appear to be moving more slowly. The mouse is perceived as moving more slowly precisely because it reflects the new possibility of action. If this were not the case, we would be subject to strange anomalies. The cat would leap leisurely; the mouse would long be gone. The cat's perception would not be ecologically valid; it would not specify the appropriate action available.

If the fly is now doing his heron imitation, flapping its wings slowly, the perception is a specification of the action now available, e.g., in reaching and grasping the fly perhaps by the wing-tip. In the case of the rapidly rotating cylinder with serrated edges (once a cube), if by raising the energy state sufficiently we cause a perception of a *cube* in slow rotation, it is now a new specification of the possibility of *action*, e.g., of how the hand might be modulated to grasp edges and corners rather than a smooth cylinder.

Again, the requirement comes to the fore for invariance laws holding across these space-time partitions of perception, in the rotating cube's case, the invariant figure of 4n-fold symmetry in any partition. The hand's modulation is guided by the same invariance information across partitions. Again we can consider the aging of the human facial profile – a very slow event in our normal partition (Figure 1.14). As Pittenger and Shaw showed, the aging transformation is a *strain* transformation upon a cardioid. We could imagine this aging event as greatly sped up, perhaps as though for a Mr. C who dwells in a much lower energy state where lifetimes pass very quickly. For Mr. C, watching another human, the head is transforming very quickly. Yet, for Mr. C, the aging event is specified by exactly the same invariance law, and his action systems will use the same information should he reach out to grasp the rapidly transforming head.

That perception is the display of possible action, that a heron-like fly specifies the possibility of grasping it by the wing-tip – this is a testable implication of the principle of perception as virtual action. The theory described here naturally generates it. I can think of no others that do, though in retrospect the implication will seem obvious. For the computer model of mind, it would merely be an ad hoc afterthought or theoretic "epicycle," not that the computer model can account for the image of the external world in the first place, let alone its scale of time. This is not to say that our current understanding of the "catalysts" at work is anywhere close or will be easy, but the prediction is testable in principle nonetheless.

AI and Real Virtuality

The deep implications of virtual action for AI should be understood. It is a standard view of AI, robotics and cognitive science that there is what is termed a "perception-action cycle." MIT Robotics professor, Illah Reza Nourbakhsh (*Robotic Futures,* 2013), describes it thus:

> We think of human intelligence as a quality that is living and interactive, embedded in the context of the world in which we function. Therefore intelligence depends on two things: being meaningfully connected to the environment, and having internal decision making skills to consider our circum-stances and then take action. The environmental connection is two-way, and we term the inputs as *perception* and the outputs back to the world as *action*. The internal decision making that

transforms our senses about the world into deliberate action is *cognition*.[54]

Thus we perceive, cognize and act, and cycle again. There is nothing exactly wrong with this – we indeed do perceive, then contemplate, then act – it just captures nothing of virtual action; the standard formulation is oblivious to this reality. The problem has already begun for AI in Nourbakhsh's statement on "being meaningfully connected to the environment." This is effected, for the human, by the fact that image of the external world is simultaneously virtual action. The image is both a display of the past and an orientation to the future. This is only achievable via a device operating within the temporal, non-classic metaphysic, a framework which, as we shall see soon enough below, supports the proper relation of subject and object.

We can put this in a context for robotics that makes the implication concrete. Place the problem in the context of the Turing Test, the nice test described by Alan Turing that he thought might be useful in determining when machine intelligence had arrived at the point where it is at least indistinguishable from the human. Turing envisioned a human asking questions of a computer behind a screen, with the computer printing out answers. But we can extend the test a bit. Thus an extended question might be, "Mr. Robot (or Mr. Human – we're not sure of course), please ingest this small pill or tablet I'm pushing under the curtain [containing a catalyst or set of catalysts of a certain strength]. Now please describe this little fly I am sending by you. Is it "buzzing," or flapping his wings like a heron, or an ensemble of whirling particles?" A Mr. Robot of course would be expected to give an answer within the understood human parameters of how the fly should appear.

Virtual Action – The Difficult Details

Bergson's selection principle – that a subset from the mass of information in the holographic field is selected via its relevance to the body's action – is the bedrock, the point where one must start in this model of vision. There must be a principle of selection. The implementation of this high level principle in the brain, therefore its precise meaning, is something that requires much more uncovering. Alva Noë, in his concept of vision as a function of "sensori-motor contingencies," seems extremely close to Bergson, if not in fact explicating virtual action more deeply. For Noë, a chair would have a set of sensori-motor actions associated with it – how we can sit on it, how it transforms as we move around it, or as we move it, and on. A ketchup bottle would have an entirely different set of actions, transforming differently as we rotate it, squeeze it, etc. It is this different set of actions, argued Noë, that underlie how the bottle looks versus how the chair looks. For Noë, there is no internal representation, no model of the chair nor of the bottle in the brain. The image of each arises because the body is in a dynamic action/feedback loop with the external field in which the bottle and chair reside, while the action contingencies set, for each, the character of the visual experience.[55]

We can see, given our discussion of Bergson, that Noë lacks the concept of the holographic field and the brain as a reconstructive wave within it – elements required to given any coherence to the notion that an image is accounted for by simply having objects in a relation to possible actions. Missing too is any consideration of the nature of dynamic form, as was discussed earlier, which indicate that transformations, laws, uncertainties and time are also part of the story. He is also simply assuming qualia via this dynamic loop, that is, he is taking a free ride on Bergson's metaphysic to account for qualia or the qualitative nature of the image.[56] He has in his theory, to my knowledge, no explicit overthrow of the classic metaphysic and its model of (abstract) time. But Noë's concept of sensori-motor contingencies appears to convey the need, when I look at the chair, for this set of potential actions to play, in some mini, reduced or virtual form, in the brain.

Andy Clark, in his attentive examination of Noë, called attention to the findings of Milner and Goodale on the role of the dorsal and ventral streams in the brain, and the phenomenal effects of damage to each stream.[57] Each "stream" is sourced originally from the optic nerve, and comprises a pathway of areas in the brain, one (the *dorsal*) branching from the primary visual area (V1) and projecting to the posterior parietal (PP) cortex, the other, the *ventral*, branching from V1 and projecting eventually to the inferior temporal (IT) cortex. The dorsal stream appears tuned with information to carry out the fine details of action, as when I pick up a letter, rotate it and put it into a mailbox slot at the post office. The ventral appears to carry representations of objects oriented to higher level operations – "comparing, sorting, classifying" or the selection of possible actions. This latter, the selection of possible actions as information in this stream, Clark now termed a "sensori-motor summarization," i.e., a high-level or virtual summary of a set of actions.

Phenomenonally, Milner and Goodale discussed a woman (identified as "DF") with damage to areas of the ventral stream, who reported that she could not "see" the orientation of a slot (like our mailbox slot), yet could rotate and insert a letter precisely into the slot. This indicates that the dorsal stream (undamaged in her case) carries information sufficient for effecting precise action, yet without conscious vision, and in fact has nothing to do with conscious vision. On the flip side, folks with optic ataxia, a condition which results from damage to areas of the dorsal stream, would be able to see the slot and its orientation, but be unable to rotate and insert the envelope, i.e., conscious visual awareness, but without the capability for finely attuned action. For Milner and Goodale (and Clark), this means that the ventral stream (and its representations of objects) is responsible for conscious vision, and of course, as Clark noted, this called into question Noe's notion of a "playing-out" of sensori-motor contingencies as the undergirding for conscious vision.

We can leave it to Milner and Goodale and to Clark to explain how the "representations" in the ventral stream – encoded in their chemical flows – mysteriously become the image of the external world. It is important to note that in Clark's notion of "sensori-motor summarizations" in this ventral stream we are still very close to Bergson's virtual action. The curious implication is, if this profound dichotomy of the functions of the two streams indeed stands, that in regards to action in varying scales of time, if one were to increase the velocity of processes in the ventral stream but not in the dorsal, i.e., not introduce a *global* change in process velocity, one would see the heron-like fly, but could only act as though it were the buzzing fly; one could not grasp the fly by the wing. But this sharp dichotomy of functions is not truly settled. Milner and Goodale allow that there must be connections between the streams, while Gallese, on the basis of his findings (which also correlate phenomenal evidence with the locations of neural damage), argues for the existence of a *ventral-dorsal* stream.[58] This pathway, part ventral, part dorsal (therefore involving action), Gallese sees responsible for the organization of actions directed towards objects (as in rotating the envelope towards the slot), but also for space and action perception and conscious visual awareness. For example, a lesion on one side of the brain (a unilateral lesion) of the ventral premotor cortex of the monkey, including area F4, (i.e., part of the ventral-dorsal stream and which controls the perception of space close to the person or our body), produces both motor deficits and perceptual deficits. Perceptually, a piece of food moved around the monkey's mouth, in the visual space opposite the side of the lesion, does not elicit any behavioral reaction. Similarly, when the monkey is fixating a centrally placed stimulus, the introduction of food in the space opposite the side of the lesion is ignored. In contrast, stimuli presented outside the animal's reach (in far extra-personal space) are immediately detected. There is a similar pattern of phenomena when there is a lesion to areas responsible for vision in far extra-personal space, that is, space beyond our near-the-body (or peri-personal) space.

Gallese quoted the philosopher, Merleau-Ponty, who noted that space is, "…not a sort of ether in which all things float.... The points in space mark, in our vicinity, the varying range of our aims and our gestures."[59] In other words, the abstract space of the classic metaphysic is meaningless to the body and perception. For Gallese, why is action important in spatial awareness?

> Because what integrates multiple sensory modalities within the F4-VIP neural circuit is action embodied simulation… Vision, sound and action are parts of an integrated system; the sight of an object at a given location, or the sound it produces, automatically triggers a "plan" for a specific action directed toward that location. What is a "plan" to act? It is a simulated potential action.

There is clearly much to be dug out regarding the implementation of virtual action and/or Clark's sensori-motor summarizations. I agree with Clark that the concept of constantly running mini-simulations of actions as our eyes scan the table with its cups and plates and silverware (and at what scale of time? Every $1/10^{th}$ second?) becomes incoherent. But there is a possibly illuminating question as to how the summarizations are initially formed. Clark's "summarizations" are not far from what is known as action "syntagms." For, example on seeing a spoon, I automatically reach out, grab and lift it to the mouth. These syntagms, formed early in development, are gradually suppressed over the course of time via neural inhibition mechanisms, but there are clinical cases of neural damage where these suppression or inhibition mechanisms are damaged, and the automatic actions take place involuntarily in the presence of an object – I can't restrain myself from reaching for and lifting the spoon when I see it. While this level of grosser action on an object is only one form of the range of actions or transformations via action envisioned by Noë, the possibility of numerous suppressed syntagms, all semi-active or resonating so to speak as we view a scene with its objects, gives a glimpse of what the dynamic state of the brain in vision might involve. We should note finally that the concept of a linear "stream" of information flow (in the dorsal or in the ventral) is likely simplistic. Again, rather, we are talking about dynamic feedback among areas and ultimately a very concrete dynamics.

The Uncertainty of Illusion

Let us do some further discussion on illusions. This subject is the great sticking point for indirect realism and the holders that "all is generated by the brain." If direct realism is construed as simply seeing "what is there" in the matter-field, this view is untenable in the face of multiple lines of evidence. As we have seen, given the inherent uncertainties of information with which it deals, the brain is in fact computing an optimal percept. On this basis alone, the brain's specification of events in the matter-field is based on probabilities. But to construe direct realism as implying that we simply see "what is there" is in fact simply an expression of what is termed *naïve* realism. Given the inherent uncertainty of measurement, nothing is simply "there." Further, as we have just seen, it is always a specification of the past, therefore, already a memory.

This aspect – that of perception already being a memory – requires me to anticipate the next chapter slightly. If the brain supports a reconstructive wave in a holographic field, then this wave is also capable of reconstructing past events in this field. The invariance laws or invariance structure of a "present" event is simultaneously creating a wave that is reconstructive of past events with similar structure. Bergson thus argued that perception is always permeated with memory experience (he saw the "flow of memories" to perception as a "circuit"). The initially indistinct words to a song, with a bit of a clue, from then on are perceived as "perfectly clear" whenever we subsequently hear the song. The "bear" near the trail in the woods, seen to be a tree stump on closer approach, would also be a reconstructed experience, now fused in the perception. This is already a form of "filling in," a phenomenon considered very problematic for direct realism. Spatial filling in can occur when a blind spot in the visual field (perhaps due to neural damage, say, a scomata) is not perceived by the subject as an empty area because the brain fills it in by completing the surrounding pattern.[60] A black line containing, in actuality, a small gap, might be seen as complete. The natural question, as asked by the philosopher, John Smythies, is how is it possible to say that the area (e.g., the line) on either side of the blind spot is seen directly, but the gap (now seen as part of the line) is constructed (or seen indirectly)?[61]

The answer is "quite easily." It can easily be both. We may call this "constructive directness" if we like. The perception is always a specification of some past state of the field. A reconstructive wave passing through a hologram can specify simultaneously in superposition, wave fronts recorded at Time 1 and Time 2. What is specified is always dependent upon a modulation pattern. This pattern may use or embody some probabilistic constraints or rules, but it is always a specification of a past form of the holographic field. It can easily include material from memory – it *always* does. This material – events of the past coalescing as images – is no more generated by the brain than the original perceptions.

Yarrow et al. experimented with viewing a silently ticking clock, where, during saccades (rapid eye movements), the second hand appears to take longer than normal to move to its next position (as though the hand briefly stopped).[62] Under such conditions, objects presented during a saccade are actually invisible. The visual system appears to be shut down for an instant, but the brain computes what we would have seen during the saccade. Smythies notes that it would be most implausible to suggest, per direct realism, that we see directly only when our eyes are not in saccadic movement.[63] But the answer is that the perception is as direct as ever. During the clock hand's motion relative to a receptive eye, information from the field is taken in, the optimal percept computed, the reconstructive wave/ specification is still to the past. During the saccade, the reconstructive wave does not cease – it continues to specify a state of the field based on the information available and the probabilistic algorithm employed by the neural architecture.

Kevin O'Regan is similar in this respect.[64] He noted that an entire page of surrounding text can be changed during a saccade without notice while someone is reading as long as the 17-18 character window the eye is focused upon is undisturbed. He opted to conceive of the environment as an "external memory store" to explain the persistence of the perceived world during saccades. However, the scale of time of this "external" store would be very problematic – would an external fly look like the buzzing fly of our scale, or be flapping his wings like a heron or be an crystalline ensemble of whirling of electrons? We can better say that the reconstructive wave and/or the pattern supporting it within the brain is not affected by a substitution of the surrounding text during a saccade with its minute information gathering capacity, the brain's specification yet being to the same states of the past.[65]

O'Regan's observation was extended under the heading of "change blindness."[66] Experiments demonstrated this dramatically. Under the right conditions, an actor in a gorilla suit could walk across a tennis court in the middle of a tennis match which subjects were observing on video, and yet be utterly invisible. Subjects were astounded when the gorilla was pointed out. This led to speculation that our perceived world, in total, is an "illusion," again, simply generated. But that the brain chooses not to employ certain information, such that the specifying reconstructive wave contains nothing about the field relative to the gorilla, is insufficient reason to call into the question the directness of perception. There is, in fact, *always* a ton of information in the holographic matter-field – the sea of real actions – that is not being used, and not part of the virtual action being specified.

I should note here how similar the "invisible gorilla" is to a form of hypnosis. The great hypnosis expert, Cleve Backster, on stage, gave a hypnotic suggestion to a subject picked from the audience such that Cleve would be invisible. To the subject, Cleve was invisible, even to the point of being completely freaked out as he observed a cigarette, which Cleve lit up, as floating unsupported with its smoke, in mid-air. Again, this can be looked at as simply a modulated or filtered specification, not something that implies the brain generates all reality.

This optimal percept, based upon invariance information in the field and probabilistic constraints, is, under ecological conditions, extremely veridical, as indeed it must be for survival. It is not nearly as illusory or unreliable as the indirect realist emphasizes. The golf ball, sent rolling by Tiger Woods across the undulating green and grain, is guided by precise specification of the world. The indirect realist is wont to emphasize the existence of illusions – the Poggendorff, the Ponzo, etc. – to enhance the constructivist implications for perception. Gibson long argued that these are artifacts, that given an ecological environment, rich with information (invariants), these don't happen, the experience being again "directly specified." In fact, some "illusions" would count as quite valid percepts from a Gibsonian perspective (e.g., the Ponzo, Figure 2.5, where the distant object would occlude far too many texture units to be the same size as the near object). Perception theorist, Irvin Rock, opposed Gibson at every turn, arguing for indirect perception.[67] Often his experiments

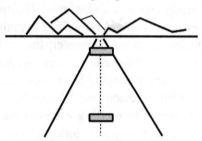

Figure 2.5. The Ponzo "Illusion." The far object on the road looks much larger than the near object, yet both are exactly the same size on the drawing and on the retina. Ecologically, in the real world, the far object would indeed be larger.

involved information-deprived experimental setups, destroying Gibson's texture gradients, for example, by forcing the observer to judge distances when looking into a darkened room through a peephole (say, the distance of two rods located at different distances on the floor, as the cups in Figure 1.4). He would then argue that inferences or mental operations must be involved. That information-deprived or ambiguous setups exist which demand reliance on probabilistic specifications is certain, in fact, as we have seen, all is probabilistic, however the specification is still to past states or transforms of the matter-field.

Subject and Object in the Temporal Metaphysic

Given the holographic properties of the field, where the state of each "point/event" reflects the mass of influences from the whole, simultaneously therefore a state of very elemental "awareness" of the whole, and given the field's indivisible motion defining a primary memory, there is implied, at the null scale of time, an elementary form of awareness, a taut web as it were, defined throughout the field. This is a field property. It is not elementary "constituents" with ad hoc intrinsic and extrinsic properties that must be "composed." This "constituent" view is the old metaphysic, itself spawned from perception's derivation of "objects" and "motions," still speaking. The brain's specification, then, is simultaneously to a time scale-specific form of this vast, taut "web" of awareness defined throughout the field at the null scale. *There is no one – no homunculus – in the brain looking at the image.* This mode of reconstructive wave specification, we should hypothesize, holds for frogs, for chipmunks and for humans.

At the null scale of time, there is no difference between subject and object. There is one continuous field, a field with *extensity* – it is not infinitely divisible, it does not consist of mutually external elements. Run the scaling transformation in reverse: The fly transitions – initially waves in the field undifferentiated from the perceiving subject, it becomes a crystalline, vibrating being, then becomes the motionless fly, then the heron-like fly slowly flapping his wings, then the buzzing fly of normal scale. Subject is differentiating from object. This is the meaning of Bergson's statement:

> *"Questions relating to subject and object, to their distinction and their union, must be put in terms of time rather than of space."*[68]

The body/brain as a modulated reconstructive wave passing through a holographic universal field, specific to a subset, to a time-scaled image of the past motion of the field's non-differentiable motion, and reflective of possible action – this is the beautifully elegant solution of the universe to the problem of specifying an image of the external world for its living organisms. Fifty years before Gabor, this was Bergson's remarkable insight.

Gibson and Bergson

What has been described here is a theory of "direct perception" or direct realism. Direct realism holds that the objects of perception are precisely where they say they are – in the external field. We are looking at the objects. They are not merely images of a very real world, but are yet only images generated mysteriously by the brain as the indirect realist holds. In its principle of "optimal specification," this is far from a naïve realism. Gibson's ecological theory is its natural complement. For Gibson, as we saw, an invariant defined only over time, e.g., over a flow field, cannot exist in an "instant," that is, it cannot exist in the mythical, frozen instant of the classic metaphysic. It is not a "bit" that can travel along the nerves. This is why he gravitated to his notion of the *resonating* brain where such invariants or complex structures of invariants are supported over the resonant feedback of the brain, i.e., over a continuous, indivisible flow.

Gibson was given to saying that this resonating brain is "specific to" the external environment. But (to Gibson) there are no representations, there are no images arising within this resonating brain, no more than there can be one (an image) in a computer, in its bit patterns or computations – unless one is committing the error of supposing or attributing the existence of an image on the basis of being an (interpreting) external observer. But yet, here is an image of the environment – what my resonating brain "is specific to" – my desktop surface with its computer and its lamp and its miniature green John Deere farm tractor. Unless one is going to dismiss this as a "delusion of introspection" – which is absurd – the origin of this image of the external world must be explained. One needs some sort of *physical mechanism or process* to explain how this image – an image of an external material field that is a vast interference pattern and which at the null scale of time looks absolutely nothing like golf balls or putting greens or buzzing flies – comes to be.

This difficulty is obscured in the Gibsonian literature. Both Anthony Chemero (*Radical Embodied Cognitive Science*) and Louise Barret (*Beyond the Brain*) have attempted to explicate Gibson's concept of direct perception. For Barret, virtually the entirety of the explanation is summed up in the statement that the brain (and body) should be viewed "as part of a loop" with the environment in the process of information pickup.[69] But an AI theorist would be quite happy to declare his robot-machine "in a loop with the environment." There is no explanation of the origin of the image here. Chemero rejects the claim that the mind is a computer or that there is any need for internal representations to explain perception. He (as does Barret) uses Gibson's notion of *affordance structures*, where an affordance is a relational property between the organism's action capabilities and information in the environment. For example, the texture gradient information specifying a stretching surface in conjunction with action capabilities of the organism may jointly result in specifying a "walk-on-able" surface, or a "slither-on-able" surface, etc. That is, there is inherent *meaning* in this relationship. It is a concept highly correlated with Bergson's "virtual action." Thus he states, ecological science is "about explaining experience," and, "our experience of the world as being meaningful [via affordances] is inseparable from our experience of it as looking (sound, smelling, etc.,) in particular ways." If this is your entire explanation of the origin of the image of the external world, and for Chemero it is, you have said how the image is meaningful, but nothing about how this experience is an image, i.e., an image of a matter-field which, as a field, looks nothing like our experience.[70] You have simply explained things away. Your embodied science doesn't need an account of qualia (as Chemero argues), yes, but only if you can actually explain the origin of the qualitative image, and only, I would add, if you have significantly altered our model of space, time and matter as opposed to the classic metaphysic. Like Gibson and those invariants in the optic array to which the brain is resonating and allowing the brain to be "specific to" the external environment, there is actually no explication of how, for a brain in which there is nothing like an image of the environment, this "specific to" actually results in an image.

This is why I am stating here that Gibson must be placed within Bergson's holographic framework. His "specific to" must be taken in the same way as a reconstructive wave passing through a hologram (which holds a myriad of recorded wave fronts) is "specific to" one selected source or a combination thereof. It is Bergson's temporal metaphysic and his holographic insight that is required to make Gibson's theory of direct perception coherent.

...And Heidegger

Let me recall my earlier comment (Introduction) on the fact that Winograd (with Flores) had moved to the concept of the "situatedness" of a being in the world, rejecting the view of cognition as symbolic manipulation of internal representations that are understood as referring to objects and properties in the "external" world. They noted Heidegger's thoughts as such:

> Heidegger makes a more radical critique, questioning the distinction between a conscious, reflective, knowing "subject" and a separable "object." He sees representations as a *derivative* phenomenon, which occurs only when there is a breaking down of concernful action. Knowledge lies in the being that situates us in the world, not in reflective representation.

There is only one way to understand this rather abstruse passage. Winograd's "situatedness" is precisely Bergson's union of subject and object "in terms of time." Heidegger was well aware of Bergson. In Bergson's model of perception, there are no internal "symbols." There are no internal symbols for the "blocks" of the external micro-world that SHRDLU (were SHRDLU a conscious being) is "looking" at; there are no internal symbols for the "buzzing" fly or the rotating cube. The "symbols" *are the objects*, precisely where they are *specified* to be, externally, in the flowing matter-field. The "symbols" *are* the blocks, right where they appear to be; the "symbol" *is* the fly right where he is buzzing; the symbol *is* the cube, right where it is rotating.

What we normally term "symbols" – the symbols or memory *images* we use in representing the world – only arise when we have to go back into memory, when we have to redintegrate, when we have to recall an event or events, when we have to "re-present" a piece of the world to ourselves via an image of memory. This "re-presenting" state is now Heidegger's "breakdown of concernful action," for we are now reflecting, not *acting* without representation on the concrete objects of the world, as when we are simply and naturally picking up the blocks, reaching for the fly or driving down the flowing road. The proponents of situatedness and the related notions of ecological psychology, embeddedness, embodiment and "extended mind" have developed many valuable concepts that must ultimately be incorporated into our theory of mind, but lacking a clear understanding of the origin of the image of the external world, they have carried the absence of representations or internal symbols in perception all the way – all the way to cognition and thought itself. In this effort, as we shall see, they fly in the face of our intuitions of how we think and remember, ignore the great problem of explicit memory, surrender any decent theory of memory recall, and along with AI place the status of the memory image in limbo, mightily confuse the subject of thought and cognition, and even confuse the AI folks (who rightly cling to some notion of representations in cognition) on the whole subject of thought.

All this is why robotics is inescapably tied to the problem of consciousness, and in turn, to the relation of subject and object, and thus to the flow of mind in a non-differentiable time.

The Requirement for a Concrete Dynamics

As a general framework for a model of the brain in perception, this has certainly been a very high level "specification." The holographic field has a decent status in physics (Bekenstein, 2003; Bohm, 1980), but obviously the work of conceptualizing the brain and its operations as forming, in toto, a reconstructive wave in this field has received no attention – no more than, circa

1945, how the brain could be a computer.[71] I will not be offering any insights into the physics of this, and physics (and engineering) it would be. My major counsel here is, and will be in the following chapters, that the model of the brain with its processes as comprising a reconstructive wave must incorporate the fact that the brain is responding to ecological invariance laws – that what must be included in any description or model is how this processing/wave is incorporating these laws for the specification of events. It is *quite useless* to be offering models such as the "quantum brain interacting with the quantum level events of the Zero-Point field and (say, via Fourier transforms) projecting an image" (though there is no "projection") and stopping there, while ignoring the mass of invariance information in the ecological event that the brain is actually processing and which *must*, ultimately, be mapped to any quantum level (and beyond) description. In the first place, by the principle of virtual action, it is this ecological invariance structure as *information* that is being used by the action/motor areas of the brain to modulate the visual areas and select, from the totality of real actions in the quantum/holographic field, that portion that is specified as virtual action (i.e., an image of the field). It *is this invariance information at the ecological level* – and ecological invariance laws are the true *information* – that we need for perception theory, memory theory and cognition.

Can such a device be artificially constructed? Yes, if what is required to create the requisite, real, concrete dynamics can be built in artificial materials, as opposed to biological materials. One does not build the real dynamics required for an AC motor out of rubber bands and toothpicks. Nor can its operative dynamics be built in the abstract space and time of the classic metaphysic. This unfortunately is the case for both the connectionist net and the symbolic computer architecture – their operative dynamics (if it can be called such) is adequately described by these abstract spatial operations, and the same operations can be carried out, as said above, by, say, an abacus or a read head and infinite tape. The concrete dynamics are irrelevant, only the abstraction is important. This is not the case for the concept sketched here.

It is this requirement for a true, concrete dynamics that has been utterly missed by Chalmers. It supports his belief in a rather soon-to-be-achieved singularity. In one thought exercise, he gradually substituted a demon for each neuron in a neural net.[72] Each demon merely noted the input to the neuron on a sheet of paper, used the weighting algorithm to determine the output, and passed the output figure to the next demon. Ultimately, all the demons were replaced by one demon racing around, writing inputs and outputs on myriads of sheets of paper. This [pure symbolic notation process], argued Chalmers, was perfectly sufficient to "maintaining the causal relations" needed for the net, i.e., its computational capacity. It is abstract computations – based in the abstract space – not dynamics, that means all to Chalmers. That the net might be part of a humming, vibrating dynamical system is not considered.

The abstract space and abstract time of the classic metaphysic are just as meaningless to the operations of Gibson's resonating brain or Bergson's modulated wave as it is to the growth processes of our aforementioned tree. The brain, like the growing tree or any other biological system, is not actually operating in the 4-d point-continuum of this metaphysic. As a physical device, the brain knows *nothing* about the continuum; it does not exist to the brain. The continuum is a conceptual derivative, a resultant from processes of the brain that a conscious being applies conceptually to external reality and its events, unfortunately often as though this continuum were indeed real. It is even applied by conscious beings to the brain and its operations, as in the computer model where, in strong AI, it is assumed that the brain is actually carrying out the operations that support perception and cognition as though simply symbol manipulations within the abstract space and time. But this supposition is wrong. The brain is working in an entirely different, yes, metaphysical structure. Therefore the brain cannot be modeled, or better and more importantly – *built or reconstructed* – as a device functioning in the point-continuum of the classic metaphysic. Thus, when a theorist drives the critical question down to the need to implement the biology of the brain (e.g., Searle), we are in fact truly entering this question of the actual metaphysic required.[73]

This vision of the role of the body/brain in perception is obviously quite different from that of the computer or robotic model of mind. This is the critical point: to support conscious perception, one needs a "device" with a real, concrete, physical dynamics. In this model, the brain is a very concrete device whose purpose is to create a reconstructive wave within or passing through the universal holographic field. It is as concrete a dynamics – as concrete a wave – as that supported by the AC motor and its creation of an electric field of force. Symbol manipulation in an abstract space and abstract time is not sufficient to support consciousness; it is not sufficient to form a wave specific to a subset of the universal field at a certain scale of time, i.e., to the external world of our experience.

This of course is anathema to current AI. The implications for a complete alteration of AI's current course are staggering. But it is worse as we shall soon see, for the operation of memory retrieval and the nature of "stored" experience are utterly different from concepts held in any current conceptions in cognitive science or AI.

Chapter II: End Notes and References

1. Bergson, H., (1896/1912). *Matter and Memory*. New York: MacMillan, p. 83.
2. Ingerman, P. (1966). *A Syntax-oriented Translator.* New York: Academic Press.
3. Gunter, P. A. Y. (1969), *Bergson and the Evolution of Physics.* University of Tennessee Press.
4. Bergson, 1896/1912, *Matter and Memory*, p. 254.
5. Strawson, G. (2006). *Consciousness and its place in nature: Does physicalism entail panpsychism?* Exeter, UK: Imprint Academic.
6. Hardcastle, V. G. (1995). *Locating consciousness*. Philadelphia: John Benjamins, p.1.
7. James, W. (1890). *Principles of Psychology.* New York: Holt and Co.
8. Robbins, S.E. (2004). On time, memory and dynamic form. *Consciousness and Cognition, 13*, 762-788.
9. Dainton, B. (2010). Temporal consciousness, *The Stanford Encyclopedia of Philosophy* (Fall 2010 Edition), Edward N. Zalta (ed.), URL = <http://plato.stanford.edu/archives/fall2010/entries/consciousness-temporal/>.
10. Lombardo, T. J. (1987). *The Reciprocity of Perceiver and Environment: The Evolution of James. J. Gibson's Ecological Psychology.* Hillsdale, N.J.: Erlbaum.
11. Crane, T. (2011). The problem of perception. *The Stanford Encyclopedia of Philosophy* (Spring 2011 Edition), Edward N. Zalta (ed.), URL = <http://plato.stanford.edu/archives/spr2011/entries/perception-problem/>.
    Siegel, S. (2013). The Contents of Perception. *The Stanford Encyclopedia of Philosophy* (Spring 2013 Edition), Edward N. Zalta (ed.), URL = <http://plato.stanford.edu/archives/spr2013/entries/perception-contents/>.
    Tye, M. (2013). Qualia. *The Stanford Encyclopedia of Philosophy* (Fall 2013 Edition), Edward N. Zalta (ed.), forthcoming URL = <http://plato.stanford.edu/archives/fall2013/entries/qualia/>.
12. Manzotti, R. (2008). A process-oriented view of qualia. In E. Wright (Ed.), *The Case for Qualia*. Cambridge, Mass: MIT Press.
13. Both Berkeley (1734/1982) and Whitehead (1920) disputed the primary/secondary disctinction. Berkeley in his idealist basis for this and Whitehead could both be seen as in essence disputing whether the classic metaphysic actually possesses any ontological status.
    Berkeley, G. (1734/1982). *A Treatise Concerning the Principles of Human Knowledge.* New York: Hackett.
    Whitehead, A. (1920). *The Concept of Nature.* Cambridge: Cambridge Univeristy Press.
14. Nida-Rümelin, M. (2008). Phenomenal character and the transparency of experience. In E. Wright (Ed.), *The Case for Qualia*. Cambridge, Mass: MIT Press.
15. Wright, E. (2008). Introduction. In E. Wright (Ed.), *The Case for Qualia*. Cambridge, Mass: MIT Press.
16. Kind, A. (2008). How to believe in qualia. In E. Wright (Ed.), *The Case for Qualia*. Cambridge, Mass: MIT Press.
    Tye, M. (1995). *Ten Problems of Consciousness*. Cambridge, Mass: MIT Press.
17. Nunn, C. (2006). Mind-matter research: Frontiers and directions. *Journal of Consciousness Studies, 13*, 90-95

18. Delvin, K. (1997). Goodbye Descartes: The End of Logic and the Search for a New Cosmology. New York: Wiley.
19. Russell, B. (1903). *The Principles of Mathematics*, London: Allen and Unwin, 346-353.
20. Simon, Herbert. (1995). Near decomposability and complexity: How a mind resides in a brain. In Morowitz, H. & Singer, J. (Eds.) *The Mind, the Brain and Complex Adaptive Systems*. New York: Addison-Wesley.
    Pinker, Stephen. (1997). *How the Mind Works*. New York: Norton.
21. Hameroff, S. and Penrose, R. (1996). Conscious events as orchestrated space-time selections. *Journal of Consciousness Studies, 3*, 36-53.
22. De Broglie, L. (1947/1969). The concepts of contemporary physics and Bergson's ideas on time and motion. In P.A.Y. Gunter (Ed.), *Bergson and the Evolution of Physics,* University of Tennessee Press.
23. Bergson, H. (1889). *Time and Free Will: An Essay on the Immediate Data of Consciousness.* London: George Allen and Unwin Ltd, p. 111.
24. Feynman, R. P. and Hibbs, A. R. (1965). *Quantum Mechanics and Path Integrals.* New York: MacGraw-Hill.
25. Nottale, L. (1996). Scale relativity and fractal space-time: applications to quantum physics, cosmology and chaotic systems. *Chaos, Solitons and Fractals, 7*, 877-938.
26. Lynds, P. (2003). Time and classical and quantum mechanics: Indeterminacy versus discontinuity. *Foundations of Physics Letters, 16*, 343-355.
27. Bergson, H. (1907/1911). *Creative Evolution*. New York: Holt, p. 308.
28. Lynds, P. (2003). Zeno's paradoxes – a timely solution. http://philsci-archive.pitt.edu/1197/
29. Dennett, D. C. (1991). *Consciousness explained*. Boston: Little-Brown.
30. Taylor, J. G. (2002). From matter to mind. *Journal of Consciousness Studies. 9* (4), p. 11.
31. Whitmann, M. (2011). Moments in time. *Frontiers in Integrative Neuroscience* 5(66).
32. Robbins, S.E. (2004). On time, memory and dynamic form. *Consciousness and Cognition, 13*, 762-788.
33. Dainton (2010) provides an excellent in-detail discussion of various philosophical stances on the consciousness of time and the experience of succession, while Whitmann (2011) reviews the research on the subject. Of Dainton's three classifications, the "cinematic" model corresponds most closely to the concept discussed here on the idea that the brain is taking a series of "snapshots" with the consequent difficulties of this position for actually explaining the experience of motion. The "retentional" model (to me, incoherent) has "episodes of consciousness which themselves lack temporal extension, but whose contents present (or represent) temporally extended intervals and phenomena," while the "extensional" has episodes of experiencing that are themselves temporally extended and are thus able to incorporate change in a quite straightforward way. As he discusses, there are philosophers, e.g., Husserl, that have insisted that the present moment must have some extent, not merely that of a mathematical point. There is not space here to embrace and fully comment on Dainton's wide ranging examination of positions. The discussion proceeds under the concept of explaining "temporal consciousness," but lurking under all these theories is, yes, the physical brain, and thus physics, and thus physics' theory of time – the theory that holds sway as our dominant theory of the subject. What I have emphasized here, and the significance

of which was missed in Dainton's brief comment on Bergson, is that we are driven always to the metaphysic of our theory of *physical motion,* i.e., the metaphysic (the abstract space and abstract time) in which *physics* itself works. This is what takes us to Zeno's paradoxes, to Notalle, and to Lynds (who is really just Bergson revisited sans any acknowledgment). Firstly, it is the structure of this metaphysic – blessed implicitly by physics and thus all of science – that we need to see is providing the iron, implicit framework in which the problem of qualia is (unfruitfully) discussed. Secondly, when it is seen that the motion over time of the universal field is indivisible, we obtain the primary continuity or memory that marks consciousness itself, derived simply from the brain's being an integral participant in the flow or time-evolution of the universal field. Our model of the physical motion of this field accounts for the experience of flow – we are not dealing (at least solely) in a realm we call temporal consciousness which is a vaguely separate realm from physics itself.

34. Robbins, S. E. (2010). Special relativity and perception: The singular time of psychology and physics. *Journal of Consciousness Exploration and Research, 1,* 500-531.

35. Bergson, 1896, op. cit, p. 255.

36. Yes, there is the law of entropy which is used to account for irreversible phenomena in physics – the impossibility of reversing the process by which the egg was broken and reassembling it. But even this law is only statistical – only a vast improbability of re-assembling the egg. It is not an instrinsic feature of (classic) time. See for example: Carroll, S. (2010). *From Eternity to Here.* New York: Penguin.

37. Robbins, S. E. (2014). *The Mists of Special Relativity: Time, Consciousness and a Deep Illusion in Physics.* Atlanta: CreateSpace.
Robbins, S. E. (2010). Special relativity and perception: The singular time of psychology and physics. *Journal of Consciousness Exploration and Research, 1,* 500-531.

38. I will not be going here into a discussion of color as an optimal specification based upon invariance in the field. I have addressed this topic elsewhere, for example:
Robbins, S. E. (2013). Form, Qualia and Time: The Hard Problem Reformed. *Mind and Matter, 2,* 1-25.
Robbins, S. E. (2012). *Time and Memory: A Primer on the Scientific Mysticism of Consciousness.* Atlanta: CreateSpace.
Robbins, S. E. (2007). Time, form and the limits of qualia. *Journal of Mind and Behavior, 28,* 19-43.

39. Hawkins, Jeff. (2004). *On Intelligence.* New York: Times Books, p. 63.

40. McFadden, J. (2002). Synchronous Firing and its influence on the brain's electromagnetic field: Evidence for an electromagnetic field theory of consciousness. *Journal of Consciousness Studies, 9,* 23-50.

41. Dennett, D. C. (2005). *Sweet dreams: Philosophical obstacles to a science of consciousness.* Cambridge, Massachusetts: MIT Press.

42. Stapp, H. (2007). *Mindful Universe: Quantum Mechanics and the Participating Observer.* New York: Springer.

43. Bergson, H. (1904/1920). Brain and thought, in *Mind-Energy,* London: Macmillan. (Originally published 1904, "Le paralogisme psycho-physiologique," *Revue Philosophique*)

44. Bergson, 1896/1912, p. 31, emphasis added.

45. Pribram, K. (1971). *Languages of the Brain.* New Jersey: Prentice-Hall.

46. Robbins, S. E. (2000). Bergson, perception and Gibson. *Journal of Consciousness Studies, 7,* 23-45.

Robbins, S. E. (2006). Bergson and the holographic theory. *Phenomenology and the Cognitive Sciences,* 5, 365-394.

47. Smythies, J. (2002). Comment on Crook's "Intertheoretic Identification and Mind-Brain Reductionism." *Journal of Mind and Behavior, 23,* 245-248.

48. Bergson, 1896/1912, p. 28.

49. Bergson, 1896/1912, pp. 31-32, emphasis added.

50. Churchland, P. S., Ramachandran, V. S., & Sejnowski, T. J. (1994). A critique of pure vision, In C. Koch & J. Davis (Eds.) *Large-scale Neuronal Theories of the Brain.* Cambridge: MIT Press.

51. Viviani, P. & Stucchi, N. (1992). Biological movements look uniform: Evidence of motor-perceptual interactions. *Journal of Experimental Psychology: Human Perception and Performance, 18,* 603-623.

Viviani, P. & Mounoud, P. (1990). Perceptuo-motor compatibility in pursuit tracking of two-dimensional movements. *Journal of Motor Behavior, 22,* 407-443.

52. Nakamura, R.K. & Mishkin, M. (1980). Blindness in monkeys following non-visual cortical lesions. *Brain Research, 188,* 572-577.

Nakamura, R. K. & Mishkin, M. (1982). Chronic blindness following non-visual lesions in monkeys: Partial lesions and disconnection effects. *Society of Neuroscience Abstracts, 8,* 812.

Weiskrantz, L. (1997), *Consciousness Lost and Found.* New York: Oxford.

53. Turvey, M. (1977). Preliminaries to a theory of action with references to vision. In R.E. Shaw & J. Bransford (Eds.), *Perceiving, Acting and Knowing,* New Jersey: Erlbaum.

54. Nourbakhsh, I. R. (2013). *Robot Futures.* Cambridge, MA:MIT Press.

55. Noë, A. (2004). *Action in Perception.* Cambridge, MA: MIT Press.

56. Robbins, S. E. (2004). Virtual action: O'Regan and Noë meet Bergson. *Behavioral and Brain Sciences.* 27 (6), 907-908.

57. Clark, A. (2008). *Supersizing the Mind: Embodiment, Action and Cognitive Extension.* Cambridge: Oxford University Press.

Milner, A., & Goodale, M. (1998). The visual brain in action. *Psyche,* 4(12), October 1998 http://psyche.cs.monash.edu.au/v4/psyche-4-12-milner.html

58. Galese, V. (2007). The "Conscious" dorsal stream: Embodied simulation and its role in Space and Action conscious awareness. *Psyche* 13(1).

59. Merleau-Ponty, M. (1962). *Phenomenology of Perception.* (translated from the French by C. Smith). London, Routledge, p 243.

60. Ramachandran, V. S., & Blakeslee, S. (1998). *Phantoms in the brain.* New York: Morrow.

61. Smythies, J. (2002). Comment on Crook's "Intertheoretic Identification and Mind-Brain Reductionism." *Journal of Mind and Behavior,* 23, 245-248.

62. Yarrow, K., Haggard, P., Heal, R., Brown, P., & Rothwell, J. C. (2001). Illusory perceptions of space and time preserve cross-saccadic perceptual continuity. *Nature,* 414, 302-304.

63. Smythies, J. (2002). Comment on Crook's "Intertheoretic Identification and Mind-Brain Reductionism." *Journal of Mind and Behavior,* 23, 245-248.

64. O'Regan, J. Kevin (1992). Solving the real mysteries of perception: The world as an outside memory. *Canadian Journal of Psychology, 46*(3), 461-488.

65. Robbins, S. E. (2004). Virtual action: O'Regan and Noë meet Bergson. *Behavioral and Brain Sciences, 27*, 907-908.

66. O'Regan, J. K. & Noë, A. (2001). A sensori-motor account of vision and visual consciousness. *Behavioral and Brain Sciences*, 24(5).

67. Rock, I. (1984). *Perception.* New York: Scientific American Books Inc.

68. Bergson, 1896/1912, p. 77.

69. Barret, L. (2010). *Beyond the Brain: How Body and Environment Shape Animal and Human Minds.* Princeton University Press.

70. Chemero, A. (2009). *Radical Embodied Cognitive Science.* Cambridge,MA: MIT Press, Chapter 9.

71. Bekenstein, J.(2003). Information in the holographic universe. *Scientific American* 289(2): 58-66.
Bohm, D. (1980). *Wholeness and the Implicate Order.* London: Routledge and Kegan-Paul.

72. Chalmers, D.J. (1996). *The Conscious Mind.* New York: Oxford University Press.

73. Searle, J. R. (2000). Consciousness, Free Action and the Brain. *Journal of Consciousness Studies, 7*, 3-22.

CHAPTER III

Retrieving Experience

We pass, by imperceptible stages, from recollections strung out along the course of time to the movements which indicate their nascent or possible action in space. Lesions of the brain may affect these movements, but not these recollections.

— Bergson, *Matter and Memory*[1]

The idea that "space" is perceived whereas "time" is remembered lurks at the back of our thinking. But these abstractions borrowed from physics are not appropriate for psychology. Adjacent order and successive order are better abstractions, and these are not found separate.

— Gibson, *The Senses Considered as Perceptual Systems*[2]

Gibson and the Abstraction

It is the unquestionable dogma of current science that our experience is stored in the brain. The brain is our storehouse of memory. The computer, in storing data in its memory, is only emulating the brain. Gibson, however, was no friend of the storehouse metaphor of memory. Comments such as the following can easily be found:

> The "image" of memory and thought is derived by analogy to the image of art. The "trace" of a percept is analogous to the graphic act. The "storehouse" of memory is analogous to the museums and libraries of civilization... But to assume that experiences leave images or traces in the brain, that experience writes a record, and that the storage of memories explains learning, that, in short, the child accumulates knowledge as the race has accumulated it, is stultifying.[3]

This metaphor, he saw, was born of a fundamental concept – the "present" is sense perception, the "past" is memory. This extends down to the elementary perception of an event. To perceive a fly buzzing by, this doctrine of sensation-based perception, as Gibson notes, assumes that a succession of items – presumably snapshots of the fly – must be stored and combined with earlier ones in a single composite. Each snapshot somehow leaves a "trace," and hence the origin of the ubiquitous – and completely vague – "memory traces" notion in the literature of memory research.

We have seen, as Gibson knew, that this picture can be pushed to absurdity. But Gibson moves further:

> The idea that "space" is perceived whereas "time" is remembered lurks at the back of our thinking. But these abstractions borrowed from physics are not appropriate for psychology. Adjacent order and successive order are better abstractions, and these are not found separate.[4]

"These abstractions borrowed from physics..." Surely the dominant memory models of the day, arch-paradigms of the storehouse – the computer or computational model, the neural network or connectionist model – see no problem with their cohabitation with physics. They have scarce paid a bit or a byte of attention to Gibson. But this "abstraction" towards which Gibson, like the apostle in Da Vinci's "Last Supper" (as we began here in the context of art), raises his finger in accusation, we have seen unmasked by Bergson. Again, it is simply an inescapable fact, as far as I can discern, that Gibson was and is operating within – is assuming – Bergson's new metaphysic.

Direct Memory

We have seen the abstraction, "borrowed from physics," Gibson so strongly accused. It is the concept of abstract space and abstract time so precisely described by Bergson. With its concept of the discrete "instant" of time, it underlies the very notion of a discrete state device. It underlies the very concept that "past," "present," and "future" are discrete "parts" of time. It underlies the concept that the "past" – a discrete part of time separate from the "present" – must be preserved by the (always "present") brain. It underlies the "snapshots" of the buzzing fly, for each snapshot again corresponds to a "point" on the fly's trajectory and therefore to an "instant." It underlies the "traces" of these snapshots somehow deposited in memory, and somehow used to construct a whole, time-scaled picture of the fly. It is indeed a framework – a metaphysic – which has done psychology, as Gibson perceived, little good. But we have also seen Bergson's alternative and the model of perception that results. Within it too is a remarkable theory of memory.

If Gibson's model of direct perception is in effect Bergson's, perception is not solely occurring within the brain. Experience, then, cannot be exclusively stored there. Bergson visualized the brain, embedded in 4-D experience, as a form of "valve" which allowed experiences from the past into consciousness depending of the array of action systems activated.

> That which I call my present is my attitude with regard to the immediate future; it is my impending action. My present is, then, sensori-motor. Of my past, that alone becomes image and consequently sensation, at least nascent, which can collaborate in that action, insert itself in that attitude, in a word make itself useful....[5]

In today's terms, we would say that in the recall of experience, the brain is yet acting as a modulated reconstructive wave passing through the four-dimensional holographic field. Just as we modulated the reconstructive wave to different frequencies to reconstruct the successive wave fronts of the pyramid/ball, cup, toy truck and candle, so it is the modulated wave patterns that the brain assumes which determine the *experiences* retrieved. Damage to the brain in various areas affects its ability to assume the complex wave-modulation patterns that might be required to retrieve certain experiences. The experiences now appear to be "lost." But the brain does not have to be our "suitcase" for experience. What is required is that it serves to assume the appropriate modulated reconstructive wave patterns within the holographic field.

> If our hypothesis is well founded, these failures of recognition are in no sense due to the fact that the recollections occupied the injured region of the brain. They must be due to two causes: sometimes our body is no longer able to adopt, under the influence of the external stimulus, the precise [motor] attitude by means of which a choice could be automatically made among our memories; sometimes the memories are no longer able to find a fulcrum in the body, a means of prolonging themselves in action.[6]

While storage in the brain is dogma, in truth it is only an hypothesis. It has never be proven. The fact that a konk on the head can cause the loss of memories does not allow us to infer, categorically, that the memories, sitting in some storage area in the brain, have been destroyed. It does not allow us to rule out the possibility that the "konk" has simply damaged the mechanisms and dynamics necessary for accessing and retrieving experience.

We should not take this to mean that no form or type of memory whatsoever is stored in the brain. To use a Bergson-like example, we may have many practice sessions at the piano, say, learning Chopin's C# minor waltz. The end result of the many practice sessions is a nice motor program – with all the modifications of neural connections this might involve – which we can unroll effortlessly as the waltz. This is clearly a form of memory "stored in the brain." In the terms of current psychology, it might be called a "procedural" memory – a memory for a sequence of actions. There are other neural storage effects. The layout of the piano keyboard, with its five black and seven white alternating keys, is experienced daily over and over. The particular black-white pattern is always the same; it is an *invariant* over these experiences. The spatial neural firing patterns in the visual cortex which respond to the layout of the keyboard must eventually be registered at some level of the neural structure or hierarchy as an invariant pattern. Jeff Hawkins (*On Intelligence*) proposes a neural network model for the formation of these all-important neural "invariants."[7] Were a different keyboard with a different white-black alternation pattern encountered one day, the difference would be detected instantly. But simultaneously every experience, every practice session or episode is retained in the four-dimensional extension of being – the day when the sun was shining brightly and the room was glowing, the dreary day when it rained, the day we had a headache. This is "episodic" memory in current terms. In principle, given the precise modulation pattern, each event is retrievable. In practice this is obviously difficult. The relation between the form of memory stored in the brain, and our experience, which is not so stored, is a complex one. Not all the aspects of it I have examined in other theoretical endeavors will be discussed here.[8]

A Rickety Dogma

Despite the storage-in-the-brain dogma, cognitive science, neuroscience, the psychology of memory, and last but not least, robotics – none have a clue how experience is actually stored in the brain. The prevailing trend has at least partial origins in the "constructivist" tradition of Ulrich Neisser (circa 1967) where memories are apparently reconstructed from vaguely specified "pieces" or elements. This is reinforced by an "abstractionist" tendency. The abstractionist sees only certain abstracted aspects of the events of experience being stored. The rotating cube would have only certain snapshots of the rotation stored. For the memory theorist, Lawrence Barsalou, the dynamic transformation of "biting" as in biting on a carrot, would be represented by three schematic states – "a mouth closed next to the object, followed by a mouth open, and then the mouth around the object" (Figure 3.1).[9]

Figure 3.1. "Biting" as an abstraction

There is no principled theory as to how or why the brain makes such a selection. *Which* snapshots of the rotating cube are stored? (We have seen that in actuality there can be no such snapshots as far as the brain is concerned.) *Which* snapshots of the biting face? In fact, there would be a flow field defining this biting transformation just as difficult to store as the flowing sides of the rotating cube. The physicist, Walter Elsasser, whose thoughts on memory we will discuss shortly, noted that, "no transcription mechanism has ever been discovered that writes these flowing events in molecular structures in real time, let alone reads them back out." Yet, say theorists Mayes and Roberts, quite confidently, "Only a tiny fraction of experienced episodes are put into long term storage, and, even with those that are, only a small proportion of the experienced episode is later retrievable."[10] It is from these abstracted elements, the principles of selection of which no one can specify, that the brain is supposed to reconstruct specific experiences.

There are only vague notions on how the brain makes this selection of elements or events, or for any particular event, which elements these would be, or how dynamic and multi-modal events are then reconstructed from fragmented pieces or static "features" of an event – as for example the ephemeral edges and vertices of the rotating cube which we saw exist only as invariants over a flow – are stored in different (unspecified) spots, frozen, as snapshots, in the brain. All theory proceeds as if it is sufficient to theorize on how the hippocampus (and/ or other structures) might store some static event, e.g., a snapshot or series of snapshots of a person with a spoon stirring our cup of coffee.

Let us remember, in the previous chapter we saw that there is no theory, in fact, not even a teensy thought of a theory, for what I termed the "primary" memory that supports the time-extended perception of the rotating cube or the buzzing fly, let alone, as Barsalou's inadequate attempt shows, of storing these dynamic, time-extended events for future retrieval. Let us note too, the question of whether the brain stores experience was Bergson's key question in *Matter and Memory* in determining whether the brain generates consciousness. If we hold that neural storage is sufficient to account for the retention of experience, it must be understood that this answer absolutely constrains *all* theories of the origin and nature of consciousness. Images, dreams, even perceptual images and perceptual experience, to include the time-extended perception of the rotating cube, *must* somehow be generated from stored elements within (or modifications of) the neural substrate. But we have seen that the metaphysic underlying this position, with its abstract homogeneous continuum and its snapshot theory of motion, is utterly, logically precluded from explaining the origin of any of these. The fact is, I repeat again, current theory has not one clue how experience is stored in the brain. Of course, it has not one clue what experience, that is to say, perception, is. Without a theory of perception, there can be no theory of the storage of experience. This is why there is no theory.

Nevertheless, despite this extreme theoretical weakness, the notion that the brain, and therefore a robot, can store experience, is a lynchpin, both in theories of consciousness, and in the robotic, machine view of mind with its view that robots can be conscious, with the philosophic mist that this generates. If the brain cannot and does not store experience, then neither will a robot, a computer or a neural network.

Elsasser's View

Not too far after the birth of cognitive science, the physicist, Walter M. Elsasser, argued that the ultimate decision between mechanistic and non-mechanistic models of the organism could begin, not in the realm of heredity and genetics, but in the data and observations of "cerebral memory."[11] The term "cerebral memory" for Elsasser was quite distinct from "storage." In the latter, we deal fundamentally with a device for writing to a suitable medium and later reading and converting the static inscription back to a time-dependent electrical message (i.e., a computer). This precise reconstruction of a past set of states he termed "homogeneous replication." Cerebral memory, however, is in his terms a function of "heterogeneous reproduction." The brain, with its myriad of neurons, he observed, is capable of an enormous number of states, in fact, so vast a number that no global state of the brain can ever be truly repeated. Heterogeneous reproduction is the creative selection from an immense reservoir of possible states, a selection occurring in such a way that the selected state is closely similar to states already existing in that class.

For Elsasser, heterogeneous reproduction spans both heredity and memory. As an agent of heredity, heterogeneous reproduction represents the common information relating parent to progeny so far as it is not fully explicated by the replication indicated in the action of the genetic code. In both cases information reappears after a period of latency. He observed that the similarity between heredity and cerebral memory was already noted by the zoologist Semon and encapsulated in Semon's notion of the "mneme" – a basic property of organisms whereby information is preserved across apparent gaps of time.[12] Homogeneous replication, Elsasser felt, was insufficient to account for the complicated mixing and superposition of memory elements as in dreams and imagination or even for the most fundamental entities of the psychological realm, namely, associations, and as well, the elementary "this reminds me of…" events characteristic of analogical remembering.

These associations and "elementary reminding" events – the very memory processes Elsasser realized cannot be accounted for by a mechanistic model – are the province of ecological psychology. This is far more so than is generally realized. The "this" of "this reminds me of" can be any *event*. As I am walking, there is a rustling in the grass on the embankment next to the road. I am suddenly reminded of an experience of several blacksnakes slithering past me down a hill. Out the window, the hanging bird feeder, over-weighted on one side with seed, is swaying at a slant in the wind. Last night's dream returns involving a large cargo ship listing and then laying on its side. The structure of perceived events is inseparably linked with the process of reminding. Long before cognitive science, at the inception of modern psychology, this basic, ubiquitous mode of reminding was called *redintegration*. An ecological model of redintegration is what we now discuss.

The Concept of Redintegration

The concept of redintegration can trace its genes back to the very origins of psychology. Thus it was Christian Wolff, a contemporary and disciple of the great philosopher Leibniz, and a mathematics professor (it took one to coin this term), who first introduced the "law of redintegration" in his *Psychologia Empirica* of 1732. In effect, Wolff's law stated that "when a present perception forms a part of a past perception, the whole past perception tends to reinstate itself." A 1912 formulation of this by Dessoir stated: "Every idea tends to recall to the mind the total idea of which it is a part."[13]

Examples of this phenomenon abound in everyday experience. Thus the sound of thunder may serve to redintegrate a childhood memory of the day one's house was struck by lightning. Perhaps, for example, we are walking down a road in the summertime and suddenly notice a slight rustling or motion in the grass along the embankment. Immediately, an experience returns in which a snake was encountered in a similar situation. Klein (1971) notes that these remembered experiences are "structured or organized events or clusters of patterned, integrated impressions," and that Wolff had in effect noted that subsequent to the establishment of such patterns, the pattern might be recalled by reinstatement of a constituent part of the original pattern.[14]

In actuality, psychology has progressed but little beyond this original formulation, though its variants appear in new form constantly. H. L. Hollingworth (1926, 1928), stimulated by his studies of traumatized World War I veterans, had defined redintegration as follows:[15]

> A complex antecedent, ABCD, instigates a conse-
> quent, XYZ. Thereafter the consequent XYZ or one belong-
> ing to the same class, may be instigated by the detail A, or a
> detail in the same class, by virtue of the historic participation
> of A in the situation ABCD.[16]

Hollingworth noted the antecedents of this principle in Locke, Berkeley, the notion of "mnemic causation" of Bertrand Russell, Thorndike's "associative shifting," and others. He also argued that the whole phenomenon of conditioning observed by Pavlov was but a special (and misunderstood) case of redintegration.

Craik and Tulving (1975) theorized in the context of the many memory studies being done with verbal materials at the time.[17] Oftentimes, people were asked to learn lists of pairs of words, where a pair might be GRASS-SNAKE. If, on reading the pair, a subject visualizes rustling grass and then the moving snake, GRASS now forms a nice "context" for SNAKE. When I see GRASS (the "cue") again, SNAKE (the "target") is very likely to be remembered. Commenting on why this case enhances memory performance, they say, 50 years after Hollingworth and 240 years after Wolff:

> One possibility is that an encoded unit is unitized or integrated on the basis of past experience and, just as the target stimulus fits naturally into a compatible context at encoding, so at retrieval, *representation of the encoded unit will lead easily to the regeneration of the total unit.* [18]

So "compatibility" of the cue with the target became the operative word here. There is little further understanding of what this means. Later (e.g., Marschark & Surian, 1992) we find explanations which state that the memory between cue and target is a function of "relational" and "distinctive" information by which the cue is related (somehow) to the target, yet made distinct from other events. But little further exploration of these "relations" is undertaken.[19]

Verbrugge (1977) performed an experiment in which he presented subjects sets of metaphoric sentences such as "The Venus fly-trap is like a prison cell, waiting for its next victim to enter," or "The dictator's treatment of people is like a boot crushing a bug." He was then able to effectively use comic strip-like cues for recall (Figure 3.2).[20] Verbrugge argued that the comic strips captured abstract perceptual relations characteristic of the event specified in each sentence. In other words, we have a more detailed attempt to warn the psychology of memory that describing the "pattern" that might define some event (ABCD) and that of the portion (A) necessary to reconstruct it might be all important.

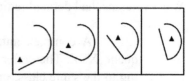

Figure 3.2 "The Venus Flytrap is like a prison cell, waiting for its victim to enter." (After Verbrugge, 1977)

The advent of mathematical models, e.g., CHARM (Eich, 1985), TODAM (Murdock, 1982), seemed to promise an insight into the inner mechanism of redintegration.[21] CHARM proposed a model for the GRASS-SNAKE type learning task using the concept that each item in the pair could be represented by a random vector of features. The vectors could simply be strings of 1's and 0's, where 1 stands for the presence of some feature, 0 for its absence.

Thus GRASS might be represented as [-1,0,1,0,-1,1,0,0,1] and SNAKE (the paired word which must be learned) as [1,1,0,0,-1,-1,0,0,0]. The two vectors are multiplied together and the result stored in a "memory vector" M. All the other pair-items in the experiment are stored in M as well. If we call our two vectors A and B, then when A (GRASS) is presented again as a "cue," it retrieves a vector B'. If B' is close enough to the original B (SNAKE), in fact closer than any other possible response, e.g., E', D', F', we have a correct "remembrance." The event/patterns however are now simply vectors of -1, 0, +1 elements with, as Murdock (1982) noted, undefined psychological significance.[22]

> Although one can make memory performance as good as desired by increasing N - the number of elements in the memory vector - what are these elements? If it takes 50, 100, 1000, or 10,000 elements to produce the necessary results, they are certainly not the cognitive features others have in mind.[23]

A small group of researchers began to leave the verbal materials in the 1980's. Zimmer and associates theorized in the context of experiments termed "subject performed tasks." In these, subjects actually perform actions such as "stir the coffee," or "bend the wire." Speculating on the mechanism behind the recall of such acted events, they use the notion of "popping into mind," as in cued recall, where "sets of features," "bound together by actions," can pop out from the noise if their "conjunctions" are sufficiently unique. These "spontaneously reconstitute" the former episode.[24]

This could go on; we shall see a few of the connectionist models for this later. I hope that it is understood that when "redintegration" is discussed here, though not currently a featured term in the literature, it is not because Wolff's law fails to be fundamental. It permeates all the above and beyond. Ignored to this point, with relatively few exceptions, has been the significance of Gibson. Yet the characterization of Wolff's "structured or organized events or clusters of patterned, integrated impressions," or event-patterns, is exactly Gibson's theory.

The Redintegrative Model

Suppose then, "stirring coffee," and to appreciate the full dynamics that might be involved, let the cup be slowly rotating, successively presenting its flow field sides and simultaneously moving towards us across the table's gradient surface. When stirring this cup of coffee, we are involving multiple areas of the brain – visual areas, motor areas, auditory areas, haptic areas. Even the action-goal of "stirring" must be supported by the pre-frontal areas. Over these, we have a resonant feedback from the multiple re-entrant projections between all areas which supports a dynamical pattern occurring over time. For practical purposes, we have a near-global, time-extended pattern supported over the brain. The dynamical pattern itself, in some form, must support the ongoing, dynamic invariance structure of the coffee-stirring event being specified in perception.

The redintegration principle I am about to state assumes a fundamental symmetry between perception and memory: the same invariance laws which determine the perception of an event also drive remembering. This implies a basic law of the fundamental operation of redintegration or direct retrieval:

(1) An event E' will reconstruct a previous event E when E' is defined by the same invariance structure or by a sufficient subset of the same invariance structure.

In essence, when the same dynamic pattern, supporting the same invariance structure, is evoked over the global state of the brain, the correspondent *experience* is reconstructed. We are essentially relying upon the same mechanism that Gibson argued supports the direct specification of an event, and this is why we can term this a model of direct retrieval or *direct memory*.

Let us put this into our event context. Imagine a drive up a mountain road. The road curves back and forth, sinusoidal, rising at a particular grade (Figure 3.3). We have then a certain gradient of velocity vectors lawfully transforming as a function of the radius of the curves and the velocity of the vehicle. Over this flow field the tau (τ) ratio is defined, discussed above, which specifies time to impending contact and severity of impact, and has a critical value in controlling action. Our driver can rely directly on the τ value to modulate his velocity to avoid

Figure 3.3. The mountainside drive.

possible impacts with structures along the road. There are other components such as the contour and texture density gradients peculiar to a mountain terrain. An integral part of this transforming field (E) is the organism (O). The transformation specifying the flow field is also that defining the values of tuning parameters for the action systems. The velocity of field expansion/directional change is specific to the velocity of the car and to the muscular adjustments necessary to hold it on the road. Therefore the state of the body/brain with respect to future possible (virtual) action as well as that actually being carried out constitutes an integral component of the E-O event pattern.

I believe it is quite common for people to have past experiences redintegrated by this form of flowing, road-driving, invariance structure. My wife tells me that every time we drive along a certain curving section of the freeway near Milwaukee, she swears she is driving on a segment of a freeway in California where she once lived. Due to the indivisible time-evolution of the matter-field, neither the original transformation of the field nor its subsequent specification by the brain as an image (of its then-past motion) have moved into non-existence. The reason that the experience is reconstructed is that the brain is thrown by the invariance structure of the present event into the same reconstructive wave pattern as that which defined the original event. This is the essence of the principle of redintegration.

The more unique this invariance structure, the easier it is to reconstruct the specific event. It is exactly as if a series of wave fronts were recorded upon a hologram, each with a unique frequency of reference wave, as when we imagined storing the wave fronts of a pyramid/ball, chalice, toy truck and candle. Each wave front (or image) can then be reconstructed uniquely by modulating the reconstructive wave to each differing frequency. This implies a second law for *sets* of events:

(2) For a set of events, E_1, E_2,...E_n, the more unique the invariance structure defining each event, the greater the probability that they will be reconstructed by E' events with the same invariance structure.

Imagine a series of perceived events, for example, a man stirring coffee, a baseball hurtling by one's head, a boot crushing a can. Each has a unique invariance structure. To create the reconstructive wave for these, i.e., to evoke over the brain the needed modulation or dynamic wave pattern, I might use as a "cue" respectively - a stirring spoon, an abstract rendering of an approaching object capturing the composite tau value of the baseball event, and an abstract rendering of one form descending upon and obscuring another.[25] But these events are multi-sensory (multi-modal) and the four-dimensional extent of experience is multi-modal. There are auditory invariants as well defined over the events. Our cues could become respectively – the swishing or clinking sound of stirring, while the steady "looming" of the approaching baseball, with its radial, expanding flow field, is proportional over a range of frequency values to the change of sound inherent in the Doppler effect, and finally, we would have the crinkling sound of collapse of a tin structure. Even the dynamics of the muscular (or haptic) component of the event has a mathematical structure we could employ to re-cue the event, namely Turvey's "inertia tensor," consisting of the mathematical specification of the forces and moments of inertia in three dimensions that describe the motion. We could cue our stirring event by wielding a "tensor object." that captures this inertia tensor (invariant) specific to spoon-stirring. Were we trying to catch the onrushing baseball, the grasping adjustment of the hand is precisely specified by the tau value, and conversely then, a specific grasping adjustment is an integral, and potentially redintegrating component of this event.[26]

Note that the invariance laws above are *amodal*. The information cuts across modalities, allowing an event specified in one modality (for example, sound), to be redintegrative of the same event in another modality (e.g., the optical).

What we are building here is this consideration for AI: If your model of memory cannot handle the invariance laws of events, your machine intelligence cannot handle the fundamental operation of memory. This in turn will preclude you from handling analogy, the fundamental operation of cognition. But as this principle of redintegration has not been fully grasped even by the psychology of memory, we are going to spend a bit more time on it, enough to see how it exists across a spectrum of memory research. The AI enthusiast may think this a bit too detailed, but it is needed and should be instructive for what actually must be accomplished. It is AI's partner, cognitive science and its deep misconception of memory that has given AI the hope it has had in equaling human intelligence via AI's present framework of thought. We will progress then from the abstract to the concrete, as research did historically, situating these principles first and briefly in the context of the much studied verbal tasks. I will move from there to imagery, then to Subject Performed Tasks (SPTs), and then view "priming" in the SPT context.

Verbal Tasks and Redintegration

In the 1970's, memory research was dominated by experiments using some form of verbal material. The initial paradigm was introduced by Herman Ebbinghaus in the 1890's. Ebbinghaus introduced the use of "nonsense syllables." He experimented with learning and remembering lists of syllables like QEZ, PUJ, KAX, etc. Another form involved lists of pairs like QEZ-PUJ or ZAK-WUX. When presented QEZ again, you had to remember that PUJ was its pair. It was therefore Ebbinghaus's attempt to remove all *semantics* from the memory task. He had found it too easy to remember pairs like GRASS-SNAKE or SPOON-COFFEE due to the "associations" already existing in his past experience. This was the drive to get at the formation of the elementary "item-bond," e.g., between QEZ and PUJ, in its formation. In essence, the attempt was being made to drive the human "device" as a far lower version of itself, what in computer terms would be called a "syntax-directed" processor. The lists of QEZ-PUJ-like pairs were sets of arbitrary syntax rules, to be laboriously associated. This was to be the primitive process of association on pure display.

My experience, in studying the vast literature on all these experiments, was one of walking deeper and deeper into a vast realm of trees grown and even sprouting everywhere. There seemed no view possible of the forest. Despite the apparent purity of the experimental verbal materials, there really was no experimental control at all over what the subject did in his head. He was free to use imagery such as the Turkish person, or his experience of snakes, and so on. Soon the research field found itself having to deal with troublesome "variables" such as "meaningfulness," and "context" in the theoretical models of the process. The mini-models of the "process" and laws of memory began to get more and more complicated and difficult to grasp. There was no sense at all that the ecological case, using real, concrete events for remembering, might be primary, or that in fact, it is in the ecological case where the greatest experimental control resides.

But as history would show, the "device" was far more powerful, and its true (holographic) properties kept intruding into these pure associationist experiments in a pesky, unwanted way. A subject might realize, awakening from his rote efforts, that QEZ could be seen as "FEZ," and PUJ stand for "pudgy," and thus become a pudgy Turkish person wearing a fez. Now he had a nice method for redintegration using the powers of his "device" the next time QEZ (now "FEZ") came along. In my graduate student days, in the 1970's, there were still tons of nonsense syllable experiments being performed (and they continue a bit today).

Consider an experiment in the verbal learning tradition, in this case the A-B, A-C paired-associate list paradigm.

List 1 (A-B)	List 2 (A-C)
SPOON-COFFEE	SPOON-BATTER
KNIFE-SOAP	KNIFE-DOUGH
BOTTLE-THIMBLE	BOTTLE-PAN

And so on......

After list 1 is learned, then the process begins again with list 2, and we must now keep the responses for list 1 (COFFEE for SPOON) separate from list 2 (BATTER for SPOON). Here, theory focuses on "inter-item" relations (or relational information) as critical to help us (e.g., Marschark et al., 1987).[27] For example, we might notice that List 2 is mostly about baking/cooking-related response words. This helps us "delineate a search set," as the memory literature terms things. We know at least, when we are dealing with list 2, that baking/cooking response words are the targets. The ecological case is far simpler and it is primary.

Let us assume these are concrete events, enacted or perceived. The subject stirs the coffee with the spoon, or stirs the batter with the spoon. He cuts the soap with the knife, or cuts the dough. He pours water from the bottle into the pan, or into the thimble. Now in the verbal case, after learning the lists, we would simply present the word "SPOON" as a cue. But this is a very vague event; it has no *specificity*. Which object, or which event will it redintegrate? Even a concrete but static spoon, placed on the table before us, would have a questionable cueing power. We have at best the classic "response competition" model which McGeoch (1942) introduced early on (Figure 3.4).[28] In the behaviorist terminology of the day, the "stimulus," SPOON, activates both BATTER and COFFEE as possible "responses." In modern terminology, we would say both words are "primed." In essence, we could say, we have sent a

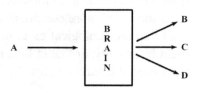

Figure 3.4. McGeoch's Interference Model (1942). Event A activates or reconstructs events B, C and D, or "responses" B, C and D. These events, B, C, D interfere with each other and make retrieving the desired memory difficult.

highly *unconstrained* wave though our holographic memory, as though we had a non-coherent wave containing frequencies f_1 and f_2, the frequencies of the original reference waves for recording two different wave fronts (or objects).

We can improve this by modulating the wave to a precise or coherent frequency, correspondent with the original reference wave, e.g., f_1, of the desired stored wave front. And concretely, in terms of events, we must put greater *constraints* on the cue event. For starters, a dynamism must be placed on the static spoon – the circular motion of stirring. But yet more precise constraint is needed to cue the proper event and object – batter or coffee. We can choose to create the greater resistance provided by the batter medium, or the larger amplitude of circular motion in the batter case assuming it was in a bowl, or both. The cue-event must force this precise modulatory pattern over the brain. Had one of the pairs been SPOON-OATMEAL, where the spoon was being used to shovel-in the oatmeal, a quite different transformation, involving scooping and lifting, and with the weight, mass and consistency constraints implied by oatmeal, would be placed on the cue-event with its spoon.

With this in mind, one can imagine an absurdly difficult paired-associate paradigm as far as verbal learning experiments are concerned. We'll call it the "A-B$_i$" paradigm. A list would look as follows:

SPOON-COFFEE
SPOON-BATTER
SPOON-OATMEAL
SPOON-BUTTER
SPOON-CORNFLAKES
SPOON-PEASOUP
SPOON-CATAPULT
SPOON-CHEESE
SPOON-TEETER TOTTER
And so on...

It is absurd since the stimulus words are exactly the same, the subject could have no clue what the appropriate response word is. But assume that the subject concretely acts out each event of the "absurd" list – stirring the coffee, stirring the batter, scooping/lifting the oatmeal, the cornflakes, cutting the cheese. To effectively cue the remembering, I have argued, the dynamics of each cue-event must be unique, and the invariance structure of an event in effect implies a structure of constraints. These constraints may be "parametrically" varied, where increasing fidelity to the original structure of constraints of a given event corresponds to a finer tuning of the reconstructive wave. (Vicente and Wang (1998) alluded to this process in a different, more advanced memory context such as chess or baseball, as "constraint attunement.")[29] The (for example, blindfolded) subject may wield a Turvey type "tensor-object" in a circular motion within a liquid. The resistance of the liquid (a parameter value) may be appropriate to a thin liquid such as coffee or to a thicker medium such as the batter. The circular motion (a parameter value) may be appropriate to the spatial constraint defined by a cup or to the larger amplitude allowed by a bowl. The periodic motion may conform to the original adiabatic invariance (frequency/energy) within the event, or may diverge. We can predict that with sufficiently precise transformations and constraints on the motion of the spoon (either visual, or auditory or kinesthetic or combined), the entire list can be reconstructed, i.e., each event and associated response word. Each appropriately constrained cue-event corresponds to a precise modulation (or constraint) of the reconstructive wave defined over the brain.

The obvious inverse is that, as the parameter values diverge from the original event, cueing/recall performance and/or recognition performance will increasingly degrade. Recognition tests are one method of testing these manipulations, employing familiarity ratings. In this case, we would present events transformed on various dimensions. The familiarity value should steadily decrease as the parameters are varied.

Parametric Variation of Cues in Concrete Events

These kinds of experiments are implicit in the literature. An example is found in a demonstration by Jenkins, Wald and Pittenger (1978).[30] Capitalizing on the notion of the optical flow field, they showed subjects a series of slides that had been taken at fixed intervals as a cameraman walked across the university campus mall. Some slides, however, were purposely left out. Later, when subjects were shown various slides again and asked if they had seen the slide shown, they rejected easily any slide taken from a different perspective and which therefore did not share the same flow field invariant defined across the series. Slides not originally seen, but which fit the series were accepted as "having been seen" with high probability. But Jenkins et al. had created a "gap" in the original set shown to the subjects by leaving out a series of six continuous slides (Figure 3.5). Thus a portion of the transformation of the flow field was not specified. Subjects were quite easily able to identify these slides as "not seen." In this case,

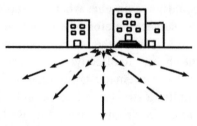

Figure 3.5. A flow field as we walk up the campus mall.

we are in effect varying parametric values defining a flow field, and more precisely here, varying the size of gaps in a flow to which we are sensitive. Other manipulations are possible, for example the slant of the gradient, the smoothness of the flow, the velocity of the flow, etc.

The many experiments of Jennifer Freyd and her associates on "representational momentum" can be seen in this light.[31] A subject may be shown three slides of a rotating rectangle. Each slide shows the rectangle rotated a little bit more. When subjects are given a recall test, they are likely to remember what would have been the fourth slide – the next rotated position or angle. A "probe" slide or memory cue of the never-seen fourth slide is rated the most likely to have been seen. The memory seems to represent the "momentum" of the moving rectangle. This however can be seen as a form of parametric manipulation of the cue-event. More straightforwardly, we could simply initially present the rectangle rotating at a certain velocity, then later attempt to cue the event, or ask for familiarity judgments, with rotations of different velocities.

On the visual side, consider, for example, presenting a simple static event of a field with a schematic tree (Figure 3.6). The trees in the figure have been grown with the precise mathematics defining real tree growth (Bingham, 1993).[32] The number of terminal branches (N) is a set function of height (H), $N=k(H)^2$, while the diameter (D) of trunk or branches at any point is a function of remaining length to the tip, $D=k(H)$. Suppose that one of the recognition items in our experiment is the leftmost or youngish tree in Figure 3.6. In the recognition test phase, the parametric values defining the structure of the trees can be varied increasingly from the original value. For example, we could re-represent the second tree, or third, or fourth tree and ask if this is recognized as part of the original set of items. Familiarity ratings should drop the further we move along the age dimension. More dynamically, a time-accelerated view of the tree's growth under certain parametric values can be used as the stimulus. For a dynamic event such as an approaching rugby ball, the time to contact value (cf. Gray & Regan, 1999) can be varied increasingly from the original value.[33]

Figure 3.6. A generated, aging tree. (Adopted from Bingham, 1993)

Even the original experiments of Pittenger and Shaw (1978), with their aging facial profiles generated via strain transformations on a cardioid (Figure 1.11), could be re-cast in this redintegration test framework.[34] Originally the subjects looked at many pairs of faces, judging each time which of the pair was the older. Changing this to a memory task, a face of a certain age can be included in a set of various items successively presented to a subject. On the recognition task, a face transformed by a certain parametric aging value is now presented. Familiarity values will be a function of the transformation. The aging transformation works for animal faces too, even for Volkswagens – it can generate increasingly aging "Beetles!" So we can have many different kinds of items in this test that eventually get aged (or un-aged) in a recognition phase.

It is good here to keep in mind the implications of virtual action relative to the previous rectangle example. We could have various possible rotation events of a rotating cube at various velocities and therefore various transitional forms - from slowly rotating, to multiple serrated edges, to fuzzy cylinder – with each transitional form conforming to a 4n-fold symmetry constraint. Each of these, by virtual action, would imply, for example, a possible modulation of the hand required to grasp either a cube, a serrated-edged object, or a cylinder. Therefore the implied muscular or haptic component of a perceived event, or parametric variation on grasping, is an equally possible cue-event manipulation.

All these are memory experiments that are either waiting to be done or implicitly have been done. They demonstrate that memory and its supporting brain dynamics are extremely sensitive to the invariance structure of events and the actual "parameter" values of the transformations involved. The importance of this is that any theory that claims to be a model of memory must be able to support this dynamic structure in events. But as we shall soon see, the major claimant to the theory of memory, namely neural networks or "connectionist" networks, is utterly incapable of this.

The Standard Concerns

Standard memory theory likes to say that it is the "distinctiveness" of events that makes them easier to remember. The distinctiveness might be a function of "sets of features" of the event. The more "distinctive" events A, B and C are, the easier it is to "encode," even "specifically encode" these events in "storage," and the easier it is to cue each event for later recall. Though there is no clue what this encoding could mean for events like stirring, theory has never gone beyond this vague equation or reference to event "features." Despite the fact that this distinctiveness/encoding formulation again represents not one step beyond Wolff's statement of 1732, memory theorists question the need for casting memory theory in terms of the invariance structure of events. They ignore that it is the precision of control of an event for modulating memory retrieval, in this case controlling a cue-event, that is the name of the game in science. And this control can only be through knowing the invariance laws or structure of an event.

To add to the reluctance, theorists note the difficulty that would exist in defining these invariance structures. Unfortunately, discovering invariance laws is also the name of the game in science. It also shows, to the chagrin of the memory theorists, that memory theory cannot be divorced from perception. Some other already studied event contexts in the ecological literature to which this parameterization of dynamic structure is extendable:

- the severity of contact between two approaching objects[13]
- volume related to perceived heaviness[35]
- acoustic information for the motion of objects[36]
- spoon handling in children[37]
- perceived relative mass in physical collisions[38]
- time-to-topple (say, of a bottle)[39]
- walk-on-able slopes[40]
- sensitivity to the relation of period and length in pendulum motion[41]
- acoustical frequency in vessel filling (where sound pitch increases lawfully as a vessel is filled with liquid)[42]

The standard theory of memory and the state of memory research has done nothing to help AI theorists understand the nature of human memory and the task they actually face. Rather they have fostered the illusion that we can easily do a model of experience as "stored in the brain" with little stored "features" and "elements" and by extension, stored in a computer memory. The complete ignoring of the role of invariance laws in the events being remembered has caused this delusion, but this ignorance is largely a function itself of the hold the computer metaphor of mind has put on cognitive science and memory theory.

Ecological psychology, I should note, has been heavily focused in Gibson's notion of the "affordance structure" of an event. The affordance structure, as noted earlier, is a relational notion tying information in the environment to actions available to the organism, or to the action capability of the organism. It is clearly very correlated to Bergson's concept of perception as virtual action. The "climbability" of stairs for humans is an example of such an affordance value. There is a dimensionless ratio, "pi," the ratio of the leg length to riser (step) height, that specifies for humans whether the stairs are "climbable." At a certain value of pi, the human perception becomes that he/she can no longer climb the stairs.[43] In the list cited above, the study on "walk-on-able slopes" is similar in concept. This concept has proven very important. Chemero, via a literature review of animal object exploration studies and via his own experiments, shows that the research literature (100+ studies) has been nearly completely confounded by its failure to consider Gibson's affordance values in regard to the objects that are commonly strewn around the area the critters are to explore.[44] However, ecological psych has done rather little to exploit the key role that invariance laws – to include affordance structures – could have in memory research, leaving the memory field to the standard approaches, that is, approaches which ignore Gibson.

Obviously, these affordance values can be parametrically varied and fit in the general redintegration law described here, and obviously they are related to the invariants structuring events. The precise meaning and interpretation of the affordance concept has generated a lot of philosophical discussion, but the effort spent in defining and discovering them seems to have simultaneously obscured their role and usage in memory research.[45] I am emphasizing the more straightforward notion of the invariance structure of events here, i.e., the key notion of the natural structure of events that drives memory, whether or not we understand the precise "affordance-related" value of this structure. This, to me, allows the clearest message for AI on what it must be considering, i.e., the dynamic, time-extended environmental structure, re the operation of memory.

Imagery and Concreteness

The introduction of imagery was perhaps one of the early things to show that there is far more going on than the laws of verbal learning, complex as they were becoming, were revealing. In introducing imagery as a variable in paired associate learning experiments, Paivio (1971) simultaneously moved to another *level of specificity*, yet closer to the concrete, ecological world of events.[46] Research more clearly delineated the "facilitative" effect of images upon memory performance. Some important aspects noted by Paivio were the following:

(1) Given a pair of objects, designated by words, or pictures, or simply the objects themselves, the more *dynamic* the image formed involving the two objects, the greater the probability of correct recall (given one object as the cue). As an example, Rowher et al. did a study in which subjects saw either, (a) two objects simply appearing side by side, (b) two objects oriented towards each other spatially in a manner corresponding to a prepositional phrase, e.g., a HAND *in* a BOWL, or a CUP *on* a TABLE, (c) two objects depicted in an action sequence corresponding to a verb phrase, e.g., the DOG *opening* the GATE. Different subjects were assigned to each type of case. After the sets of pairs were presented to each subject, there followed a test in which the experimenter named each stimulus object, e.g., HAND or DOG, and the subject was asked to recall the object paired with it. Performance was best in

case (c) where the objects were in motion, followed by (b) where they were at least spatially related, and then by (a) or simple juxtaposition.[47]

(2) What forms in effect a corollary to the above is the finding that *interactive* images are more effective than non-interactive images. Again it was found that subjects produced better performance when told to create interactive images, rather than simply being told to image. To visualize a "jar *on* a table" was better than simply a "jar *and* a table."[48]

(3) The *concreteness* effect. Given a pair of words, it is the *specificity* of the *stimulus* (cue word) that is most crucial for recall. Paivio referred this "specificity" to the *concreteness* of the cue word. Paivio (1971) tested four conditions involving stimulus-response word-pairs which varied in abstractness-concreteness:

   a) Concrete stimulus, concrete response (house-shoe)
   b) Concrete stimulus, abstract response (house-truth)
   c) Abstract stimulus, concrete response (furniture-carrot)
   d) Abstract stimulus, abstract response (furniture-vegetable)

Learning was best in (a) where both members of the pair were concrete, followed by (b), then (c), and lastly (d) where both members of the pair were abstract. Ultimately this finding was dubbed the "concreteness effect" and has been considered one of the strongest or most "robust" effects in memory research.[49] Only the most special conditions seem able to destroy it.

Given the preceding discussion of redintegration, the reason for the effectiveness of imagery in paired-associate learning, particularly dynamic imagery entailing some event, should be quite clear. The creation of a mental image of an event firstly comes a step closer to the level of specificity of a concrete, perceived event. It inherently will possess some degree of invariance structure. Suppose for a moment our word-pairs were:

SPOON-WATER
KNIFE-SOAP
TURTLE-BOARD
HAMMER-ROCK
BOAT-CUP
And so on....

For these we envision the spoon stirring the water, the knife cutting flakes from the soap, the hammer crushing the rock, etc. These imaged events are a series of unique event structures along the time dimension. Uniqueness could also be termed "distinctiveness," but this term, used very vaguely in the literature (cf. Schmidt, 1991, for a critical review), now carries a very "distinctive" and precise meaning in this model – *it is the dynamic structure of transformations, invariants, and constraints defining each event.*[50] Again, when we present simply the word SPOON as a cue, we are not using a very powerful cue. The relation of the cue to these event structures is clearly critical as we have seen. The cue-event gains its power by establishing the structure of constraints that are specific to the precise event. Simultaneously, the invariance structure of each cue (event) should be unique, for this corresponds to the unique reconstructive wave. This is why the "specificity of the stimulus" (cue) is so important. But at least, in these imagery experiments, we have the uniqueness of event structure.

To dig down a little deeper, we can ask why "prepositional" type imagery is less effective than the "actional" type. Consider "the hand in the bowl" versus "the hand stirring in the bowl." Here the "hand in the bowl" is but a snapshot of several possible events – a stirring hand, a hand moving up and down, a hand grabbing a goldfish, etc. The perceptual relations or mathematical structure supported over such a static scene are not as specific and therefore the resonance states not so sharply differentiated from states appropriate to a hand in relationship to some other object, e.g., a can, a cup, a briefcase. Given this it can be said that the dynamic image-cue by nature creates a more specific modulation pattern for our "reconstructive wave" such that the possible scenes that can be reconstructed are intrinsically constrained. To specify an event of a spoon-in-motion is already to constrain the scenes that can be reconstructed, while to restrict it to a spoon-in-a-circular-motion involving a force of a given strength is to constrain the (to-be-stirred) object – relative to the event invariance structure – to an equivalence class of objects, each stage, as we have seen, corresponding to a finer tuning of the reconstructive wave.

Craik and Tulving (1975), in interpreting such results, would have been led to say that the more dynamic image leads to a "richer, more elaborate encoding," and the achievement by target and cue thereby of a greater "compatibility" with the structure and rules of "semantic" memory.[51] But now we have insight into what "compatibility" means – the precise sharing of mathematical invariance defined over cue and target – and of what the rules of "semantic memory" actually consist, i.e., invariance laws, and how "richness" of encoding is actually to be described via the mathematics of events.

We must consider briefly the source of the concreteness effect itself. In essence, the abstractness of a word represents an increasingly higher order of invariance.[52] Intuitively we understand that the higher the order of invariance a phrase specifies, the more difficult it is to instantiate that structure as an image of a particular event. When we start from the specification, "A utensil is interacting with a piece of furniture," rather than "A knife is cutting the wooden top of the table," we have complicated the modulatory task. From this perspective, the concreteness effect is very real, but it is in one sense an artifact, created by the intrinsic difficulty of transducing these stimuli to something nearer the concrete, ecological events with invariance structures allowing redintegrative laws to operate effectively.

Subject-Performed Tasks

There is a line of memory research on what is known as subject-performed tasks (SPTs).[53] The research has generally shown that simple action phrases such as "break the toothpick" are better recalled when participants perform the actions themselves as opposed to simply hearing or reading the action description.[54] The large memory effect of the SPT relative to the largely predominant verbal tasks (VTs) has been called the SPT effect. Tasks performed by the experimenter and simply observed by the subject, i.e., experimenter performed tasks (EPTs), have virtually the same effect as the SPT with relatively short (18-20 item) lists. The SPT gains an advantage over the EPT for very long (e.g., 48 items) lists.[55]

SPTs are also impervious to the "generation effects" of VTs. As we just saw, in a verbal task, if the subject is given the word BALL and asked to generate (imagine) an event, e.g., imagining a bouncing ball, he tends to do better in later recall than a subject who was simply presented the phrase, "The ball is bouncing." In an SPT, it makes no difference in later recall if the subject thought up the act of bouncing the ball and performed it, or merely performed it upon the supplied command, "Bounce the ball." Similarly, in verbal tasks, it can make a difference if the subject is told to check a word for spelling, or imagine its use in a sentence. The spelling check is a "shallow encoding" of the word, the sentence is a "deeper encoding." These types of instructions are virtually meaningless and have no effect in an SPT.[56]

For the redintegration model, these findings are fully expected. Purely from the ecological perspective, a subject performed task, e.g., "break the match," or "stir the coffee," is a completely specified multi-modal invariance structure. It sits at the highest level of an order of *completeness of specification*, which is to say completeness of specified event constraints. Whether the event is self-generated or performed on command, there is little difference in the invariance structure defining the event, or in the "modulated wave" required to reconstruct the event. The event carries none of the baggage of variability that abounds in purely verbally based experiments where subjects' mental operations are generally uncontrolled. In the purely verbal case of the presentation of the event (a sentence), we have very little idea what the "event" actually is. It may involve a visual image, it may not; the sentence may have been comprehended, it may not. Therefore the actual structure of event constraints is unknown. The use of imagery instructions comes closer, attempting to create an imaged, concrete event. But we are unsure of the veridicality of the image with respect to the concrete event; we are unsure that the complete structure of transformations and invariants was produced or to what extent.

I'll note the implications of this understanding of redintegration for just a few specific aspects of the SPT research.

1) The transitve-intransitve pattern

In the SPT experiments, there has been some controversy over the role of objects.[57] The Swedish group used real objects in their experiments, while the Saarbrücken group had the subjects perform actions with imaginary objects. The latter group still found an effect from acting out the event, but found the effect got a boost when real objects were used. While action was clearly seen as important, the question became, why? Zimmer considered the concept of brain-embedded programs for action or "action schema." For example, the action schema for "lifting" has a "slot" for *something to lift*, and in this sense action programs might be the units that "bind" events together.[58] In this respect, he noted an experiment using actions with transitive vs. intransitive verbs (push the refrigerator vs. sit by the desk).[59] Only the actions were re-performed in recall, with care taken to constrain the specifics of the action. If the original action involved pushing a refrigerator, then as a recall cue, the subject pretended to push something difficult to move. The cueing effect was stronger for transitive verbs. The subject was much more likely to remember that the action involved pushing a refrigerator. But just "sitting by" something, even if sitting in exactly the same way, was less likely to retrieve the fact that it was a desk one was sitting by.

We have seen now that the "transitive-intransitive" effect holds for SPTs, EPTs, VTs and imagery. This indicates that there is a memory mechanism or law that cuts across all modes of experiencing an event. It cannot be a purely motor effect; it is a more general effect than the SPT, yet applies to the SPT.

The principle acting must be more general and deeper than "action as the glue of events." The concept of a reconstructive wave faithful to, or supportive of, the invariance structure of events, to include their virtual motor component, is such a general principle.

2) *The role of objects*

The role of actual objects in the events, noted above, indexes how the SPT research efforts have exposed the concept that there are obvious levels of specificity. From worst to best:

- Verbally specified events
- Imagined events
- Observed events (as in EPTs)
- Imitated, concretely acted events (as in SPTs)
- Concretely acted events (as in SPTs).

The presence of objects – their actual usage in the event – can only aid more precise specification of the invariance structure and its constraints, and therefore the differentiation of events. This is because "specificity" *corresponds precisely to the degree of instantiation of the full dynamics supporting the perception of an event.* In cued recall, as we have reviewed, this becomes increasingly important. The discussion of the fine tuning of memory performance that is possible via the parametric manipulation of invariance structures highlights this. With respect to the role of action, *enactment guarantees the specificity.* The precise action constraint, used as a cue, again is a precise constraint on the reconstructive wave. Based on the invariance structure in which the cue is normally embedded it specifies, if not the actual event, an equivalence class of objects. Perhaps we should say, just as in McGeoch's model, that a set of past events has been "primed." In a reconstructive wave, we are dealing with something more dynamic and concrete than an abstract "slot" or argument for an object in an action schema.

3) *Verb to Verb failure*

In this context, it can also be seen why one should not have expected the attempts of SPT researchers to associate verbs to verbs (actions to arbitrary actions) in SPTs to be particularly successful (they were not), e.g., "lifting the book" as a cue for "tapping the wall."[60] There is nothing in the invariance structure of E' capable of redintegrating E. This was in effect a nonsense syllable PA task imported into the context of SPTs.

4) EPT vs. SPT performance

Why is the performance on EPTs so nearly equal to that of the SPT? If action or motor encoding is the primary principle operating in the SPT effect, why is there not a greater difference? In truth, there is no truly principled reason within the current SPT/motor action framework of theory for the supposed EPT episodic-relational advantage, nor especially for the larger question as to why the EPT is within a hair of SPT performance. The redintegrative model makes perfect sense of the virtual equality of EPT performance. We have seen that the EPT, as a concrete, ecological event, is highly specific of the invariance structure of events, and especially when coupled with the principle of perception as virtual action, the redintegrative model described would fully predict very strong memory performance in this very concrete, ecological context. The SPT, at the greatest level of specificity, would be expected to eventually prove superior.

Priming

Priming is considered to have major implications for the structure of memory. The concept will be important in the discussion of explicit (conscious) memory in Chapter V. In one experimental paradigm a word is presented briefly, e.g., "spoon" followed quickly by another word or non-word, e.g., in the word case, "coffee." The subject's task is usually a simple one like indicating whether "coffee" is a word or a non-word. In the SPOON-COFFEE pair, there would be an expected priming effect since SPOON is a close "associate" of COFFEE and has prepared the way in some sense for the response. In a pair like SPOON-BOOK we might expect little or no priming effect as BOOK is not a close associate of SPOON.

Figure 3.7. A semantic activation network for the concept "sleep." The words shown are the 15 highest associates to sleep. (After Roediger et al., 2001)

A major theoretical explanation for the priming effect has been the "spreading activation" model (Anderson, 1983).[61] Here memory is conceived as a network of "nodes" consisting of concepts related by semantic links or associative links. Consider the concept of SLEEP with its semantic network (Figure 3.7). Roediger et al. describe the classic, spreading activation-explained phenomenon, where the subjects hear fifteen of the surrounding concepts/ words (bed, rest, awake, tired, etc.).[62] Though "sleep" is not presented, on a later recognition test, the subjects are extremely likely to recognize it as having been part of the original list they heard.[63]

"Stirring" is no less a dynamic invariance structure than "sleep." On seeing SPOON, activation would be conceived to spread through the network of nodes related to SPOON, ultimately reaching COFFEE and facilitating response time to COFFEE. But what is stored at these nodes? If our node is STIR, is it the dynamic, time-extended, multi-modal invariance structure we have described for a coffee stirring event, or a yet higher order invariance defined across many forms of stirring? But how is this invariance, which has no reality other than as an invariant defined across concrete *experience*, stored "at a node?"

Another competing model is the compound cue theory. Here the SPOON (prime) –COFFEE (target) pair is viewed as forming a compound cue in short-term memory which is used to create a match to information in long-term memory. This joint-cue is a more powerful cue, providing the basis for a familiarity or parallel matching process to all items in memory. Facilitation of a response then is considered a function of "familiarity." A pair like MOTHER-CHILD is more familiar than MOTHER-HOSPITAL.[64] The familiarity value is conceived to relate directly to the response time required to categorize CHILD or HOSPITAL (as a word or non-word).

The SPOON-COFFEE pair is really but a compacted version of an experimental paradigm where sentences are presented such as:

(1) The spoon stirred the [COFFEE].

or

(2) The spoon stirred the [BOOK].

There is again a quicker response time in categorizing COFFEE (as word/non-word) in (1) than BOOK in (2). Again, (1) is presumed to have greater "familiarity" than (2), enhancing the response process. McKoon and Ratcliff however rejected the usefulness of this type of experimental material because they saw no way to get "familiarity" values from the sentences, whereas as with single words they could use associative frequency norms, e.g., the frequency that MOTHER appears as an associate to CHILD as opposed to HOSPITAL, or SPOON with COFFEE as opposed to BOOK.

Yet, with the sentence paradigm, we begin to approach the ecological case – real, specified events. Again we have extremely little control over the events in the subject's mind when we present word pairs like SPOON-COFFEE or DEER-GRAIN. Suppose we had this set of sentences:

(3) He stirred the coffee with the [spoon].
(4) He stirred the coffee with the [knife].
(5) He stirred the coffee with the [orange peel].
(6) He stirred the coffee with the [truck].

Here we are clearly in the case of an event invariance structure. "Coffee stirring" specifies an equivalence class of objects that can participate in the event, and that can fill in the blank. We have sent, in effect, a reconstructive wave through memory defined by the constraints of the invariance structure. Sentence (3) is the level of invariance defining normal (global) context. It is most "familiar." Sentences (4), and (5) begin defining a dimension of possible substances and structures which can participate in the event given they support certain structural invariances. Sentence (6) sits way at the end of this dimension, if at all. Nevertheless, with proper (global) context, for example a pre-discussion of childhood play, I could likely bring up the response time on (6). "Familiarity" or networks of "associates" are only a poor approximation to describing the effect of the dynamic patterns of activity and invariance structures involved here.

Priming is a another case of redintegration with its inherent reliance on event invariance structures. This means that priming is also subject to the parametric variation of these structures. This can then be kept in the very ecological dimension where it must be initially understood. Therefore we might have the equivalent of a "priming sentence" such as:

(7) The spoon stirred the _____.

But let the event be concretely acted out, e.g., the (blindfolded) subject actually stirs with the spoon within standard spatial constraints, where the substance stirred has liquid properties, thus resistance, similar to coffee. Now we present words/non-words (or better, concrete objects/events?) for recognition reaction time. Again in this case, we must reckon with normal context, i.e., coffee as normally stirred, as providing the shortest time. But there should eventually be some equivalence class of liquids which have been primed. As we vary the parameters of the substance, for example, now moving to a thick, batter-like substance, this effect should become more pronounced. Now something like "batter" should be primed more quickly, or "dough," etc. Conversely, as parameters diverge from the coffee stirring event, for example, the diameter of the circular motion grows too large, or the periodicity too different, etc., categorization times to associate words such as "coffee" will increase.

There are cross-modal invariants that may be manipulated. Let the event be pouring water into a glass, an event of rising water normally accompanied by a lawfully related increasing rise of pitch.[65] In this case the pitch may be manipulated to actually fall, or rise in a manner not coordinate with the invariance law. This, we can propose, should disrupt or lower categorization response time of words, e.g., POUR.[66]

Admittedly, we must be careful. "Martini" may be in the equivalence class of substances when taken relative to the resistance of the liquid to the stirring-spoon, but not when viewed from a larger perspective - relative to the complete experience of the wielding of the object. The martini-stirring event is characterized by a different stirrer (a stirring stick), a different container (a martini glass), and therefore a different dynamics. This is a context law for this kind of event and priming "martini" may then require this event structure. In fact, then, it is the complete dynamics of the event, i.e., the full invariance structure that is determining what is being primed. Again we are visualizing a brain-supported wave through our "holographic memory," the dynamical pattern supporting this being determined by the invariance structure of the (stirring) event. To complete the hypothesis then, we would say that, firstly, all the normal components ("associates") of the invariance structure are primed, to include visual, auditory, haptic invariants, etc. Secondly, as in the stirring case, objects or substances within an equivalence class are primed.

Priming a 4-D Memory

The totality of 4-D experience is a vast whole, with no true seam or break. What happens then in such a system when there is presented a word, e.g., CANOE? If the person has taken several canoe trips, we have just entered this memory with a key that will "activate" the whole in a particular mode, just as a wave of a particular frequency "activates" a hologram in a certain mode. CANOE is an integral element in these events, but it is always part of a whole event. There is the paddling, the paddles, the water, its sky-blueness, the muscles straining, the portaging, the portage, the lakes, the pines, the waves, the wind, the loons, the rapids, the campfires, the cooking, the fish, the fishing, the rods, the reels, the lines, the hang-ups... All these are aspects of a canoeing event or events. Because the *events* can be reconstructed via CANOE, these things are "activated." A spreading activation model, we can note, will always appear to have some validity, though it is only a shadow of the truth.

I am not attempting here to create a complete theory of priming. Certain kinds of priming effects last for many days and are modality specific, suggesting a form of "biasing" of a dynamic system to reproduce a pattern. In the situations above, our intuitions have been that if I follow CANOE with PADDLE (asking whether PADDLE is a word or non-word) I will obtain quicker reactions than if I follow it with TABLE. At the same time the compound cue theory will work – CANOE-PADDLE is more "familiar" than CANOE-TABLE. At the same time, however, a context can have been arranged beforehand which enhances the response time to TABLE, e.g., a picture of the canoe on the table being scraped and cleaned. This would destroy the normal familiarity standards and the "distance" of "links" in memory as well. So all is clearly event dependent, i.e., dependent on the precise invariance structure which defines the modulatory pattern evoked and therefore the reconstructive wave sent through 4-D multi-modal memory.

But simply discussing this in terms of static words such as "canoe" or "spoon" is relatively meaningless. We still are far from the ecological case with which we must begin. What is the "priming" effect of just the lexical "spoon?" How can we truly know? It is an ambiguous event, taking on whatsoever transformation the subject chooses to place upon it. What then is the priming effect of a spoon visually moving in a stirring motion? In a scooping motion? In a shoveling motion? Now we start to constrain the reconstructive wave towards an equivalence class of events defined by a certain invariance structure. Such a class should show the strongest priming effect. If we are interested in priming as a phenomenon, such an approach might begin to tease out some laws of "priming."

There are many other applications of this redintegrative model to current memory research – many aspects of the findings in Subject Performed Tasks, or imagery effects, or the famous concreteness effect involving the superior memory for concrete words over abstract words, or Vicente and Wang's implicit use of these priniciples (using the notion of "constraint attunement") in the context of remembering larger events such as baseball games (in *Psychological Review*, 1998), and more. "More" would also include a series of experiments by J. J. Asher on second language learning, where remarkable learning results were obtained using the ecological case – actually coordinating second language learning with performing concrete actions, that is, the subject performed tasks taken in the context of language learning. To Asher, first language learning, on which the learning of a second language should be modeled, takes place in an environment of linguistic commands to which the body/brain becomes attuned – "Johnny, wipe your nose!" or, "Johnny, pick up your spoon!" I have discussed some of this elsewhere.[67]

Elsasser and Bergson

For Elsasser, the book on cerebral memory has already been written. It is Bergson's *Matter and Memory*. For Bergson, the question of whether experience is stored in the brain is the absolutely critical question, the answer to which determines the relation of mind to matter. This is yet true; it is simply not understood by the current discussants on the problem of consciousness. As he explored the physiology and memory research data of his day, particularly on amnesias and aphasias, he, like Elsasser, came to the conclusion that a mechanistic model cannot account for the preservation of experience. Bergson, in perfect accord with his model of time and its indivisible flow, opted for a four dimensional model of being.

Elsasser, hoping to rely instead on his concept of the immense reservoir of possible brain states, chose to disagree with Bergson, noting that the concept of a dimension implies an *order*, and that the mixtures and the arbitrary and out-of-order intrusions of memories (that redintegration itself instigates) militate against this. Nevertheless, there are cases such as Sacks' retardate twins, who, given any date in their past, reel off every detail – the items of their lunch, detailed conversations, news items – as though they are seeing a panorama unfold before their inner eye.[68] These indicate there is indeed an order.

There is a great deal of evidence that all experience is indeed "stored." Just a small bit of this evidence is discussed in some of my other efforts.[69] We will not go into it here. For Bergson, the very essence of this memory is "to have date." The real difficulty, once one recognizes the nature of our perception of time-extended events, i.e., the origin of the image of the transforming external world, is that there is no principle by which this flowing experience could be jumbled, disordered, or rearranged. Retrieved in various chunks arbitrarily, or at will, yes. Disordered, no.

Intro to Analogical Reminding

Continuing his thoughts on the difference between the computer and the brain, Elsasser noted that psychology's central concept of *association* subsumes the ability of one thought to evoke other thoughts related by either spatiotemporal proximity of the objects, or by analogy of form, or of history, or numerous other similarities. "A computer," he remarked, "is quite unable to produce any kind of association in the psychological sense of that term; it could never say, "this reminds me of....".[70] The implication here is that there is a fundamental memory retrieval operation, namely redintegration, that underlies the fundamental cognitive operation of analogy. Using his spoon, little brother launches a pea at big sister across the dinner table. I say, as an analogy, "The spoon is a catapult." What has happened here is the insertion of a possible component (spoon) within an event invariance structure (catapulting). The spoon, under the dynamic catapulting transformation, now evidences new "features" or "properties" which support the invariance structure of the event. Redintegration, then, underlies the fundamental operation of thought – analogy.

Hofstadter and Sander, in *Surfaces and Essences*, have recently created a large and brilliant tome devoted to proving that analogy is such – fundamental, basic – even unto being the operation that creates *categories, classes and concepts.* One cannot get more fundamental, more basic. Without this ability to create analogy, one cannot even approach creating the equivalent to human thought. We will explore the current attempts to achieve this by symbolic programs and connectionist networks in the next chapter. But redintegration is the basis, i.e., redintegration based on the retrieval of experience via the invariance structure of an event. Without being able to support this retrieval operation, AI has already lost the battle to build an equivalent to human intelligence.

Chapter III: End Notes and References

1. Bergson, 1896/1912, *Matter and Memory*, p. 88.
2. Gibson, J. J. (1966). *The Senses Considered as Visual Systems.* Boston: Houghton-Mifflin, p. 276.
3. Gibson, J. J. (1966). *The Senses Considered as Visual Systems.* Boston: Houghton-Mifflin, p. 277.
4. Gibson, J. J. (1966). *The Senses Considered as Visual Systems.* Boston: Houghton-Mifflin, p. 276.
5. Bergson, H. (1896/1912), op. cit., p. 180.
6. Bergson, H. (1896/1912), op. cit., p. 132.
7. Hawkins, Jeff. (2004). *On Intelligence.* New York: Times Books.
8. Robbins, S. E. (2009). The COST of explicit memory. *Phenomenology and the Cognitive Sciences, 8,* 33-66.
9. Barsalou, L. W. (1993). Flexibility, structure and linguistic vagary in concepts: Manifestations of a compositional system of perceptual symbols. In A Collins, S. Gathercole, M. Conway, & P. Morris (Eds.), *Theories of Memory,* New Jersey: Erlbaum.
10. Mayes, A. R., & Roberts, N. (2001). Theories of episodic memory. In A. Baddeley, M. Conway, & J. Aggleton. *Episodic Memory.* New York: Oxford University Press, 86-109.
11. Elssaser, W. (1987). *Reflections on a theory of organisms.* Baltimore: John Hopkins University Press.
12. Semon, R. (1909/1923), *Mnemic Psychology* (B. Duffy, Trans.). Concord, MA: George Allen & Unwin.
13. Dessoir, M. (1912), *Outlines of the history of psychology.* New York: MacMillan Co.
14. Klein, D. B. (1970). *A History of Scientific Psychology.* New York: Basic Books.
15. Hollingworth, H. L. (1926). *The Psychology of Thought.* New York: Appleton and Co. Hollingworth, H. L. (1928). *Psychology: Its Facts and Principles.* New York: Appleton and Co.
16. Hollingworth, H. L., 1926, op. cit. pp. x-xi.
17. Craik, F., & Tulving, E. (1975). Depth of processing and the retention of words in episodic memory. *Journal of Experimental Psychology: General, 104,* 268-294.
18. Ibid., p.291, emphasis added.
19. Marschark, M., and Surian, L. (1992). Concreteness effects in free recall: The role of imaginal and relational processing. *Memory and Cognition, 20*(6), 612-20.
20. Verbrugge, R. (1977). Resemblances in language and perception. In R.E. Shaw & J. D. Bransford (Eds.), *Perceiving, Acting and Knowing.* New Jersey: Lawrence Erlbaum Associates.
21. Eich, J. (1985). Levels of processing, encoding specificity, elaboration, and CHARM. *Psychological Review. 92* (1), 1-38.
22. Murdock, B.B. (1982). A theory for the storage and retrieval of item and associative information. *Psychological Review, 89* (6), 609-626.
23. Ibid., p. 625.
24. Zimmer, H. D., Helstrup, T., & Engelkamp, J. (2000). Pop-Out into Memory: A Retrieval Mechanism That is Enhanced with the Recall of Subject-Performed Tasks. *Journal of Experimental Psychology: Learning, Memory and Cognition, 26,* 3, 658-670.

25. Craig, C. M., & Bootsma, R. J., 2000. Judging time to passage. In M. A. Grealy and J. A. Thomson (eds.), *Studies in Perception and Action V,* New Jersey: Erlbaum.
    Verbrugge, R. (1977). Resemblances in language and perception. In R.E. Shaw & J. D. Bransford (Eds.), *Perceiving, Acting and Knowing.* New Jersey: Lawrence Erlbaum Associates.

26. Savelsbergh, G. J. P., Whiting, H.T., and Bootsma, R. J. 1991. Grasping tau. *Journal of Experimental Psychology: Human Perception and Performance* 17: 315-322.

27. Marschark, M., Richman, C., Yuille, J., & Hunt, R. (1987). The role of imagery in memory: On shared and distinctive information. *Psychological Bulletin, 102,* 28-41.

28. McGeoch, J. A. (1942), *The psychology of human learning.* New York: Longmans, Greene.

29. Vicente, K. J., & Wang, J. H. (1998). An ecological theory of expertise effects in memory recall. *Psychological Review,* 105 (1), 33-57.

30. Jenkins, J. J., Wald, J., & Pittenger, J. B. (1978). Apprehending pictorial events: An instance of psychological cohesion. *Minnesota Studies of the philosophy of science,* Vol. 9, 1978.

31. Finke, R. A., & Freyd, J.J. (1985). Transformations of visual memory induced by implied motions of pattern elements. *Journal of Experimental Psychology: Learning, Memory and Cognition,* 11, 780-794.
    Finke, R. A., Freyd, J. J., & Shyi, G. C. (1986). Implied velocity and acceleration induce transformation of visual imagery. *Journal of Experimental Psychology: General,* 115, 175-188.
    Freyd, J.J. (1987). Dynamic mental representations. *Psychological Review,* 94, 427-438.
    Freyd, J.J., & Finke, R. A. (1984). Representational momentum. *Journal of Experimental Psychology: Learning, Memory and Cognition,* 10, 126-132.
    Freyd, J. J., Kelly, M. H., & DeKay, M. L. (1990). Representational momentum in memory for pitch. *Journal of Experimental Psychology: Learning, Memory and Cognition,* 16, 1107-1117.

32. Bingham, G. P. (1993). Perceiving the size of trees: Form as information about scale. *Journal of Experimental Psychology: Human Perception and Performance,* 19, 1139-1161.

33. Gray, R. and Regan, D. 1999. Estimating time to collision with a rotating nonspherical object. In M. A. Grealy and J. A. Thomson (eds.), *Studies in Perception and Action V.* New Jersey: Erlbaum.

34. Pittenger, J. B., & Shaw, R. E. (1975). Aging faces as viscal elastic events: Implications for a theory of non rigid shape perception. *Journal of Experimental Psychology: Human Perception and Performance* 1: 374-382.

35. Amazeen, E. (1997). The effects of volume on perceived heaviness by dynamic touch: With and without vision. *Journal of Ecological Psychology, 9,* 245-263.

36. Jenison, R. (1997). On acoustic information for motion. *Journal of Ecological Psychology, 9,* 131-151.

37. Steenbergen, B., van der Kamp, J., & Carson, R. G. (1997). Spoon handling in two-four year old children. *Journal of Ecological Psychology, 9,* 113-129.

38. Flynn, S.(1994). The perception of relative mass in physical collisions. *Journal of Ecological Psychology, 6,* 185-204.

39. Cabe, P., & Pittenger, J. (1992). Time-to-topple: Haptic angular tau. *Journal of Ecological Psychology*, 4, 241-246.
40. Kinsella-Shaw, J., Shaw, J., Turvey, M. T. (1992). Perceiving "walk-on-able" slopes. *Journal of Ecological Psychology*, 4, 223-239.
41. Pittenger, J. B. (1990). Detection of violations of the law of pendulum motion: Observer's sensitivity to the relation of period and length. *Journal of Ecological Psychology, 2*, 55-81.
42. Cabe, P. A. and Pittenger, J. B. (2000). Human sensitivity to acoustic information from vessel filling. *Journal of Experimental Psychology: Human Perception and Performance* 26: 313-324.
43. Warren, W. H. (1984). Perceiving affordances: Visual guidance of stair climbing. *Journal of Experimental Psychology*: Human Perception and Performance, 10, 683–703.
44. Chemero, A. (2009). *Radical Embodied Cognitive Science*. Cambridge, MA: MIT Press.
45. One can see Chemero Ibid.) for this disucssion or:
    Chemero, A. (2003). An outline of a theory of affordances. *Journal of Ecological Psychology*, 15, 181-195.
46. Paivio, A. (1971) *Imagery and verbal processes*. New York: Holt, Rinehart, and Winston.
47. Rowher, W. D. Jr. (1967). Pictorial and verbal factors in the efficient learning of paired-associates. *Journal of Educational Psychology*, *58*, (5), 278-284.
48. Wollen, K. A. (1969). Variables that determine the effectiveness of picture mediators in paired-associate learning. Paper presented at the Meeting of the Psychonomic Society.
49. Marschark, M., Richman, C., Yuille, J., & Hunt, R. (1987). The role of imagery in memory: On shared and distinctive information. *Psychological Bulletin, 102*, 28-41.
50. Schmidt, S. R. (1991). Can we have a distinctive theory of memory? *Memory and Cognition*, 19(6), 523-542.
51. Craik, F., & Tulving, E. (1975). Depth of processing and the retention of words in episodic memory. *Journal of Experimental Psychology: General, 104*, 268-294.
52. Robbins, S. E. (2002). Semantics, experience and time. *Cognitive Systems Research*, 301-335.
    Robbins, S. E. (2006). On the possibility of direct memory. In V. W. Fallio (Ed.), *New Developments in Consciousness Research.*. New York: Nova Science Publishing, 1-64.
53. For reviews of this research:
    Engelkamp, J. & Zimmer, H. D. (1994), *The Human Memory: A Multi-Modal Approach*, (Seattle: Hogrefe & Huber).
    Engelkamp, J. (1998). *Memory for Actions*, East Sussex: Psychology Press.
54. For reviews:
    Cohen, R., Peterson, T., Mantini-Atkinson, T. (1987). Interevent differences in event memory: Why are some events more recallable than others?, *Memory and Cognition*, **15** (2), 109-118.
    Nilsson, L. G. (2000). Remembering actions and words. In F.I.M. Craik and E. Tulving (Eds.), *Oxford Handbook of Memory* (pp. 137-148), Oxford: Oxford University Press.
55. See Engelkamp, 1998, pp. 55-59.
56. Two views have competed for the explanation of the effect. The multi-modal view (Backman & Nilsson, 1985; Backman, Nilsson, & Kormi-Nouri, 1993) has emphasized the multi-modal nature of enacted events, arguing SPTs activate the verbal-semantic content

of the action as well as information from perceptual cues. This combination, it is felt, accounts for the improved retention. Engelkamp (1998; Engelkamp & Zimmer, 1985, 1997) focused on the motor component. Central to the encoding of actions is the fact that they must be planned and initiated. Rather than all sensory and motor features contributing to the effect, only the motor features contribute to the enactment advantage.

57. Zimmer, H. D., & Cohen, R.L. (2001). Remembering actions: A specific type of memory? In H. D. Zimmer & R. L. Cohen (Eds.), *Memory for Actions: A Distinct Form of Episodic Memory?* Oxford: Oxford University Press, pp. 3-24.

58. Zimmer, H. D. (2001). Why do actions speak louder than words?: Action memory as a variant of encoding manipulations or the result of a specific memory system? In H. D. Zimmer & R. L. Cohen (Eds.), *Memory for Actions: A Distinct Form of Episodic Memory?* Oxford: Oxford University Press, pp. 151-198.

59. Ratner, H. H., & Hill, L. (1991). The development of children's action memory: When do actions speak louder than words? *Psychological Research*, 53, 195-202.

60. See Engelkamp, 1998.

61. Anderson, J. R. (1983). A spreading activation theory of memory. *Journal of Verbal Learning and Verbal Behavior*, 22, 261-295.

62. Roediger, H. L., Balota, D., & Watson, J. (2001). Spreading Activation and Arousal of False Memories. In H. L. Roediger III, J. Nairne, I. Neath, A. Surprenant (Eds.), *The Nature of Remembering: Essays in Honor Robert G. Crowder*. Washington, D. C.: American Psychological Association.

63. Roediger, H. L, & McDermott, K. B. (1995). Creating false memories: Remembering words not presented in lists. *Journal of Experimental Psychology: Learning, Memory and Cognition, 21*, 803-814.

64. Shelton, J.R. and Martin, R.C. (1992). How semantic is automatic semantic priming? *Journal of Experimental Psychology: Learning, Memory, and Cognition*, 18(6), 1191-1210.

65. Cabe, P. A. and Pittenger, J. B. (2000). Human sensitivity to acoustic information from vessel filling. *Journal of Experimental Psychology: Human Perception and Performance* 26: 313-324.

66. This model has affinities to a response competition model of priming (cf. Klinger & Burton, 2000) already precursed, as noted, by McGeoch, though obviously extended here beyond the S-R formulation. Interference is intrinsic in such a model, but theory has for some time held that priming is not subject to interference. Lustig and Hasher (2001), in a recent review, have effectively shown that priming is indeed subject to interference – in consonance with this model. Neither spreading activation nor compound cues have anything inherently within their theoretical structure that supports or predicts the parametric manipulation of invariance structures proposed here.
Klinger, M. R. & Burton, P. R. (2000). Mechanisms of unconscious priming I: Response competition, not spreading activation. *Journal of Experimental Psychology: Learniing, Memory and Cognition*, 26(2), 441-456.
Lustig, C., & Hasher, L. (2001). Implicit memory is not immune to interference. *Psychological Bulletin, 127*, 618-628.

67. Asher, J. J. (1965). The strategy of total physical response: An application to learning Russian. *International Review of Applied Linguistics*, 3, 291-300.

Asher, J. J. (1966). The learning strategy of total physical response: a review. *The Modern Language Journal*, 50, 79-84.

Asher, J. J. (1972). The child's first language as a model for second language learning. *Modern Language Journal,* 56, 135-150.

Asher, J. J., & Price, B. (1967). The learning strategy of total physical response. *Child Development*, 38, 125-137.

68. Sacks, O. (1987). *The Man Who Mistook His Wife for a Hat.* New York: Harper and Row.
69. Robbins, S. E., 2006, op. cit.

Robbins, S. E. (2012). *Time and Memory: A Primer on the Scientific Mysticism of Consciousness.* Atlanta: CreateSpace.

70. Elsasser, 1987, op. cit., p. 86.

CHAPTER IV

AI and Analogy

…analogy is the fuel and fire of thinking.

— Hofstadter and Sander, *Surfaces and Essences*[1]

AI and the Problem of Analogy

Analogy is the fundamental basis of thought and language. The just previous sentence relies on analogy; it is invoking the concept of a basement or foundation underlying and supporting a structure, in this case the structure of thought. Metaphor, which is simply another form of analogy, is the cognitive basis of language. Language is littered with "dead" metaphors that are simply not recognized as such, for example, "He grasped the concept," or "He jumped right on the task." If you cannot support analogy, you have no theory of intelligence. You cannot support thought. You have no theory of cognition.

AI comes in two major flavors. One can be termed the "symbolic manipulation" paradigm. This was the first to be developed, starting roughly in the 1960's. The other is the connectionist (or neural network) model, initiated with seriousness roughly in the very late 1970's. Connectionist models are considered more near the biological and have the advantage of a natural learning process through their weight adjustments. Both approaches continue to vie for position; in some camps they are seen as complements, though no one knows how the symbolic manipulation model can use the output of a neural network, i.e., how there can actually be a complementary relationship. It doesn't actually matter. Neither can support analogy. Both end at the same place.

If I were to pick a year when the symbolic computer model of mind and brain swept into the University of Minnesota where I was in graduate school, I would say 1972. In this year the Carnegie-Mellon computer scientists, Alan Newell and Herbert Simon, published *Human Problem Solving*. My primary advisor in psychology, Paul E. Johnson, held a seminar on just this book, and the graduate students in the class, including me, poured over its chapters and discussed it. To Newell and Simon, the brain is just another form of computer. Its essence is to *manipulate symbols*, just like the symbols – the little a's and b's and c's – that are moved around in an algebraic equation using the proper rules:

> It can be seen that this approach makes no assumptions that the hardware of computers and brains are similar, beyond the assumption that both are general purpose symbol-manipulating devices, and that the computer can be programmed to execute elementary information processes functionally quite like those executed by the brain.[2]

In the book, Newell and Simon described a computer program, General Problem Solver (GPS), which could successfully solve problems in three subjects – logic theorem proving, chess, and cryptarithmetic. An example of the latter type of problem is, DONALD + GERALD = ROBERT, where one must find a unique number value (0-9) for each letter, where we are given initially only that the letter D has the value 5. Real human subjects were recorded, with their ongoing comments, as they solved these problems – a verbally expressed thought-trail termed a "protocol." The protocols of the human subjects and the steps they took towards a solution were "compared" with the "protocol" of the steps the computer took, and the authors claimed reasonable similarities. That the two "protocols" with their rather vague similarities might represent two completely different underlying processes or forms of thinking "devices" wasn't much worried about. This very loose form of "scientific" comparison still carries on today, both with this form of AI and with the neural network models.

In essence, the solution method of GPS was the exact form of what would eventually become "expert systems." Paul Johnson was extremely impressed. Along with his psychology doctorate, he had a masters degree in physics, and as his research assistant, I had been helping him do experiments on physics students, attempting to model the structure of their knowledge of physics concepts. Newell and Simon gave a new, concrete approach to modeling knowledge. I played for awhile with constructing one of these "expert systems" to solve elementary physics problems. The program would be given as input a language-based statement of the problem, for example: "The truck traveled for three hours at 10 miles/hour. How far did it go?" But handling all the possible variants of even these simple forms of problem, I soon saw, was a lost cause. This requires knowledge of the physical world, in fact, the form of knowledge that computer modelers ultimately began to call "common sense knowledge," the basis for which we have been discussing.

Other works like Newell and Simon's were appearing or had already, for example, MIT theorist Marvin Minsky's collection of computer programs which solved problems ranging from geometry proofs to rudimentary "language comprehension." B. F. Skinner, his rats and his Skinner boxes were being swept aside. The new model of the brain, leaping into the pent up vacuum created by Skinner, for Skinner had no model in actuality, was that the brain was in essence a digital computer – a symbol manipulation device. We only needed to discover the cool software programs necessary and we would soon have language understanding programs, programs for vision, for mathematics, for chess, and of course, walking, perceiving robots. Secretaries would take dictations from their boss in English and translate them to fluent Japanese. The computer now presented a very concrete tool to implement what was in fact a deep, long held metaphysical position on the nature of mind, a position that went all the way back to Plato. The achievement of all this, given we now had an absolute lock on a device to implement this long held, implicit conception of the nature of mind and intelligence, was thought by its proponents to be very, very imminent, i.e., it should have happened thirty years ago.

Shaw's Analysis

In this year, 1972, I attended a seminar on this new subject led by Dr. Robert E. Shaw. Bob Shaw was my doctoral thesis advisor. He was a student of Gibson. Bob would later found *The Journal of Ecological Psychology* – *the* academic journal for the Gibson school of perception theory. At Cornell (where Gibson taught), Bob had been a post-doc in abstract automata theory for two years. Automata theory is the abstract, theoretical basis of all computing. Bob Shaw was well armed for the subject.

In the seminar, largely keying off Feigenbaum's book, *Computers and Thought*, we went through a large array of computer models at the time which dealt with some aspect of mind, be it logic problem solving, language, vision, whatever. Each was found wanting. The "want" was not a matter of persnickety detail; it was on a general principle: the computer modelers were always giving away the problem. The brain could not possibly be pre-programmed with the advantages the computer modelers were giving themselves.

What do I mean by "giving away the problem?" Consider a problem solved by Newell and Simon's GPS termed the "monkey and the bananas" problem. The problem states that the monkey is in a room with a box, the bananas hanging from the ceiling. The monkey's problem is to grasp the bananas which are out of reach – a problem solvable by moving the box beneath the bananas and climbing up. GPS, as always, follows a "means-ends" analysis. The concept behind means-ends analysis is simple. If I want to go to the grocery store (my goal), and currently I am in my house (my current state), there is a series of "sub-goals" I need to achieve.

- To get to the store, I have to drive the car.
- To get to the car, I have to get to the garage.
- To get to the garage, I have to get out of my chair.
- To turn on the ignition, I have to put in the key.
- To put in the key, I have to have the key in my hand.
- And so on.

So we move to a specified goal by achieving (through various "means" or actions) a series of sub-goals. In the monkey's case the goal is "bananas in hand" and a series of sub-goals are given by "differences." The relevant differences (defined to the program) are the monkey's place (D1), the box's place (D2), the contents of the monkey's hand (D3), and the differences are furthermore ordered in degree of difficulty from D3 to D1. This is what is termed an *object language* – a language or symbol set defining the problem environment. The operators given the program are "climb," "walk," "move box," and "get bananas." The program must discover the proper sequence of operators required to reduce the differences successively to the point where the bananas are in the monkey's hand. This is in essence simply creating a *proof*, namely, a proof that we can get from A to B. It is a proof procedure carried out within a fixed theory of the monkey's world.

The object language, then, defines a *frame of fixed features* in which the solution is carried out. But, as GPS did, giving the monkey "move box" as an operator, i.e., the *mobility* of the box, is equivalent to giving away – or better, giving away the discernment of – a fundamental feature and thus the solution path to the problem. Given this "mobility" or "move box" as an operator, it is only a matter of solving for the right sequence to apply the operators to resolve the "differences" and thus get a meal of bananas. For Gutenberg, the inventor of the printing press, it was quite a different story. In contemplating how to produce books in mass, the "mobility" of type as an intrinsic feature or operator in the problem of creating a printing device was not at all apparent. This emerged only over *analogy*.

Gutenberg's Analogical Press

Gutenberg also happens to have left us with a "protocol" of his solution processes. His problem existed originally, he stated, in the form of a desire to write "in a single instant, by a single effort of my thought, everything that can be put on a large sheet of paper, lines, words, letters, by labour of the most diligent class for a whole day, nay for several days."[3] His first suggestion as to the means came when he noticed how playing cards were made. The card images were carved on a block of wood, ink applied to the engraving, a thin sheet of paper placed over it, then rubbed and polished, and removed, leaving the image. This method had the advantage of being able to reproduce thousands of cards by repetition of a single operation and the multiplication of the blocks. But it had the disadvantage of being useable only on one side of the paper. Gutenberg wished to generalize this method "for large pages of writing,

106

for large leaves covered entirely on both sides, for whole books, for the first of all books, the Bible...," but he did not see how.

In his letter to Frere Cordilier, he tells of his noting the method of creating coins:

> Every coin begins with a punch. The punch is a little rod of steel, one end of which is engraved with the shape of one letter, several letters, all the signs which are seen in relief on a coin. The punch is moistened and driven into a steel plate, which becomes a hollow or stamp. It is into these coin stamps, moistened in their turn, that are placed the little discs of gold, to be converted into coins by a powerful blow.[4]

In his fifth letter he tells us:

> I took part in the wine harvest. I watched the wine flowing, and going back from effect to cause, I studied the power of this press which nothing can resist.[5]

Having already noted the punch, he saw that the pressure created by the wine press could be exercised also by lead:

> To work then! God has revealed to me the secret that I demanded of Him... I have had a large quantity of lead brought to my house, and that is the pen with which I shall write.[6]

At this point there occurred the relation to a seal:

> When you apply to the vellum of paper the seal of your community, everything has been said, everything is done, everything is there. Do you not see that you can repeat as many times as necessary the seal covered with signs and characters?[7]

And the whole process:

> One must strike, cast, make a form like the seal of your community, a mould such as that used for casting your pewter cups, letters in relief like those on your coins, and the

punch for producing them like your foot when it multiplies its print. There is the Bible.[8]

From the eighth letter:

The letters are moveable. The mobility of the letters is the true treasure which I have been searching for along unknown roads.[9]

The imagination is sorely tested when we try to place this process within the framework of a match of pre-defined, fixed features. Gutenberg begins with a general formulation of the goal, a general desire to print things quickly, in quantity, in great amounts at once. He has noticed the "repetitive" feature of card-making and the "multiplicative" feature of the blocks. Being tied to the concrete transformations defining card making, they are very *specifically* defined. As they stand, these features have only their particular meaning in their particular case. Notice that it is not even clear to Gutenberg that these are particularly important features. The "features" involved in coin-making – the rigidity and force provided by the steel punch are likewise tied to the particular event.

These events were fused in Gutenberg's mind with yet a third event – the wine-pressing. There are invariants defined over all three, particularly the application of great force and the repetitive application of the force. These features can now approach the abstract generality which the feature matching framework envisions, but they do so only by virtue of their definition across concrete events.

Gutenberg was *defining* the features of the world in which he would solve the problem. He was *creating* the object language. The features were being defined through analogy – he was seeing analogies to seals, to moulds, to stamping coins. As we start as infants, no less later as inventors, the brain is initially confronted with a world in which it must define the features. It is the *problem of the definition of features* that must be solved. Said differently, it is, as Narasimhan (1969) noted very early in the game, *creating* the object language that is the problem.[10] The computer modelers were simply ignoring this, surreptitiously solving the problem, defining features (the object language) and then creating a logic system in which the computer could do that which it is capable of doing – manipulating the nicely pre-defined features as symbols.

The computer modelers, are still trying to explain how the brain does *analogies* in this very same way – by defining fixed features of the world, and then creating a proof procedure which "finds the analogy." We begin with the latest form of these attempts, as found in connectionism.

Connectionism and Its Assumption

The realm of connectionist theoretical effort is vast. The subjects to which it has been applied span object recognition, categorization, sequential action learning and disorders thereof, semantic cognition and disorders in semantic memory, also for consciousness, analogy, and much more. Virtually nothing in the sphere of mind seems out of its reach. Indeed, a famous critique was made by Fodor and Pylyshyn (1995), but it seems only to have provided a challenge for obstacles to be overcome. Connectionism is the 800 pound gorilla on the block where cognitive science lives.[11] It is in connectionsim that AI's hope for achieving an equality with human intelligence largely lives, as it is the most "brain-like" of architectures. I am going to draw a limit here on the spheres of mind into which connectionism can even possibly advance. I am not arguing that connectionism, or better, some form thereof, is inapplicable everywhere, but the limit is a very harsh one.

One source of the limit is in a fundamental supposition that is employed to begin modeling. This is that the ecological world can be partitioned into various categories of entities which a network will connect in appropriate ways. The entities are objects, properties of objects, "features," relations, "events," "actions." This fundamental starting point is justified as a simplifying assumption to get the dynamics of the models in motion; it is considered of little consequence.

In essence, these various types of entities are all abstract "objects," and the objects are being manipulated in an abstract space to form appropriate connective juxtapositions. In a word, this fits the definition of syntax earlier noted in its most elemental form: rules for the concatenation and juxtaposition of objects. The firing frequencies of the set of neurons in the brain at a particular instant of time can be visualized as a set of, or vector of, firing values, for example, the vector for a brain of six neurons might look like [.3, .5, .3, .7, .2, .4] – a "six-dimensional" vector for our n=6 neurons. The syntactic rule view is perfectly consonant then with a major underlying principle of connectionism, namely, any mental state can be represented by a n-dimensional vector of numeric activation values of the neural units in a network – for any such state simply represents a particular configuration or status of these rules relating objects. A second major principle, that memory is a function of the connection strengths of these units to each other via a (NxN)-dimensional matrix of connection weights, is consonant as well, expressing again the effective, current status of any rule relating these objects.

This abstract view will cause no alarm to the connectionist. In fact, it will be familiar. In essence, it is the basic point of Searle's famous "Chinese Room" argument applied directly to connectionism.[12] To remind us briefly, Searle had envisioned himself in a room in which he took in statements in English, translating them into Chinese, and sending the translation back out. The translation was effected by Searle himself acting as a computer, simply using a translation algorithm, substituting symbols for symbols, creating eventually a statement in Chinese. It is mere manipulation of syntax rules, argued Searle; no understanding of Chinese is arising at all in this process. It is the source of Searle's oft-repeated rejoinder: "Syntax is not sufficient for semantics."[13] The controversy here has been enormous, but even the standard, non-connectionist symbolic approach to AI has long and successfully resisted a negative (to itself) conclusion to the debate.

I intend to take the debate to a deeper level: I intend to show *why* syntax cannot support semantics, why this approach cannot support the background of "common sense knowledge" necessary for understanding, and why syntax, no matter what the "implementation" or system it is embedded within – be it robot, be it digital computer, be it quantum computer – is not capable of supporting the perception of, and therefore the understanding of, events. The deep core of this, to anticipate, is that dwelling within the above abstract view is this fact: *connectionism begs the description of change.* The change of position of abstract objects in an abstract space is not change. It is neither real motion nor real time. It is the same old abstract "time" that is simply another form of an abstract space. In essence, this means that connectionism is precluded from embracing the concrete *events* of the ecological sphere.

I hasten to say that by "event" I do not refer to the learning of sequential actions. Botvinick and Plaut, for example, provided a connectionist model of multistep actions such as making tea or making coffee – events requiring a series of steps, the order and elements of which can be disrupted by diseases like Alzheimers.[14] This is the syntax of a complex action, where its components can be treated as objects, ordered by a syntactic rule. This is perhaps appropriate grist for connectionism. But any of these components, say, stirring the coffee with a spoon, is as we have seen, a complex transformation of the matter-field over concrete time with optical structure (invariance), acoustic structure, kinesthetic structure, physical forces, moments of inertia, energy frequency ratios. It is this information, defined over the flow of time, to include the flow itself, that is unavailable to connectionism. But this information is the heart of semantics. When the strategy is taken to discretize it into objects amenable to syntactic manipulation, the result is systems that are brittle, arbitrary, and riddled with the hallmark failures of reference emerging when semantics is reduced to syntax. The semantic cannot be so reduced.[15] This simplifying assumption is inescapably sacrificing any ability to deal with the realm of the semantic, and it is obscuring the fact that with respect to certain forms of memory and cognition – forms that are not essentially syntactic – nothing real that the brain is actually doing is being modeled.

But sub-serving memory, we have seen, is the fundamental retrieval operation of redintegration, for redintegration is driven by the invariance structure of events. Again, these events cannot be reduced to properties, features, or "invariants" inherited from perception as connectionist models use this term. The very processes of perception – unusable by connectionism – are already the basis for, and operating in, memory retrieval, long before connectionist networks even engage in the subject with their simplifying assumptions. It is this retrieval process, i.e., redintegration, that underlies the fundamental operation of cognition of analogy. If analogy rests upon a highly ecologically-based redintegration, an attempt to syntacticize it will create an artificial, brittle system. It is a signal that the limits of connectionism have been crossed, in fact, that connectionism has simply crossed over into the same problems as the earlier, symbolic manipulation model of AI.

A Connectionist Model

The first model we will look at, appearing in the highly prestigious journal, *Behavioral and Brain Sciences*, is by the network theorists, Rogers and McClelland.[29] Rogers and McClelland employ a multi-layer network where the input units correspond to an item in the environment, for example: ROBIN, or SALMON, or FLOWER. The units in the relationship layer correspond to contextual constraints on the kind of information to be retrieved, for example: IS, CAN, HAS. The input pair, ROBIN CAN, they state, corresponds to a situation in which the network is shown a picture of a robin and asked what it can do. The network is trained to turn on the correct attribute units of the output layer, in this case: GROW, MOVE, FLY, SING (as opposed to SWIM, DIVE, FLOP for the salmon). The input pair, ROBIN HAS, will elicit WINGS,

FEATHERS, BEAK, LEGS, as examples, from a trained network, as opposed to BARK, BRANCHES, LEAVES, as examples, for TREE.

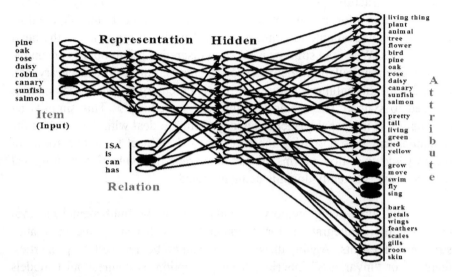

Figure 4.1. Connectionist model of semantic memory. Where connections (arrows) are indicated, every unit connects to every other unit. Adapted from Rogers and McClelland.

As the connection weights are initially random, the output units of the network must be adjusted gradually via a *backpropagation* algorithm based upon the amount of error relative to the desired output state. This adjustment, to obtain the correct response sets, often requires many hundreds of epochs of training. For Rogers and McClelland, the fundamental principle operating to achieve the correct output unit states is *coherent covariation*. The fact, for example, that *flying* and *singing* tend to occur consistently with robins, while the color *red* may occur with good likelihood for both flowers and robins tends to pull the weights apart in the appropriate direction.

Rogers and McClelland hold that this network is perfectly at home in the ecological world. The input units can be construed as receiving perceptual input, for example the observation of a robin sitting on a branch, and the output units are predicting possible events or outcomes, say, the robin flying away.

The Network Versus the Invariance Structure of Events

Let us situate another ecological learning situation within the Rogers and McClelland framework. Given the object, SPOON, in the context of CAN, the network would be trained to respond with the set of things a spoon can do, for example, STIR (as in coffee), SCOOP (as in cereal), CUT (as in grapefruit), BALANCE (as on the edge of the coffee cup). If we focus on the first of these, STIR, we are aware that we are in the realm of events, in this case *stirring* events, in which a spoon is being used. But this event has a structure. Let us remind ourselves...

Remember our event: stirring coffee in a cubical cup, using a spoon. The (ongoing) event has a time-extended invariance structure. The swirling coffee surface is a radial flow field. The constant size of the cup, as one's head moves forward or backward, is specified, over time, by a constant ratio of height to the occluded texture units of the table surface gradient. Over this flow field and its velocity vectors there is the value, τ, (tau), specific to the time to impending contact with an object or surface, and has a critical role in controlling action. As the coffee cup is moved over the table towards us, this value specifies time to contact and provides information for modulating the hand to grasp the cup. As the cup is cubical, its edges and vertices are sharp discontinuities in the velocity flows of its sides as the eyes saccade, where these flows specify, *over time*, the form of the cup. The periodic motion of the spoon is a *haptic* flow field that carries an adiabatic invariance – a constant ratio of energy of oscillation to frequency of oscillation. There is another aspect to this motion of the spoon, as the use of the spoon is a form of "wielding," described under the concept of the "inertia tensor." This entire structure and far more must be supported, globally, over time, by the resonant feedback among visual, motor, auditory, even prefrontal areas. In other words, *it is this entire informational structure that must be supported, in ongoing fashion, by the neural dynamics supporting the perception of the coffee stirring event.*

Now we can imagine that we have trained the network of figure 4.1 with yet other terms. For example, as input terms, we might have had SPOON, FORK, HAMMER, SAW. As output terms, we could have STIR, CUT, STICK, POUND, TOOL, UTENSIL, etc. In Rogers and McClelland's formulation, I would present SPOON in the context, CAN, and the network is trained, looking at errors in the responses and making the needed connection weight adjustments, to respond with STIR. In the causal "interpretation" of the network's response, after the example of the robin on the branch, the network is predicting the accompanying events we'd expect on seeing a SPOON moving within the cup of coffee, for example, the circular motion of the coffee liquid, the clinking sound, the haptic or muscular feel of the periodic motion, etc.

But what sense is this? This is a remnant of the supremely non-ecological verbal learning tradition, its roots in the semantics-eradication program of Ebbinghaus, which ultimately bifurcated events arbitrarily into components, e.g., SPOON and STIR, or JAX and WUK, then asked: how do we learn these components as a paired-associate pair? In reality, we are perceiving the spoon as an integral part of a stirring event, with all the event's ongoing invariance structure. Where is the "error?" We need no weight adjustments to "link" the event "components" to a proper output pattern. The "components" are already integrally "linked" in the dynamic physics of stirring. For there to be a stirring at all, there must be a liquid, its resistance, an instrument moving the liquid, a force behind it, a spatial constraint on the liquid (such as a cup), a periodic motion, etc., etc. These are not "components" that must be laboriously associated.[16]

A spoon scooping and lifting oatmeal is yet another event with an integral and complex set of forces and auditory/visual patterning. A spoon stirring pancake batter is yet a different complex invariance structure. A spoon digging into and cutting grapefruit is yet another. A spoon balancing on the edge of the coffee cup another. Now we have the set: SPOON CAN: [stir, balance, scoop, cut]. Again we can ask, if I re-present SPOON, which event will it redintegrate? Again, SPOON is roughly equivalent to a static event, a resting spoon. There is little structure to this cue-event; it is underspecified, yet common to all. It is like sending an imprecise reconstructive wave with little coherence through a hologram – we reconstruct a composite image of multiple recorded wave fronts, in this case, spoon-related events. It is the classic interference of McGeoch. The brain's neural network does not require "error-training" to specify this set.[17] This is a completely misguided, Ebbinghaus-like concept of the neural network theorists.

But, as we have seen, we can retrieve specific events. The cue must have the same invariance structure or a sufficient subset. For the coffee stirring, we re-present an abstract rendering of the coffee's radial flow field, or simulate the inertial tensor of the wielding. We are creating, globally throughout the brain, a more constrained, more coherent "reconstructive wave." To reconstruct the batter-stirring event as opposed to the coffee-stirring, we must constrain our wielding cue differently to capture the larger amplitude of the stirring motion and/or the greater resistance of the batter.

The "coherent covariation" that these networks detect is essentially a low order form of invariance, what I shall term a *syntactic* invariance. Syntactic invariance is of a very low order; as low an order as facts like the nonsense syllable QEZ always occurs with PUJ, or WUX with GEK. This is but a simple spatial conjunction of objects. Object X is always found by Y. Again, this is the very definition of syntax: *laws for the legal concatenation or juxtaposition of objects.* It is a purely *spatial* operation – in the sense of the classical abstract space. The lists of nonsense syllables invented by Ebbinghaus were nothing but low order syntax rules. To the neural network, its inputs and outputs are just as meaningless – pure syntax rules. This level or form of invariance is utterly insufficient to capture the dynamic transformations, forces, fields and invariance involved in time-extended events like coffee stirring. This is where the *semantics* resides.

The connectionist will wish to invoke *recurrent* networks as the answer to handling dynamic events with invariance defined over time. There are many complex variants of recurrent networks, but taking recurrence at its most elemental beginning, it is clear that if we begin with our standard network (as in Figure 4.1) with its input layer, output layer and hidden (the middle) layers, and simply add a "context" layer of units which holds the previous state (or weight) values of the hidden units, this does not change the basic pattern – we are still learning syntax rules and in a discrete state model of time. Recurrence, in and of itself, has nothing that intrinsically allows it to represent the dynamics of these events and the forms of invariance existing over their time-extension that we have discussed. If perchance it does, if recurrent nets can support wielding, stirring, and rotating cubes, this needs to be explicated explicitly relative to the ecological laws of events.

I will reemphasize the previous sentence. Ecological psychology is a *science* doing the appropriate work of a science. It is discovering invariance laws. Taking a function of mind such as semantic learning and creating a mechanistic model that approximates this function – and, just as we have seen with Newell and Simon's General Problem Solver (GPS), an approximation is essentially what connectionist models generally achieve – is not all there is to science. It is incumbent upon connectionism to show how its mechanistic networks meet science, particularly the science of ecological psychology. Connectionism must show how its networks support the invariance laws defined over the concrete events of the ecological world. I, for one, hold that they cannot. The burden of proof is on connectionism.

Neural Networks versus the Turing Test

It is a simple fact that we have no problem understanding, "A SPOON can CATAPULT (a pea)," for the spoon, we know, can be inserted in, and support the forces/invariance structure of, catapulting. Does this mean that the network would have to be trained, specifically, with CATAPULT as an output unit/term?

Absolutely, for according to the Rogers and McClelland model, without the appropriate connection weights being trained up, the network would have no "knowledge" about this fact. Does this mean that the network has to be trained for events like, "A spoon can hammer," or "A spoon can mash," or "A spoon can make music," etc? Yes, it does. What this means is that the network would have to be trained for every possible, unforeseen event in which a spoon might participate, or in which we might decide a spoon could participate.

Here we have entered the realm of a critique by the computer scientist, Robert French, on the possibility of computers ever passing the Turing Test. The "Turing Test" is a well known procedure devised by Alan Turing, one of the pioneers of computing. Its purpose, as noted earlier, is to test present and future computers (and their software) to determine if the computer has arrived at the point where it is indistinguishable from a human. The procedure is for the tester to ask written questions of a computer placed behind a screen. The answers are returned in written form. Many think it inevitable that a computer will someday pass this test. For Ray Kurzweil, this should be well before 2045, the year when robots eclipse us.

French gave a devastating critique of this possibility.[18] He argued that no computer will ever pass a test where its answers were compared to humans for questions such as:

- "Rate purses as weapons,"
- "Rate jackets as blankets,"
- "Rate knives as spoons,"
- "Rate banana splits as medicine."

Humans easily can determine whether a purse can make a weapon (for self defense) or a jacket can be a blanket. Some of these depend on the transformation. Knives can stir coffee just fine, but are lousy for eating soup. But computers would need to store the experience of the human being. For this, symbols, syntax rules and data structures will not do. Nor will neural networks. The problem equally holds for evaluations of statements such as:

- "A credit card is like a catapult"
- "A credit card is like a fan."

The list is endless.[35] Says French, "...no a priori property list for 'credit card,' short of all of our life experience could accommodate all possible utterances of the form, 'A credit card is like X'."[19] But what is experience? What is it other than perceived events, ongoing over time, which have an invariance structure? Without the ability to support the invariance structure of events, the neural network models have no chance of "storing" the requisite experience. Lacking this, as French too noted, ultimately these networks, yes, the very networks of Rogers and McClelland, would have to program (or train the connection weights) for *all possible pairs* of objects and actions – and even this massive syntactic rule pairing would still be woefully insufficient. Re this critique, effectively an impossibility proof for connectionist networks, the connectionist theorists' response has been: Insert head in sand.

What is happening, then, when we rate "a knife as a spoon?" It can be described as this: *it is the projection of the transformational dynamics of an invariance structure upon a possible component.* We place the knife within a coffee-stirring event and see if it can "hold up," that is, see if has the requisite structural properties to move the coffee medium. So too, when we rate credit cards as spoons (under a stirring transformation) or as fans (under breeze generation), or spoons as catapults (under a catapulting transformation). The list is endless because the card or the spoon is fair game for an infinity of transformations under which new structural invariants can emerge. More precisely, each is fair game for insertion into an infinity of invariance structures.

The Analogy Defines the Features

Note that these statements – a credit card is like a catapult, a credit card is like a fan, a spoon is like a catapult – are *analogies*. To account for analogy, one cannot begin with a preset list of features. The features emerge under the transformation. We have already glimpsed this with Mr. Gutenberg. In effect, *the analogy defines the features.*

Consider being asked to design a mousetrap. We are provided with several components: a piece of cheese, rubber bands, a 12" cubical box, pencils, a razor blade, toothpicks (the strong kind), a rubber eraser, string, tacks. (At one time, I believe, this was used as a creativity test for future engineers.) One AI program that considered something like the problem was Freeman and Newell's.[10] This program had a list of *functional requirements* and *functional provisions* for various objects. For example, to design a KNIFE, the program discovered that a BLADE *provided* cutting (a functional provision), but *required* holding (a functional requirement). A HANDLE *provided* holding. By matching the requirements to the provisions, the program "designed" a knife.

One can try mightily to imagine how such a program would work in the mousetrap problem. There are many possible designs. I might make a form of crossbow, where the ends of the rubber band are attached to the outside of the box, the pencil (as an arrow) drawn back through a hole in the side, a paperclip holds it via a notch in the pencil, and a trip mechanism is set up with the paperclip, the string and cheese (Figure 4.2). Or I might devise a sort of "beheader," where the razorblade is embedded in the pencil as an axe,

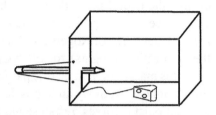

Figure 4.2. The Crossbow Mousetrap

the pointed pencil-end lodged in a corner, the whole "axe" propped up by a toothpick with downward tension from the rubber band, string attached to the toothpick for a trip mechanism, etc.

What, one can ask, would the database of functional provisions and requirements look like? To make the story short, any hope for this scheme is quickly abandoned. The problem is far larger. One rapidly starts to entertain the storage of "features." Noticing the "sharpness" of the pencil was integral to seeing it as supportive of the killing-function within the crossbow architecture. It is doubtful that "killing" or "piercing" would have been listed in the database as "functional provisions" of a pencil. The corner of the box provided "holding" for the pencil-axe, and while it is doubtful this would have been listed as a functional provision of box corners, it seems a type of feature. Note, meanwhile, that in the axe case, the pencil "provides" something quite different from the pencil as arrow, while a certain feature of strength and rigidity has emerged in this context.

So do we envision a list of pre-defined "features" for each object in our database. At a later date, as we will see shortly, in essence this would be the approach of well-known AI "analogy making" programs. But features are very ephemeral. Just like the "vertices" and "edges" of the rotating "Gibsonian" cube, they are functions of *transformations*. A fishing rod can be flexible under one transformation, sufficiently rigid under another. A floppy sock, under the appropriate "swatting" transformation, gains the rigidity and mass to become a handy fly-swatter. The pencil's rigidity under one transformation may change to just enough flexibility to support the launching of spit wads. A box may preserve its edges and corners invariant under various rotations, but lose them completely under a smashing transformation applied by the foot. And precisely the latter may be done to turn the small box in the potential components list

118

above into a temporary dustpan. Thus we would need to store all possible transformations upon any object.

What actually happens then in thought? Like Gutenberg, our goal is a general one: our aim may be killing the creature, but there is no useable content in a purely abstract "killing." Killing *is* an invariance across concrete forms of killing. So when I contemplate crossbow shooting, this places the potential components within a dynamic transformational structure. The stretchability and force of the rubber bands emerges, the sharpness and straightness of the pencils, the "anchoring" potential of the side of the box to which I will tack the rubber bands, etc. These features become the "object language" I could provide a solution program. Or, contemplating beheading by axe, the length and requisite strength of the pencil emerges. I can groove the pencil and wedge the razorblade in to make an axe. The "container" property of the box corner emerges, as I can prop the raised pencil-axe in the corner, a toothpick will prop it up, a rubber band tied to the pencil and tacked to the "anchoring" feature of the floor will provide downward force, etc.[20]

These "features" or "properties" of the objects dynamically emerge as a function of the transformations placed upon them via the invariance structure and the constraints naturally specified by the proposed structure, e.g., the crossbow requires anchoring points for the bowstring – the rigidity of the box can provide these. They cannot be all pre-set. New ones will always emerge. This is the problem with any approach that holds that the features define or determine the analogy. What is required is a "device" which can support the dynamic transformations of experience unfolding in a non-differentiable flow of time.[21]

The Symbolic Programming Approach to Analogy

The symbolic programming method has proffered several models for analogy making, the most famous of these being the Structure Mapping Engine (SME).[22] To SME, as in all AI, the *features* define the analogy. Thus SME treats analogy as a mapping of structural relations relative to pre-defined features. The solar system, for example, and the Rutherford atom both have specific features and their relationships described in predicate calculus form, e.g., Attracts (sun, planet), Attracts (nucleus, electron), Mass (sun), Charge (nucleus), etc. Douglas Hofstadter (author of *Gödel, Escher, Bach*), with his former students, yup, Robert French and David Chalmers, level a heavy critique upon this approach, noting the helplessness of SME without this precise setup of features and relations beforehand, and with this setup given, the purely syntactical, nearly "can't miss" algorithmic or proof procedure that follows. The resultant discovery of analogy is, to quote these critics, a "hollow victory."[23]

BACON, as another example, attacks Kepler's problem of discovering the law of planetary orbits. It quickly solves the problem with a precise, tabular representation of the solar system showing a primary body (Sun), a satellite body (planet), a time T the two objects are observed, and two dependent variables – the distance D between primary and satellite, and the angle A found by using the fixed star and the planet as the endpoints and the primary body (Sun) as the pivot point.[24] Kepler, French notes, took 13 years to sift through the data and flawed concepts of the solar system to find the relevant features. Yet SME, he notes, uses an entirely different representation of the solar system, exactly suited to its programmatic purpose, to find an analogy to the Rutherford atom.

The features on which the analogy is based cannot be preset, pre-defined. As noted, it is the analogy that defines the features. Analogy is a transformation. This is to say that it is a process that occurs over an indivisible, non-differentiable flow of time. It is supported only over concrete experience or the remembrance thereof, i.e., it is carried only over the transforming images of the figural mode. AI – based in an abstract time and without a theory of perception – can support neither of these requirements for analogy. It has, therefore, not a prayer as a theory of cognition.

An AI theorist, Eric Dietrich, in an essay (2001) wherein he arrived at the principle that it is the analogy that is defining the features, discussed what he termed "analogical reminding."[25] Walking in an alley, he spots a configuration of garbage cans. Instantly it becomes "Garbagehenge." In essence, the static structure of the garbage cans has driven recall of past experiences of Stonehenge, whether visits or pictures; the lowly garbage cans are now exalted in what we can call an "analogic" event. In this little example, Dietrich was struck by the fact that at the basis of analogy is an apparently instantaneous operation of memory retrieval that, of itself, is inherently analogic. As a computer theorist, Dietrich had no idea how this could be implemented. We have seen that this operation is redintegration. The lowly garbage cans were simply a "static" event. We have been dealing with events that are far more dynamic – continuous transformations or change in the external field. Connectionism begs the description of this change. It starts after it has crystallized and frozen this change into objects and "properties." But it is real, concrete, changing events that drive the brain. Events have a structure and the neural architecture must respond to this structure. It is the invariance laws of events that drive the fundamental memory retrieval operation supporting analogy.

DORA - Another Connectionist Model

Doumas, Hummel and Sandhofer (2008) present a model (DORA, or the Discovery of Relations by Analogy) for the learning of relational concepts.[26] The model is ambitious and wide ranging, attempting to support the fundamental basis for cognition, namely, analogy, and embodying thereby a model of memory. The model begins with what the authors term an "holistic representation of objects." A "cup" would have an associated set of features, represented by semantic units (Figure 4.3a). Propositions are represented in four layers (Figure 4.3b), with the just-noted bottom layer of semantic units encoding features such as visual invariants (round, square), relational invariants (more, less, same), dimensional invariants (size-3, size-5, color-red), complex perceptual/cognitive properties (furry, barks), category information (apple, dog). The crucial aspect here is that these units are independent, representing separable properties. A unit coding for "red" will become active in response to any red object.

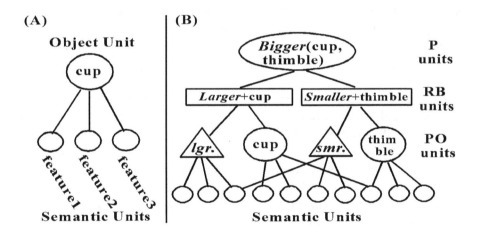

Figure 4.3. The structure of propositions in DORA

The units of the second layer – predicate and object units (PO) – code for (or are tokens of) individual predicates (relational roles or attributes) and objects. A token for the object *cup* in the proposition *bigger* (cup, thimble) is connected to a set of semantics corresponding to the features of *cup* (round, handle, shiny) while the token for the relational role *larger* is connected to a set of semantic units corresponding to its (the relational role's) features. The next layer, the role-binding (RB) units, encodes the bindings of relational roles to their fillers. Thus, in the proposition *bigger* (cup, thimble) there is an RB unit representing the binding *larger*(cup) and an RB unit for *smaller*(thimble). The final layer is comprised of a set of proposition (P) units which binds RBs in multi-place relations.

I am not going to describe the dynamics of the formation of these connections and/or retrievals. What I wish to note immediately is that the authors acknowledge that while the model is explicated and developed almost solely in the context of dimensional relations such as *larger* or *smaller*, they insist that the model will equally hold for the relations involved in *events*, in their example, the event of *chasing*. The model is built on the principle that any multi-place relation is formally equivalent to a linked set of single-place predicates.[27] A "relation" such as *chasing,* they argue, differs from one such as *bigger* only in the semantic features composing it. When a child chases a dog or a butterfly, he can compare the experiences and "predicate what it feels like" to be a chaser. The semantic features attached to the feeling are likely to include those of motion, running, excitement, a sense of pursuit, and the chaser role thus gains semantic content. The same will hold for experiences (and the role) of being chased, and thus the child has the opportunity to learn, via a key operation for the model, namely the operation of *comparing* these experiences/events, that *chase* is a two-role relation in which both objects are in motion, both experience excitement, but one wishes to catch while the other wishes to escape.

The model, the authors note, does not speak to where the semantic invariants underlying *chases* come from, but it does speak to the question of how they eventually become predicates that can take arguments and can therefore support complex relational reasoning. Their claim is that human cognitive architecture, starting with the invariants or regularities in its environment, isolates these invariants and composes them into relational structures, and that DORA's learning mechanisms can convert these into explicit predicates and relations that make reasoning possible.

This claim is the critical issue. The claim, we saw, can equally be found, in only slightly less explicit form, in the extensive connectionist model of semantic cognition of Rogers and McClelland. Doumas et. al state explicitly what has been an implicit assumption of connectionism, namely this: a connectionist cognitive/memory architecture can simply inherit the results of perceptual processing – the "semantic invariants" – and begin from there. This, is not the case. An "invariant" has been trivialized here. It has become merely a static feature connectionist theory presumes it can use as an abstract object in a rule system.

Connectionism and the Semantic Units of Events

In the architecture of DORA, a complex event such as *stirring a cup of coffee* is considered a multi-place relation which can be treated as a linked set of single-place predicates or equivalently, role-filler bindings. Presumably, we would have predicates such as *stirrer*(spoon), *stirred*(coffee), *circling*(spoon), etc. I have given my rendition of this in Figure 4.4. The objects such as the cup, the spoon, or the coffee have attached sets of semantic units, and the firing of units that happen to be common to various pairs or sets of objects spawn the predicate units. Extrapolating from the *chasing* example noted earlier, this structure of linked units would be held to represent the stirring event. The process of linking semantic units to the objects (into which the component events feeding this structure are partitioned) is in effect the focus of the connectionist mechanism we viewed by Rogers and McClelland.

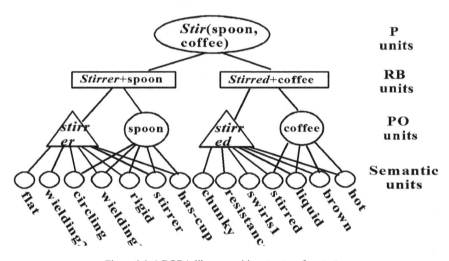

Figure 4.4. A DORA-like proposition structure for *stirring*

Before addressing this "appearance" of the semantic units, it is relevant to revisit the notion of the wielding of the spoon in our stirring event. DORA would assign this aspect of the stirring experience to a semantic unit tied to the abstract relation unit of "STIR." What would the nature of such a "unit" possibly be? Let us remember again the dynamics behind this. The person wielding his pendulums (or spoons) settles into a steady state; the information specifying this state (dependent on the lengths and masses involved) is provided by kinematic information based in the kinetics of muscle/tendon stress/strain distortions propagated globally via the nervous system - ultimately *haptic* flow fields. This information also serves as a source of constraint for the fields that produce it, and it guides the wrist-pendulum to its stable attractor state.

Kugler and Turvey, we noted, described how change in periodic timing is brought about by change to internal parameters (stiffness, resting length, etc.) that preserve the amount of energy degraded as a constant over varying frequencies of oscillation, namely, an *adiabatic* change (invariant), i.e., a transformation according to the earlier noted ratio (Energy of Oscillation/Frequency of Oscillation = k). Here the proportionality constant that relates frequency to energy in turn scales as a function of the moment of inertia of the oscillator.

Connectionist theory would like to simplify the "output" of this haptic flow with its underlying adiabatic invariance as registering as some value in a semantic unit. These are the "complex perceptual properties" of DORA (e.g., *furry, barks*). But there is no single output value, say "wielding-1." Like the edges and vertices comprising the form of the rotating cube, there is only the invariance over this complex haptic flow field over time. This greatly complicates whatever could be meant by a "semantic unit." Further, even could a single value characterize this, there would be an infinite number, one for every variant corresponding to the form and weight of the stirrer used and the resistance of the medium – "wielding-2" for martini stirring, "wielding-3" for cereal-stirring, "wielding-4" for beef-barley soup stirring, "wielding-5" for tomato soup stirring, "wielding-6" for cake batter stirring, etc. But, again, a single value cannot express this – it is carried only over the full dynamics of the system.

The brain is specifying dynamically complex physical fields. The spell of computationalism, under which connectionism currently dwells, implies that the physical is unimportant, only abstract computations bear the theoretical load; we can start with the "semantic invariants" treated as abstract objects. But these forces are all-important. This is where semantic invariants live. They are essential to something as simple as stirring.

Event Geons

The *spoon-stirring-coffee* event is a dynamic transformation of a portion of the ecological world. Something would be required to accomplish the work of partitioning it into the semantic features with which connectionism begins. Rogers and McClelland imply it has been partitioned into STIR and

124

SPOON, with SPOON partitioned into features it HAS and IS. But STIR is a higher order concept covering a very complex transformation. Under this, the spoon is "creating a force," it is "pushing the liquid," the liquid "is moving in a radial, complex pattern of motion," the spoon is "clinking" against the side of the cup, it is "constrained" to a certain radius, it has a "periodicity," it is "rigid," it has a certain "flatness," but has a "cup-like quality," it is "shiny." All these are complex patterns, for the visual motion as complex as a flow field, or for the hand's motion as complex as "wielding." The above is an arbitrary set. None are truly separate, the *event* does not happen without the spoon, the force, the liquid, the container.

Meanwhile, across the table, big sister is using the spoon to scoop cereal. Again, another complex transformation. The spoon is applying different forces, a different motion, a different visual transformation; the Rice Krispies are parting, piling into the spoon, falling off. Or the spoon is ladling-soup – another complex transformation. Yes, it makes sense to ask, given a SPOON, what can it do? But it makes no sense to be attempting, via weight adjustments, to *re-link* spoon to stir, or spoon to scoop, or spoon to ladle. These are already inseparably whole events. What does make sense is to ask how SPOON, *as a cue*, can redintegrate a set of *events* in which it participated. But this is an entirely different operation, as we shall discuss.

Now we imagine a set of stirring events – a spoon stirring cereal, a spoon stirring soup, a spatula stirring cake batter, a board stirring cement. Considering just the general visual form – the radial flow field – there will be an invariant form across all these events. But to obtain it, there is first an important and disturbing implication for memory, as exemplar theory (Crowder, 1993; Goldinger, 1998) insists upon: all these stirring events must be stored.[28] The abstract invariant, *stirring-motion*, does not exist unless the separate events also exist across which the invariance can be defined. Given this stack of events, we could obtain an abstract feature, call it "swirl" – in truth, merely a higher order invariance across the radial flow patterns of all these events. This we could "attach" or link to an abstract STIRRED relation-unit (or STIRRER? Both?), though the notion of a "link" between it and sub-units becomes clearly a bad misrepresentation of the reality here – it is already inextricably part of all the events over which it emerges as an invariance. So also we could "attach" an abstract "wielding," an abstract "clinking," an abstract "constrained-to-a-circle" motion of an abstract instrument, an abstract "resistance to the motion," an abstract "immobility of the container," etc., etc. And how could this operation, defining an invariance across the "stack" of events, happen?

We require an operation that takes an entire stack of events, much like Gelernter (1994) envisioned, collapsing them such that the invariants stand out, the variants becoming noise.[29] As we have seen, the classic, concrete embodiment of such an operation is exemplified by the recording of a succession of n wave fronts on a hologram. In Figure 2.3 we used different objects – a pyramid/ball, a cup. Now we imagine using simply different cups, where each cup is of a different form. With each object wave reflected from a given cup, we pair a unique reference wave of frequency, f_i, creating a unique interference pattern for each recorded object-wave/reference wave pair. By then modulating a reconstructive wave passing through the hologram to each successive frequency, f_i, we reconstruct the image of each cup uniquely. But if we employ a less than coherent reconstructive wave, a composite of f_i thru f_n, we will reconstruct a fuzzy image. The invariants across all the cups will yet stand out, the variants being confused. In this operation, we did not begin with separate features of the cup – the cups were a whole – and only through the operation did separate "features" stand out.

These higher order invariants – in essence, classes – emerging via our reconstructive wave operation, are the "invariants" DORA intuitively assumes exist, and which it can use. But these exist only over the complex invariance structures and dynamic time-extended patterns we have discussed. Their emergence is dependent, in this scenario, on a form of redintegrative memory operation, retrieving sets of whole events and their structures, that is radically different from the memory operations DORA envisions (and which we will see it subsequently employ). Even with such an operation, we would yet question how or why a separation operation now occurs to carve the invariants into independent "feature" units that are now linked to a "relation" in a loose conglomerate.

Curiously, Doumas et al. approvingly invoke the JIM or "geon" model (see Chapter I, Figure 1.5) as a prime example of one of connectionism's "successes," in this case in the realm of object recognition. We have seen that this is absurd; Shaw and McIntyre's wobbly cube destroys this static model. Further we noted that the geon turned out to be a handy way to hold the features of the cube together as a whole, else the separately stored features could be put back together in all kinds of ways, none looking like the original cube. The "geon" here was the handy picture on the top of the puzzle box that gives us a clue on how to fit the puzzle pieces together. Yet we have the same problem for the "events" of connectionism in general. Even if we had this set of complex features linked to the relation, we are in the same shape as in the decomposition of the cube and cone into features.

Now we need "event geons," and particularly here, a *stirring geon*, for in the decomposition of the stirring event (both arbitrary and with no definable limit to the number of "features") into static feature units attached to an abstract "relation" unit, we have lost the global picture of the transformation.

If you have lost the global picture of the transformation, you have lost the ability to form analogies. You can no longer place a pencil in a coffee stirring transformation or stirring event and see if it will work, that is, see if the requisite "features" will emerge. Nor can you place a spoon in a catapulting event. You have no events. You have no analogies.

The DORA Comparator

DORA employs a comparison process across events, or better, partial fragments of events, but it starts this higher up its hierarchical chain. As it assumes there is a feature-fragmentation accomplished (somehow) by perception, let us consider this further for a moment. At this level, DORA envisions comparing object units, finding common features and creating single place predicates. Thus we might bring *spoon* and *spatula* into memory, and find a common "feature," namely, "stirrer." This stimulates the birth of the explicit property, "stirrer," and this can be bound to each object, such that we have *stirrer*(spoon), or *stirrer*(spatula). Every feature in common between the two objects, according to DORA, is also linked to this relation.

This is the first problem: If "stirrer" is a feature of these two objects, how can this "feature" possibly be other than a full stirring event with its invariance structure? Just what is a "partial" stirring event such that we only have a "stirrer" as a feature? Now, to find these two "features" of the two objects the "same," we must be implicitly comparing the two *events*. But the two events – spatula stirring of a cake batter, and coffee stirring – have similar but different radial flow fields, different values of wielding, periodicities, acoustics, etc. How does the model determine these two "features" are the "same?" The second problem: Figure 4.4 shows the dilemma, for there I attached features to spoon such as wielding1, circling, rigid. Are they part of the object, or part of the event in which the object participated? In reality, they are part of stirring. If they are part of the spoon, how are they the "same" as the spatula's? The third problem: In DORA, all features the two objects share in common are attached to the newly formed *stirrer* relation. The spoon occasionally sits on a surface, so does the spatula. Both are occasionally washed. DORA contains a "pruning" process to rid predicates of such extraneous features, but unless two objects are compared where one object stirs but is never washed nor rests on a surface, these features could not be pruned and would remain with *stirrer* forever. This is nonsensical. How could these features possibly have been part of a stirring event in the first place?

The origin behind these dilemmas is the "simplifying assumption," whereby the ecological world is viewed as objects, and properties, with properties attached to objects. But objects are simply special cases of an event, an event relative to a scale of time, a scale that happens to be imposed on the material field by the brain. In turn, an object-event is always itself nested in some event – the spoon at rest is an event, or the spoon is stirring, it is scooping, it is cutting cheese, it is catapulting a pea. Its "properties" emerge over the specific event. It is events that are primary. And events have a structure over time that is resolutely ignored only with the consequences above. Therefore, when Rogers and McClelland (2008) state that, "…the main function of the semantic system is to support performance on tasks that require one to generate, from perceptual or linguistic input, properties of objects and events that are not directly apparent in the environment," it is actually an appeal to this primacy.[30] The cheese-cutting spoon, the soup-stirring spoon, the pea-catapulting spoon – all show different properties that are not "directly apparent" in the resting spoon. "Properties" of objects are always functions of events. In the norming tasks that these models use to provide the "properties" assigned as patterns in a visual input layer (cf. Rogers et al., 2004), where a subject looks at a picture of an object and is asked to list its properties, it would seem a good hypothesis that s/he is but implicitly recalling various events in which the object takes part.[31] Now, when we turn around and "link" these properties to an object, we are doing nothing less than very laboriously linking back to the object, strange fragments of events in which the object took part – with the strange logical consequences just observed.

Failure of Reference

Though I wish to try to derive and comment later on some implications from DORA in the context of analogy, I can take the analyses of DORA relative to actual, ecological events no further, for other than the brief comments on *chasing*, the model's mechanism for actually engaging concrete events is in fact very unspecified. At present there is no algorithmic engine to create the proposition *stirring*(spoon, coffee) from the single place predicates (which themselves have the strange origins noted). The current engine is a comparator that operates on propositions which have a dimensional value. If DORA "thinks" about a DOG of size-6 and a CAT of size-4, the comparator, detecting the dimensional value, links a "more" relation to the size-6 (or "*more*+size-6") related to the DOG and a "*less*+size-4" for the CAT. If this pattern reminds DORA of a previous comparison of the same type between a BEAR (more+size-9) and a FOX (less+size-5), a further operation now compares the CAT and DOG units to the similar setup for the BEAR and FOX, eventually spawning a new unit, BIGGER, bound to BEAR and FOX or *Bigger*(BEAR, FOX). Note that what is lurking behind this engine – coded into it and making it work – is the implicit knowledge of the reciprocity of Less-More.

Given the difficulty of the subject of analogy, this is like popping the hood on your new Porsche expecting to find a 450 Hp. engine, and discovering forty chipmunks winding up a rubber band. Obviously a quite different engine is needed to create an ecological "predicate" such as *stir*(spoon, coffee). There are no simple dimensional values to rely upon. I will submit that any system proposed will have, lurking in the background like the Less-More symmetry, the implicit (coded) knowledge of the structure of each event (e.g., *stirring*) it is dealing with. Without such constraints, what would prevent DORA from thinking about *stirrer*(spoon) and *chased*(Mary), and being reminded of a previous comparison, *stirrer*(spatula) and *chased*(Joe), thus deriving *stirring*(spatula, Joe)? And what would such a constraint amount to other than rigging the system to always "compare" (even if it could) two halves of the same event (stirrer/stirred), with what sense?

The proposition, *stirring*(spatula, Joe), is the essence of a syntactic "failure of reference." As a sentence, it takes its place with other sentences that are syntactically correct but seem to have no semantic justification:

1. The leaf attacked the building
2. The shadows are waterproof.
3. The spatula stirred Joe.
4. The building smoked the leaf.

Katz and Fodor (1963), early in the game, tried to solve this problem by "semantic markers" assigned to each lexical item in the deep structure.[32] These were simply syntactic rules trying to represent physical constraints – rules attempting to do the work of the invariance structure. The "leaf" in (1) would thus receive a marker denoting it as *inanimate* among other things, while "attack" would receive a marker requiring its use with an *animate* object. Having incompatible semantic markers, such a system brands the sentence as meaningless. "Stirring" would have been tagged with a marker requiring its object to be, say, liquid. Joe, having no such marker, would have thus been seen as illegal in (3) and the string also branded as meaningless. Unfortunately such sentences can appear very meaningful. Sentence (2) would also have incompatible markers, yet is perfectly interpreted as meaning that we can throw as much water on shadows as we like and they will be unharmed. As for (3), we *can* easily make sense of this sentence, "The bad architecture of the system is like a spatula, stirring Joe, the programmer, into an anxious mess." Such facts quickly lead to "rules for relaxing the rules," but the rule system quickly ends in anarchy, being so flexible that it is useless as an explanatory device.

The apparent meaningless could only be avoided by a constraint, but this constraint is equivalent to having –– stored somewhere and acting – the complete invariance structure of the event (of stirring, of pouring)! The invariance structure is what prevents Joe from "being stirred" given the normal context of a stirring event. But *this* structure cannot be syntactically represented. You are begging an entirely different form of knowledge to apply the constraint to prevent this. The fact is that this is a matter of perception, i.e., of the specification of events via invariance laws. When we assign a meaning to a sentence such as (2), it is because the perceived event of water pouring upon a shadow shares an invariant with other events of water pouring over waterproof materials, namely the undamaged state of the material substance of these objects under this transformation. It is the event invariance structures that are prior in explaining these linguistic cases.

In other words, the phenomenon of language is simply not going to yield to the vision of the brain as a manipulator of abstract symbols in an abstract space. Language is a sister of perception and of the invariance laws defining it. This requires a "device" which can represent the multi-modal time-extended experience over which events take place.

The application of DORA to the concrete events of the ecological world, other than a vague note about "chasing," has been left a promissory note. I have taken it as an object lesson on what must actually be addressed. There is no theory as to how these base level semantic units can possibly represent ecological events and their invariance structures or how such structures could truly be "compared." The implications of this will emerge in the reference failures of the syntactic rule systems these architectures actually embody. DORA is built upon the hope that it will escape such a fate due to its anchoring in the base level "semantic invariants," but the formation of relations, especially via analogy, is at the level of the invariance structure of events, not at the syntactic level to which this formation has here been taken.

DORA vs. French's Impossibility

In the model, the creation of BIGGER rested on the setup of the dimensional features, e.g., size-5, feeding its comparator. Ignoring for the moment that DORA lacks such a comparator for ecological events, let us suppose we have formed single place predicates (SPs) such as *stirred*(coffee), *stirrer*(spoon), and *stirred*(paint), *stirrer*(paint-stick). According to the model, a pair of single place predicates enters working memory, in this case *stirred*(coffee) and *stirrer*(spoon). These are mapped as a unit onto other SPs, in this case *stirred*(paint) and *stirrer*(paint-stick). This mapping serves as a signal to link the SPs into a larger predicate structure, thus *stir*(spoon, coffee) and/or *stir*(paint-stick, paint).

This is simply a syntactic mapping. It is, as we saw Narasimhan note, simply a proof procedure carried out in a fixed "object language" or categorization of the world. It has nothing to do with analogy.[33] It was based on the fact that we attached "stirrer" as a feature to spoon, and "stirred" as a feature to coffee. Given the precise setup of the SPs, the mapping might occur via an algorithm. Without this precise setup, the process is helpless. The network has no ability to recognize the validity of, or create, multi-place predicates such as *stir*(knife, coffee) or *catapult*(spoon, pea) without this setup. There is nothing in the network, unless it has been specifically trained, that would support these relations, for the knowledge which supports these resides in the invariance structure of events, and these structures are nowhere near representation in this model.

We have already noted the helplessness of these kinds of analogy models without this "precise setup," for example, SME's treatment of the solar system and the Rutherford atom with the features of each nicely predefined, and with this setup provided, the purely syntactical, nearly "can't miss" algorithmic procedure that follows, and, as noted, the resultant "hollow victory." In essence, connectionism has now moved into precisely the same critical, problematic area and taken on the same ills as the symbolic manipulation paradigm. This is to say that it is equally helpless before the problem of *common sense knowledge*.

The frame problem is but a variant of this general problem: As the robot observes the spoon while it stirs, the coffee cup bulges in and out and the coffee makes a "snap, crackle, pop" sound. Are these expected aspects of the event? Must the robot check its list of frame axioms for a stirring event? Or does this anomalous event, sharing enough of the invariance structure to serve as a concrete, redintegrative cue for a stack of stirring events, simply fail to *resonate* with a stirring event's invariance structure as defined over the retrieved stack? Analogy too is an aspect of this general problem. The ability to see that purses can be weapons, or spoons can be catapults is part and parcel of this general problem.

This "failure to resonate" is seen in a little example from the authors of the experiment we saw which used a walk up the campus mall with its flow field. Jenkins, Wald and Pittenger also described an experiment which used multiple slides of a room. While examining one of these, they had the experience of a vague feeling that it did not "fit." Ultimately they discerned the reason to be that all the slides shared a common invariant, that of the *shadow angle* – all but this one slide which was immediately sensed as not being a fit. Again, note that this implies that the room displayed by the slides was "stored" in all its detail.

Note that this is a "felt" interference. We (or Jenkins et al.) *are* this "device" with its interferometric, resonant properties.[34] It is both a *quality*, inherently time-extended, demanding a 4-D consciousness, and a knowledge. To remind us of Bergson's example, so the qualitative aspect is clear, consider hearing six notes played successively in a given tempo. The six notes successively permeate one another, in all building a qualitative whole. Now the same series is played with one note held slightly longer. The *qualitative* difference between the two series is instantly detected.[35]

If at first glance this "felt" knowledge appears a weakness in this framework, I would submit that this unease is an index of the mistaken mindset that the computer model, with its disembodied comparisons of abstract symbols, has gradually engendered. In fact, this "felt" knowledge is the basis for an *intrinsic* intentionality.[36] The basis for this is in a being dynamically participating in the indivisible motion of the field, and thus comprising a 4-D extended consciousness capable of registering quality. The observer relative intentionality characteristic of the computer model, i.e., the ascription of human-like consciousness to discrete computations of a program (e.g., "the program understood the difference between the two patterns") comes precisely from surreptitiously ascribing 4-D extent to discrete, syntactic operations. We are applying our consciousness and its inherent continuity to the syntactic operations.

Failure to Net Quality

Consider the concept of "mellow." The word has manifold meanings: we can talk of a wine being mellowed with age, a dimension of the word we apply to taste. We speak of a violin being mellow or of a song being mellow, a dimension applying to sound as well as mood. We speak of the interior of a house or room being mellow, referring to the visual. We can say "mellow" of a soil. The concept of "mellow" expresses a very abstract qualitative invariance defined *across* many modalities. At the same time *within* each of these dimensions it is a quality that emerges only over *time*, within the experience of a being dynamically flowing over time. "Mellowness" does not exist in the instantaneous "instant." This quality can only become experience for a being for whom each "state" is the sum and reflection of the preceding "states," as a note in a melody is the reflection of all those preceding it, a being whose "states" in fact permeate and interpenetrate one another. If we take this to heart, we should say that the meaning of the word "mellow" is an invariant defined within and across modalities and over time. It is not a homogeneously represented invariant, nor can it exist in space, when space is defined as the abstract, three-dimensional, instantaneous cross-section of time.

Yet, this instantaneous, homogeneous representation is exactly what AI, in either of its flavors, would propose. The data structure supporting a symbolic program would consist of "nodes" with abstract links to "mellow," as for example in Figure 4.5. We can easily imagine the network of Rogers and McClelland being extended to incorporate "mellow." We would see things like VIOLIN IS {mellow}, ROOM IS [mellow], or SOIL IS [mellow]. That these syntactic structures have nothing to do with the meaning of mellow is obvious.

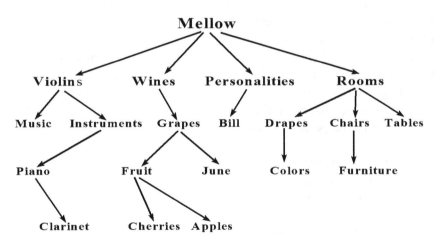

Figure 4.5. A Network Representation of "Mellow"

Rogers and McClelland presumably believe that VIOLIN and MELLOW are somehow related to other parts of the brain's neural net as it processes an event involving a mellow violin. But then we are back to the question, where is the "error." Why would the net need training to adjust its weights to "associate" violin and mellow? The mellow quality of the violin is an intrinsic aspect of the event, just as we said in regards to all the aspects of the coffee stirring. Again, these "components" of an event don't need to be "associated." Further, there are untold numbers of these components in an event – nameless invariants – that have no "symbol" but whose existence can suddenly become quite obvious. I say, for example, "As he stirred, the coffee went snap, crackle and pop." This is obviously a violation of an invariance law in coffee stirring. It happens to be the source of humor; one can imagine this scenario causing laughs in an animated cartoon. But what is the "node" or symbol for the nameless invariance being violated here that we would link something to in our neural net? And again, this network cannot possibly account for the emergence of analogy, where suddenly, for example, a culture, as in the 1960's, decides it is cool to apply this quality of mellowness to a *personality*, as in "Joe is mellow."

Change and Memory

Connectionism, in essence, begs the description of change. But it is real, concrete events that drive the brain. Events have a structure and the neural architecture must respond to this structure. It is the invariance structure of events that must drive the fundamental memory retrieval operation – implicitly residing even in DORA – redintegration. It is the description of change – the invariance structure of the event – that is all important for memory retrieval. What static "properties" shall we link to the facial profile to support such a memory retrieval? What "properties" are we attaching to the campus mall? What "properties" are we linking to the *spoon* such that it can redintegrate, depending on the transformation in which it is placed, either soups, or batter, or catapults, or teeter totters, or cheese, or coffee, or Rice Krispies....? How can we expect static properties to substitute for the dynamics of the event? It now becomes incumbent on connectionist theory to demonstrate how networks can be sensitive to such parametric variations and such dynamics, how this change is specified and detected in its input patterns, keeping in mind that this extends to the complexities of things like "wielding."

McClelland et al (1995) provided a model which they felt would account for paired-associate learning. Like the Rogers and McClelland architecture, to which it is a near cousin, it proceeds by epochs of weight adjustments to obtain the appropriate output patterns. This again is more syntactic rules. If it is to handle the "A-B_i" paradigm, its input patterns must be capable of capturing the patterns and dynamics of the ecological cue event. If the model is considered to be limited to modeling a purely rote, semantic-less form of PA learning, then it belongs at best in a form of memory fitting under or near the "procedural." It describes the development of a "mechanism" for the rote learning of the pairs. But we saw that it was the continuous intrusion of semantics that caused the ever increasing epicycles in the verbal learning models. Faced with learning QEZ-PUJ, the smart subject considered that QEZ could stand for FEZ and that he could imagine a pudgy Turkish person wearing the FEZ. Faced with learning DOG-GATE, he imagined a dog opening a gate. "Imagery" became yet another of the many "variables" in the models. But the subject is simply using the event-driven memory with which he was ecologically equipped by evolution; he is not simply and only a syntax-driven machine. The large body of recent research on Subject Performed Tasks, where the subject recalls (with extremely high performance levels) lists of events s/he physically enacted such as "break the pencil," or "bend the wire," and whose findings have undercut most of the "laws" of verbal learning, only emphasize the primacy of this event-driven memory.

Perhaps such an event-driven memory sounds like the content-addressable memory long ago described by McClelland and Rumelhart (1986).[37] But again, just as noted above, the input patterns of such a model (and the output patterns), which is to say the network itself, must support the invariants of events defined over a non-differentiable flow. Such an architecture should be radically different. Until we can support this, we have at best an artificial approximation. The same comment would apply to the proposition that we can simply insert the term "properties" for "invariance structure" in the essential formula I have given: *An event E' will reconstruct a previous event E when E' is defined by the same invariance structure or by a sufficient subset of the same invariance structure.* "Properties," we have already noted, are simply derivatives of events in the first place, and seem safely antiseptic and amenable "objects" for syntax rules only by the fact that we are ignoring the invariance structure of the events from which they emerge and without which they do not exist.

Rogers et al (2004) in their modeling of semantic dementia, employ properties of objects (as activation patterns in visual units), linking them to units representing names and units for verbal descriptors, and train the network such that given a name, it responds with the properties/descriptors, or inversely, given the properties, it reflects the name.[38] Increasing lesions (removal of weights) reflects an observed clinical pattern of name loss or category confusions. Rogers et al. may have indeed captured a mechanism linking objects to names. But its use of "properties" does not justify the method as a general model of event retrieval; it is not capturing the dynamics of the events. There are at least indications that semantic losses are sensitive to the dynamics of things as well, for example visual agnosias where the name is "lost" when the subject is presented a static object, and retrieved when the object is put in a normal motion.[39]

DORA, we noted, envisioned a pair of single place predicates entering working memory, say, *stirred*(coffee) and *stirrer*(spoon), coming under the control of the "driver" component of the model. As other propositions in permanent storage (or what is termed "Long Term Memory") share the semantic units such as *stirred*(paint) and *stirrer*(paint stick), these are retrieved into the recipient component, and are now available for mapping. Therefore, at DORA's heart is a theory of redintegration. It is based on activation of the "same" problematic, semantic units – the stirring-n's, the wielding-n's – which must bear the entire description of change. There is no explication of what "same" could possibly mean other than begging the work of ecological psychology in describing these aspects of the event.

DORA is but one of several implementations of connectionist architectures which aim to implement the construction of analogy.[40] Experience has taught me that connectionist theorists, invariably unable to grasp the general point here on invariance structures and the necessity to actually engage them, will simply point out some other model, this being the "answer." The Vector Symbolic Architecture, as one example of one of these "answers," is an effort to implement a more biologically plausible, more efficient architecture without using the troublesome backpropagation method of, say, Rogers and McClelland.[41] Nevertheless, the fundamental view of analogy is exactly the same, i.e., analogy depends on a systematic substitution of components of compositional structures. The systematicity and compositionality are considered the outcome of two operations, namely, binding and bundling, where binding associates fillers (Spoon, Coffee) with roles (Stirrer, Stirred), and where bundling combines these role/filler bindings to produce larger structures. Therefore the very elements of the composition, i.e., the features of objects, must be predefined, the values set, the relations fixed – all for the sake of allowing a syntactic process to unroll.

The Chinese Room

I noted early in this chapter that the critique of reliance upon syntactic rules begs comparison to the Chinese room argument. In other words, there are theorists that, having again missed everything so far, including the problem of the origin of the external image, will attempt to dismiss everything by saying, "All this is just Searle's argument. Nothing here. Move on."[42] Searle's argument relied on one simple point, namely an appeal to the implausibility of any understanding arising (in any mysterious space) from Searle's mere manipulation of symbols as Searle translated statements in his room.. As to what "understanding" actually might be, other than it might require, a) consciousness (with no theory of this), and, b) common sense background knowledge (with no theory of this), the Chinese room argument had not a great deal to offer, and this lack has been a source of the voluminous controversy ever since, leading to a famous quip by Hayes that the field of cognitive science ought to be redefined as "the ongoing research program of showing Searle's Chinese Room Argument to be false."[43]

Searle was dealing with understanding language, but language, like the sentence, "The man stirred the coffee with the spoon," is at minimum a vehicle for expressing perceived events. We begin then with the "understanding" of events, which is to say, the perception of events. More precisely, *language is a mediating device to move the brain into the appropriate modulation patterns to reconstruct an event.* And the argument here is devoted, beyond what Searle discussed, to just what events are – in terms of their perception as an external image in the first place, in terms of their definition over a non-differentiable flow and of the invariance laws defined over this flow, and simultaneously then, in terms of surfacing exactly why their perception and their use in cognition cannot be supported by syntactic rules.

Surfaces and Essences: **What Lies Beneath**

Hofstadter and Sander recently produced a large work on analogy (*Surfaces and Essences*, 2013), arguing that analogy is the very basis of cognition. There is a profound change represented in this book, a change at least trying to occur in the minds of proponents of cognitive science. Hofstadter and Sander propose that analogy is the fundamental operation of thought, that categories or concepts are in fact made (continuously and ubiquitously) via the operation of analogy. This little statement, we have seen, is in fact deeply contradictory to current models of analogy (either connectionist or symbolic manipulation). These start with the "features" of two realms, say the planetary system and the Rutherford atom, mapping them to one another, i.e., the (pre-defined) features are used to define the analogy. "Features" here is just another term for categories or concepts. Hofstadter and Sander are in effect saying that it is the reverse – the analogy defines the features, i.e., the analogy brings them into existence. This is a deep, critical insight, not that it has not been seen before.[44] It happens to be the death-knell of the computer model of mind. Its adherents, as we have seen, have in other words being giving away the problem in their computer models of problem solving and analogy since its inception.

The authors explicitly scope-limit themselves, refusing to deal with any implications for the underlying questions on the nature of the brain and consciousness (they say with "biological models") that their thesis cries for. This extends to complete silence on current connectionist and computer models of analogy. Yet, as we have seen, Hofstadter and his students (Chalmers, Robert French) have written incisive critiques on some of these models, calling the "success" of these models "hollow victories." While in the book the authors note that current computers are utter dummies when compared to the human ability to make analogies and that the inadequacy of machine language translation stem from this, they still leave the possibility floating in the ether that somehow, someday, computers will be programmed to perform analogy as well as humans, propping open the door for theorists like Kurzweil to continue to promulgate concern for the imminent singularity. I think we have seen, already at this point, why this door is closed.

The lack of a theory of perception/memory, as per usual, is a major point of vitiation in the book. Is it concepts that are stored or "encoded," or is it experiences that are stored? Their answer is that it must be concepts – experience can't be stored.

> It may not be obvious why we need to encode our
> experiences at all – that is, why we need to reduce them to a
> tiny fraction of their entirety.[45]

This theme of the need for "reduction," abstraction, or "selection of elements" out of the flow of experience should be familiar. As usual, too, the authors have no principles by which this reduction is effected, but the authors cannot bring themselves to believe experience(s) can be stored in the brain (and we have seen that experience cannot be). But the reason they use is that this would be like storing massive, un-indexed videos of events. If we observed a coffee-stirring event where a wet noodle was the stirring instrument, we would have to search thru all the videos to find a similar event – a computationally intensive, costly, slow, useless procedure. In other words, the program would have to start "watching" every video stored to find something similar. Obviously, the brain is not storing "videos" in the first place – remember Bergson's rejection of "photographs" being developed by the brain or Elsasser's note that no such real-time molecular transcription method has ever been discovered.. The authors, being torn by their intuitive sense that we indeed do need these "videos," i.e., the entirety of experience, nevertheless feel forced to vote that events are not stored, rather there must be some form of "conceptual encoding" (abstraction/reduction) for every event remembered and stored.

This leaves a strange bootstrap problem as without concepts already pre-encoded in infancy, how does the process of finding new analogies (remindings) ever get going? Nor can Hofstadter and Sanders bring themselves to believe that the conceptual skeletons (or deep, abstracted essences) of every event are always instantly pinpointed and encoded for later use in a future analogical reminding event. But without the experience(s) available to memory, how then are all these new concepts/categories being continually generated/perceived? We could only have creative combinations of already stored concepts. The authors struggle with this core problem in their need for a model of analogical reminding (pp. 171-176). Their discussion obviously trails into vagueness. It is a symptom of, a) the ignorance of Gibson and the intrinsic structure in perceived events, and, b) a lack of any theory of the fundamental operation of redintegration, and of course, c) a missing theory of the perception of the external world, i.e., of experience, in the first place.

There is another lack. In all of this we are relying on a developmental trajectory requiring roughly our first two years of life that ultimately gives birth to what Cassirer termed the "symbolic function." This is another very real, concrete, *dynamical* function that is being developed. It is yet another physical dynamic AI has not even begun to conceive. When Piaget's two year old daughter, Jacqueline, sees a blade of grass and it reminds her of playing with a grasshopper several days earlier, Piaget (*The Construction of Reality in the Child, 1954*) has gone through great pains to describe the gradual development of an interrelated complex of base concepts, requiring the brain roughly two years to achieve, that bring the child to this culminating, critical point, namely this new ability to use a piece of grass – now as a symbol and yet equally as an analogy – to simultaneously represent a past event and now an explicit memory.

It is to this problem – explicit memory – that we now turn.

Chapter IV: End Notes and References

1. Hofstadter, D., & Sanders, E. (2013). *Surfaces and Essences: Analogy as the Fuel and Fire of Thinking.* New York: Basic Books, p. 3.
2. Newell, A., & Simon, H. (1961). Computer simulation of human thinking. The Rand Corporation, p. 2276, April 20, 1961, 9.
3. Montmasson, J. (1932). *Invention and the Unconscious.* New York: Narcourt-Brace.
4. Ibid., p. 272.
5. Ibid., p. 273.
6. Ibid., p. 273.
7. Ibid., p. 273.
8. Ibid., p. 273-274.
9. Ibid., p. 274.
10. Narasimhan, R. (1969). Intelligence and artificial intelligence. *Computer Studies in the Humanities and Verbal Behavior*, March, 24-34.
11. Fodor, J. & Pylyshyn, Z. (1995). Connectionism and cognitive architecture. In C. Mac Donald and G. Mac Donald (eds.), *Connectionism: Debates on Psychological Explanation.* Oxford: Basil Blackwell.
12. Searle, J. (1980). Minds, brains and programs. *The Behavioral and Brain Sciences.*3, 417-424.
13. Searle, J. (1984). *Minds, Brains and Science: The 1984 Reith Lectures*, Harvard University Press.
14. Botvinick, M. & Plaut, D. C. (2004). Doing without schema hierarchies: A recurrent connectionist approach to normal and impaired routine sequential action. *Psychological Review, 111*, 395-429.
15. Robbins, S. E. (2002). Semantics, experience and time. *Cognitive Systems Research* 3: 301-335.
16. The integral reciprocity of "event components" sketched here is certainly correlated with Turvey's (2004) notion of "impredicativity." The concept of the "invariance structure" is intended, however, to explicitly call to attention the multiple invariance laws comprising, in total, a given multi-modal event, and this for the precise reason, as we have already seen, that this formulation has the greater utility in constructing a model of memory retrieval or redintegration.
    Turvey, M. (2004). Impredicativity, dynamics and the perception-action divide. In V. K. Virsa & J. A. Kelso (eds.), *Coordination Dynamics: Issues and Trends.* New York: Springer.
17. Robbins, S. E. (2008). Semantic redintegration: Ecological Invariance. Commentary on Rogers, T. & McClelland, J. (2008). Précis on *Semantic Cognition: A Parallel Distributed Processing Approach. Behavioral and Brain Sciences*, 726-727.
18. French, R. M. (1990). Sub-cognition and the limits of the Turing Test. *Mind, 99*, 53-65.
19. French, R. M. (1999). When coffee cups are like old elephants, or why representation modules don't make sense. In A. Riegler, M. Peshl, & A. von Stein (Eds.), *Understanding Representation in the Cognitive Sciences*, New York: Plenum, p. 94..
20. It may be felt that I have excluded the possibility of imagining never-experienced events, but note that the entire discussion of analogy thus far involves precisely this aspect of

"never before experienced" – spoons becoming catapults, credit cards becoming fans, pencils becoming arrows.

21. I note that the mousetrap design problem as posed by Behe (1996; 2007), as an analog for evolution's problem in the creation of biological machines, has deeply concerned evolutionary biologists (e.g.., Miller, 2003; Miller, 2008). Deciding that if, for evolutionary processes, there are available components that each have an independent function (as they do above, e.g., the pencil, the toothpick), the biologists assert an understanding of, and an ability to specify, the mechanisms underlying such a design achievement. In other words, they are claiming a solution to the problem of common sense knowledge. If so, the biologists should be sharing, as neither AI, nor connectionism, nor ecological psychology yet have a theory of the "device" required.

22. Gentner, D. (1983). Structure-mapping: A theoretical framework for analogy. *Cognitive Science, 7*(2), 155-70.

23. Chalmers, D. J., French, R. M., & Hofstadter, D. (1992). High level perception, representation and analogy: A critique of artificial intelligence methodology. *Journal of Experimental and Theoretical Artificial Intelligence, 4*(3), 185-211.

24. Langley, P., Simon, H., Bradshaw, & G., Zytkow, J. (1987). *Scientific Discovery: Computational Explorations of the Creative Process.* Cambridge: MA: MIT Press.

25. Dietrich, E. (2000). Analogy and conceptual change, or you can't step into the same mind twice. In E. Dietrich & A. B. Markman (Eds.), *Cognitive Dynamics: Conceptual and Representational Change in Humans and Machines*, New Jersey: Erlbaum.

26. Doumas, L., Hummel, J., & Sandhofer, C. (2008). A theory of the Discovery and Predication of Relational Concepts. *Psychological Review*, 115, 1-43.

27. Mints, G. E. (2001). Arithmetic, formal. In M. Hazewinkel (Ed.), *Encyclopedia of Mathematics* (pp. 63-64). Berlin, Germany: Springer.

28. Crowder, R. G. (1993). Systems and principles in memory theory: another critique of pure memory, in A Collins, S. Gathercole, M. Conway, P. Morris (Eds.), *Theories of Memory*, New Jersey: Erlbaum.
    Goldinger, S. (1998). Echoes of echoes? An episodic theory of lexical access. *Psychological Review, 105*(2), 251-279.

29. Gelernter, D. (1994). *The Muse in the Machine: Computerizing the Poetry of Human Thought.* New York: Free Press.

30. Rogers, T., & McClelland, J. (2008). Précis of: Semantic Cognition: A Parallel Distributed Processing Approach. *Behavioral and Brain Sciences, p. 693.*

31. Rogers, T., & McClelland, J. (2004). *Semantic Cognition: A Parallel Distributed Processing Approach.* Cambridge: MIT Press.

32. Katz, J. J., & Fodor, J. A. (1963). The structure of semantic theory. *Language, 39*, 170-210.

33. Narasimhan, R. (1969). Intelligence and artificial intelligence. *Computer Studies in the Humanities and Verbal Behavior*, March, 24-34.

34. The analogy is to the *interferometric* property of holography. For example, a hologram can be made of a tire at t_1, the tire then subjected to stress, then a hologram made at t_2, and superimposed on the first. An interference fringe would indicate a defect in the tire.

35. Bergson, H., 1889, op. cit.

36. Crockett, L. J. (1994). *The Turing Test and the Frame Problem.* Norwood, N.J.: Ablex.

37. McClelland, J. L., & Rumelhart, D. E. (1986). A distributed model of human learning and memory. In J. L. McClleland, D. E. Rumelhart, & the PDP Research Group (Eds.), *Parallel distributed processing: Explorations in the microstructure of cognition* (Vol. 2, p. 170-215). Cambridge, MA: MIT Press.
38. Rogers, T., Lambon Ralph, M., Garrard, P., Bozeat, S., McClleland, J. L., Hodges, J., & Patterson, K. (2004). Structure and deterioration of semantic memory: A neuropsychological and computational investigation. *Psychological Review*, 111, 205-235.
39. Turvey, M. (1977). Contrasting orientations to the theory of visual information processing. *Psychological Review, 84*, 67-88.
40. Eliasmith, C., & Thagard, P. (2001). Integrating structure and meaning: a distributed model of analogical mapping. *Cognitive Science, 25*, 245-286.
     Halford, G., Wilson, W., Guo, J., Gayler, R., Wiles, J., Stewart, J. (1994). Connectionist implications for processing capacity limitations in analogy. In K. Holyhoak & J. Branden (eds.), *Advances in Connectionist and Neural Computation Theory, Vol. 2, Analogical Connections*, 316-415. Norwood, NJ. Ablex.
     Hummel, J.E., & Holyhoak, K. J. (1997). A theory of analogical and access mapping. *Psychological Review, 104*, 427-466.
     French, R.M. (2002). The computational modeling of analogy-making. *Trends in Cognitive Science*, 6, 200-205.
41. Gayler, R.W. (2003). Vector Symbolic Architectures answer Jackendoff's challenges for cognitive neuroscience. In Peter Slezak (Ed.), ICCS/ASCS International Conference on Cognitive Science (pp. 133-138). Sydney, Australia: University of New South Wales.
42. I am not joking on this. Indeed, this was the essence of a review on a paper that comprised all the arguments in this chapter.
43. Lucas, M.M. & Hayes, P.J. (Eds.) (1982) Proceedings of the Cognitive Curriculum Conference. University of Rochester.
44. See my *Time and Memory* book for a discussion on this.
45. Hofstadter and Sanders, 2013, op. cit., p. 171.

CHAPTER V

Why Robots Need Explicit Memory

They believed that they had understood and explained an
intellectual act if they could break it down into its simple
components – and they held it to be evident or dogmatically
certain that these components could consist in nothing other than
simple sense impressions…But it was precisely this fundamental
vision which inevitably removed them in theory from the peculiar
principle and problem of the symbolic.

— Cassirer, *The Philosophy of Symbolic Forms, Volume III*, p. 215

The Phenomenon – Loss of the Explicit

Perhaps nowhere is the problem of explicit memory better exemplified than in the cases of H.M. and Clive Wearing. The case of H.M. emerged in the 1950's and is now very well known. In 1956, William Scoville removed the medial portions of both H.M.'s temporal lobes in an attempt to control an epileptic condition.[1] After this operation, the nature of his conscious experience changed markedly. He displayed a severe Amnestic Syndrome, appearing unable to retain any further long-term memories. H.M. cannot remember events from one day to the next, in fact for far briefer intervals. He could retain a string of three digits, e.g., 824, by means of an elaborate mnemonic/rehearsal scheme for perhaps fifteen minutes. Yet five minutes after he had stopped and explained the scheme to experimenters, the number was gone. Remarkably, his same examiners can come into his room day after day, yet from day to day he does not remember ever having seen them. It was Milner who discovered that H.M. could learn perceptual or motor skills such as mirror-tracing. But, though steadily improving from session to session, he insisted, upon entering each practice session, seeing the mirror-tracing apparatus, etc., that he had never done this before. For H.M., by his own description, each day is "a day unto itself," without history.

Clive Wearing lives perhaps in an even shorter temporal frame. I first saw Clive discussed in Gray's paper modeling the hippocampus after a "comparator" of present vs. past event.[2] Clive is another individual, similar to H.M., with extensive bilateral damage to the hippocampus, amygdale, etc. Clive, as H.M., is unable to remember previous events. He feels constantly that he "has just woken up," and keeps a diary in which this feeling is repeatedly recorded at periods of hours, even minutes. Statements are made such as, "Suddenly I can see in color," "I've been blind, deaf, and dumb for so long," "Today is the first time I've actually been conscious of anything at all." To Wearing, the environment is in a constant state of flux. A candy bar, even though held in his hand, but covered and uncovered by the experimenter, appeared to be constantly new.

While Clive Wearing and H.M. are at the extreme end of the Amnestic Syndrome, it is in such cases that the problem of the explicit is shown in stark relief. Clive and H.M. are the epitome of a consciousness whose scope is limited to the present. The fundamental dynamics are operative that support the specification of the "world-out-there," the multi-modal world of present experience – conscious perception. As in H. M. and "824," there is even extremely short-term memory. But as soon as we move to the slightly more remote past, beyond the time-scale of perception and events held by rehearsal, a whole set of higher harmonics as it were, beyond the fundamental, are no longer part of the "chord" supported by the dynamically transforming brain. It was Wolff, we saw, in 1732, who coined the termed "redintegration," stating that "when a present perception forms a part of a past perception, the whole past perception tends to reinstate itself." The full mechanics of redintegration, it seems, must include some of these overtones, beyond the fundamental, to explain direct recall of events as explicitly *past* events, i.e., to *localize* these events as events in one's past. H.M. approaches for the *nth* time the mirror tracing apparatus. The same flow field is specified as he moves to the device, moving across the same texture gradient specifying the same floor, the same table surface, the same optico-structural transformation of the device as he moves towards it, the same action being carried out. Everything required for redintegration appears present – the same event pattern, the same perceptual information. The redintegrative dynamics should be perfectly supported. The phenomenon of priming indicates that it is. But there is no *explicit* memory of ever having done, seen or experienced this before. For a theory of consciousness, the problem is startling, with strange symmetries to the problem of perception. We have all the neural dynamics supporting perception and redintegration operating, yet there is a mysterious ingredient missing – the ingredient that makes the past event consciously remembered.

Weiskrantz argued that in the case of the amnesic, a wide range of skills is capable of being learned and retained, not just the procedural (as in mirror tracing), in fact, nearly anything.[3] The list includes:

- New rule learning for verbal paired associates[4]
- A new artificial grammar[5]
- Classification of novel drawings relative to drawings previously seen[6]
- Mathematical problems[7]
- Even the answers to anomalous sentences, e.g., "The haystack was important because the cloth ripped." Answer: parachute.[8]
- Word processing (computer) skill and its associated vocabulary.[9]

There appears to be no limit, no limit, that is, as long as the task does not require the amnesic to place an event in the past. Weiskrantz expressed these amnesic-capable tasks as tasks which do *not* depend on a "joint product" relating present to past (current event x stored event). The amnesic simply cannot perform this product, this fundamental comparison – *present x past*.

The Problem of the Explicit

The memory ability that a Wearing, H.M., or amnesic in general does indeed preserve is generally subsumed under the concept of the *implicit*. Since the first coining of the now ubiquitous explicit/implicit distinction (circa 1985), I think it safe to say that there has been relatively little theory on the true nature of the difference, i.e., on the nature of the *past x present* product of Weiskrantz.[10] In a journal for which the subject should be extremely relevant (*Consciousness and Cognition*), Light and Kennison (1996) and McKoon and Ratliff (1996) focused narrowly on identifying implicit versus explicit influences upon memory performance on a task requiring forced choice identification of words, while Bower (1996) argued that amnesics have a selective deficit in forming novel associations to contexts.[11] In this, he neglected both the problem of retrograde amnesia (loss of memory for events which were experienced *before* any injury) and the reason why association+context is consciously experienced as an event in one's past, i.e., why association+context is still not just implicit memory? These were the first and last approaches near the subject of the explicit in this particular journal. Dienes and Perner (1999) attempted a detailed philosophical analysis of the distinction, but their primary objective was, "to create a common terminology for systematically relating the somewhat different uses of the implicit-explicit distinction in different research areas," and they stayed within this scope.[12] In general, the explicit is associated with consciousness, the implicit is not. Little is discussed beyond this, with emphasis generally on conditions or variables inducing or affecting implicit memory performance.[13] In general, it seems to be the view that loss of explicit memory is the result of damage to an explicit memory "system," generally considered to involve the pre-frontal, cortical areas and medial-temporal lobes, but just why its proper functioning yields a *conscious* remembrance is vague. The critical difficulty, for consciousness, is why – even in a fully functional "explicit memory system" in which all retrieval mechanisms are fully operative, be they connectionist neural nets with their firing patterns, or the operations of cognitive symbolic programs – should these operations result in a consciously experienced remembrance as opposed to yet another "implicit" operation. This is the question: Just what is required for a past event to be consciously experienced as an event localized in one's past? What must such a system actually involve?

The question is extremely difficult. Perhaps this is why it has scarcely been addressed at all. Consider (ignoring this book, i.e., without the theory presented here) what is the current state of affairs. The question rests firstly on the hard problem, and goes beyond it. Before me, on the patio,

146

are wind chimes waving and tinkling in the wind. As I look on them, I am reminded of a past event wherein I gave other such chimes to my wife. In this simple case resides all the problems. There is no theory on how the wind chimes are even perceived, that is, how they are seen in volume, in depth, externally, in space, as an image of the external world with all its inherent qualia. Because we have no theory of conscious perception, which is to say, of *experience*, our theory of memory is ungrounded – we do not truly know how experience is stored or just what is being stored. Therefore we cannot truly know how it is retrieved. Inherent in the wind chimes are their waving motions, therefore the perceived event has an ongoing time-extension. Current cognitive science does not have a theory of the memory that supports this elementary or primary time-extension in perception, further adding to the first problem of what is actually being stored. Now we add the dimension of explicit memory. The past event of viewing the just-given wind chimes is retrieved as an image – a phenomenon (the image), the origin of which, and worse, the need for which – given all knowledge is supposedly held in data structures – as we shall see Pylyshyn argue (next chapter), there is no theory.[14] Finally, and most difficult, the present event (the wind chimes) now functions within what I shall term an *articulated simultaneity*, for it serves both as itself and as a symbol of a past event, assuming both one meaning and another, yet within a global, temporal whole or state of consciousness. Explicit memory, then, is bound to the development of the symbolic – the ability to employ a form (the wind chimes) abstracted from our experience to represent another aspect of experience (the event of the gift) – what Cassirer would term the "symbolic function." The symbolic function, we shall see, carries this aspect of an articulated simultaneity – this "oscillation" between two elements within a temporal whole. This tells us that the symbolic itself is a problem in the relation of mind to time.

The subject of explicit memory, then, is for good reason ignored in current psychological theory. It is no wonder that AI theorists are under the impression they do not need to consider it a problem at all. Yet a theory of explicit memory is the very answer to this question: *why does cognition require consciousness?* The fact is, cognitive science with its major models – connectionism, the computer simulation of thought, AI – seems to work fine without consciousness. So it has convinced itself. We will see what is required for the explicit here, starting with the true complexity of this *past x present* "product." It is in general underestimated, again, if discussed at all. The ability does not develop overnight. The literature of childhood amnesia sees the child requiring at minimum two years to achieve explicit memory. But this literature, we shall see, rather underestimates, in fact vacillates on, what is involved. Thus, in the last decade and more, there has been an extensive effort to show that children evidence "access consciousness" (Block, 1995) considerably earlier than this two year figure.[15] Access consciousness, in its definition as "the ability to use previously stored representations to direct thought" is certainly subsumed in the developing ability to establish the *past x present* product. Rakison, in his review of these attempts, has shown that in every case, this (earlier development) thesis can be rejected.[16] The two year figure holds; the dynamic trajectory is developing a complex ability; it requires a certain time to unfold. The robotics theorist should be asking why so long a trajectory? and what is being accomplished? Here, we will view this product as the end result of the developmental trajectory Piaget described which supports a simultaneous and interrelated group of concepts – causality, object, space and time. Simultaneously and integrally with this, the ability to symbolize emerges. Therefore we will be re-examining Piaget.

A word on some necessary limits in the ensuing discussion is needed. I will not be addressing the role of imitation, pretense, play or language in the developmental story we will follow in Piaget. The appeal to imitation, pretending and play as part of developing a "sense of self" is common in the developmental literature in explaining the escape from childhood amnesia into the explicit, but it entirely misses the point of the truly critical development of causality, object, (classical or constructed) space and time underlying both cognition and this very sense of self as an "object" in a field of causal forces among other objects. Language will be neglected precisely because, as we shall see, it is not language that underlies the birth of the explicit, rather, it is the general ability underlying language itself, and this is a base set of concepts on space, time and causality, and the symbolic function. Though it is a somewhat common conception that it is language that gives rise to access consciousness,[17] and by implication explicit consciousness of a past event, the developmental trajectory supporting the explicit about to be reviewed nowhere relies on language; it is language that relies on the dynamic we are about to explore.

Explicit Memory in Piaget

Let us begin at a more advanced point on the developmental trajectory, a point which illustrates what can be termed the *dynamical lens on events* inherent in Piaget's view. Piaget describes a simple memory experiment with children aged 3 to 8.[18] They are shown a configuration of ten small sticks (Figure 5.1 [A]). They are asked to have a good look so they can draw it again later. A week later, without having seen the configuration again, they are asked to draw what they were shown before. Six months later they are asked to do the same thing.

In the one week interval case, the reconstruction of the event is dependent, in Piaget's terms, on the operational schemata to which the child assimilated the event. The memory is dependent, in other words, on the child's current ability to coordinate actions. At around 3-4, the series is reproduced as in Figure 5.1[B]. Slightly older children (4-5) remember the form in Figure 5.1[C]. Figure 6.1[D] is a slightly more advanced reproduction, while at 6-7, the child remembers the original series. After six months, as Piaget

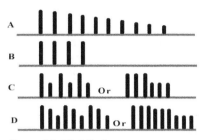

Figure 5.1. Stick Series

describes, children of each age group claimed they remembered very well what they had seen, yet the drawing was changing. The changes generally, with rare exceptions, moved in small jumps, e.g., from A to C, or from C to D, or from D to A.

The drawing of a series – the process of seriation – requires concrete operations. To order a simple series, A, B, C (where A is longer than B, B longer than C), one must simultaneously relate or coordinate the height of B relative to A, the height of B relative to C. This is fundamentally based on the inter-coordination of action. As the child follows this developmental trajectory, Piaget argues, the available dynamics supports successively different "de-codings" of the memory, i.e., the events are reconstructed with an increasingly sophisticated logical structure. The past event is seen through this dynamical lens. But simultaneously then, when the series is a perceived event, it is being perceived through this same dynamical lens. The events gain increasingly complex *symbolic* structure.

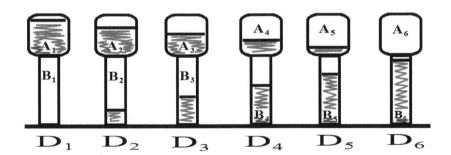

Figure 5.2. Two flows at different velocities. In a series of stages, the water is gradually emptied from the top beaker (I), while the lower beaker (II) gradually fills.

149

This is but one of a large number of such examples of events treated by Piaget where we see this developing dynamical lens, and the need for a *simultaneous* relation of magnitudes. In another, more dynamic event (*The Child's Conception of Time*, 1927), the experimental apparatus consists simply of two differently shaped flasks, one placed atop the other, with a tap or valve between the two (Figure 5.2). The top flask is initially filled with liquid. The child (age 5-9) is provided with a set of drawings of the two flasks (with no liquid levels filled in). At regular intervals or stages a fixed quantity of liquid is allowed to run from the top flask into bottom until the top is empty. Because the flasks are differently shaped, the one empties at a different velocity than that at which the other fills. At each stage, starting at the beginning, the child is asked, using a fresh drawing, to draw a line on each flask indicating the level of the liquid.[19]

The drawings are now shuffled and questions ensue:

1) The child is asked to reconstruct the series, putting the first drawing made down, the next to the right, and so on.
2) Every sheet is now cut in half and the drawings shuffled. The child is again asked to put them in order.

The children again go through stages. At first they cannot order the uncut drawings (the D's of Figure 5.2). Then they achieve this (uncut) ordering but fail ordering the cut drawings. The child may come up with an arrangement of the cut drawings such as I_3, I_1, I_2, I_5, I_6 above II_1, II_5, II_6, II_3, II_2. Even with coaching, he cannot achieve a correct order. Beneath these failures lies a certain mental rigidity. The child is required here to move mentally against the irreversible, experiential flow of time. Regardless of the irreversible flow of the water, they must perform a reversible operation. They must construct a series A -> B -> C... where the arrows carry a *dual or simultaneous meaning* standing for "precedes" as well as "follows." *It is a pure problem of representation.* The child must also grasp the causal connections within and between the two flows. Ultimately, the children will surely and securely order this double series with its causal link as the operating principle. The operations involved in this coordination of two motions, participating in the logic of objects we call causality, underlie our "schema" of time. This schema, supporting our memory operations, our retrieval of events, is again a lens upon our experience. It is a cognitive capability that develops over several years, based on the coordination of actions, first sensori-motor, then mental – and something that must be subject to disruption via a traumatic injury or disease.

I have alluded to the fact that over this developmental trajectory, events become increasingly symbolic. The nature of the symbolic is key to explicit memory. Within Piaget is a theory of the symbolic, and somewhat buried there as well, a vision of the development of explicit memory in the child. The "explicit" in Piaget goes by his phrase, "the localization of events in time," and we will be asking if Piaget is describing the growth trajectory of a cognitive structure, even before the latter point of this trajectory we have just been viewing involving the advent of "operations," that supports this "localization."

The Stage Growth of the Explicit

Perhaps some from the cognitive science world are wondering why I am focusing on this particular subject, namely, Piaget. To a certain extent, it is fair to say that he has been written off by cognitive science. Gopnik, in a piece entitled "The Post-Piaget Era," expressed an apparently common view that Piaget's theories are increasingly implausible, and explored the various contenders for alternatives, to include the information processing approach.[20] Yet in the same year, Lourenco and Machado published a strong defense of Piagetian theory, arguing that its critics had approached the theory "from without, rather than from within," or to be more straightforward, that there was insufficient grasp of the theory and its implications, and that elementary mistakes in interpretation were being made.[21]

Piaget is, in vast proportion, phenomenology. There is not a great deal of mechanism underlying his theory, mainly his insistence on the importance of action (assimilation, accommodation), and the growth and ability of inter-coordinated actions to support mathematical group relations. It is a search for a *"law of evolution,"* and as Piaget notes, "It is only in relation to such a law of evolution that an attempt at differential analysis of behavior patterns acquires some meaning."[22] This apparent reliance on phenomenology would generate criticism that the theory is merely a "redescription" of manifest behavior with no explanatory value.[23] Yet all this is being superseded by the awareness that in his "stages," Piaget is describing the necessary result of the evolution of a system characterized by non-linear dynamics with its natural bifurcations. We are looking at the natural result of a self-organizing system.[24]

We are going to review Piaget's stages. I apologize if for some it is the nth time, but I must presume that not many have perused Piaget for his implicit theory of explicit memory.

The First Two Stages (0-4 months)

In the first two stages identified by Piaget, everything, he argues, takes place as though time were completely reduced to impressions of expectation, desire, success or failure. The world virtually emanates from one's actions. "Objects" do not yet exist. There is the beginning of *sequence* linked with the development of different phases of the same act. But each sequence is a whole isolated from the others. *Nothing yet enables the subject to reconstruct his own history,* and to consider these acts succeeding one another. Each sequence consists in a gliding from the preliminary phase of desire or effort, experienced as a present without a past. Finally, he argues, "this completely psychological *duration,* is not accompanied by a seriation of events external and independent of the self – since no boundary yet exists;"[25]

He comments then:

> The only form of memory evidenced by the behavior patterns of the first two stages is the *memory of recognition* in contradistinction to the *memory of localization* or evocation. ...it is not proved that recognition transcends a global sensation of the familiar which does not entail any clear differentiation between past and present but only the qualitative extension of the past into the present.[26]

This latter comment on recognition – the "qualitative extension" – I would presume, derives from Piaget's mentor of sorts, Bergson, who saw recognition as the familiarity produced by an "automatic motor accompaniment" (as when we walk up our own driveway for the nth time). The "duration" in which the child dwells also is an invocation of Bergson's "duration" – the qualitative, non-differentiable flow of time which cannot be defined as a series of "instants."

Stage 3 (5-7 months)

Piaget describes in the next stages how actions lead to *localization in time.* Thus he describes Laurent (at 8 months):

> Laurent sees his mother enter the room and watches her until she seats herself behind him. Then he resumes playing but turns around several times in succession to look at her again. However there is no sound or noise to remind him of

her presence. Hence this is the beginning of object formation analogous to what we have cited in connection with the third stage of objectification. This process is on a par with a beginning of memory or localization in time.[27]

Piaget sees here an elementary concept of before and after. But Laurent's turning around is not yet "evocation," for it is by virtue of the movement of turning around in order to see that the child forms his nascent memory. But however "motor" and however little representative, it is the beginning of localization.

But is there an orderly arrangement of memories relating to external events? The child yet fails to note anything regarding the sequential positions of objects – the object has no spatial permanence.

Laurent immediately, after the behavior pattern [noted above] reveals an action which clarifies its meaning. His mother having risen and left the room, Laurent watches her until she reaches the door, then, as soon as she disappears, again looks for her behind him in the place where she was at first![28]

Laurent's mother is not yet a permanent object, moving from place to place, but rather a memory image capable of reappearing precisely where it was previously perceived. The order is a function only of Laurent's action, as though, using Piaget's example, having laid my watch on the desk, then covered it with a manuscript, and now having forgotten these displacements of my watch, I look for it again in my pocket where I always reach for it. In essence, the child perceives the order of phenomena/events only when he himself has been the cause. *A universe without causality externalized in things cannot comprise a temporal series other than those relating to acts of the subject.*

Stage 4 (8-11 months)

In this stage, the before-after relation begins to be applied to the object, not just actions. The object disappears behind a screen, but while perceiving the screen, the child retains the image of the object and acts accordingly. The child is now recalling events, not merely actions. But this is extremely unstable. The object is hidden originally at A, and found by the child at A (e.g., under a pillow). The object is then moved in full view to B, and hidden, under another pillow (B). The child goes to B, but if the object is not found immediately, goes back to A, where the *action* was originally successful. The child's memory is now such that he can reconstruct short (but only short) sequences of events independent of the self.

The searching phenomenon described above is commonly termed the *A-not-B* error in the developmental literature, and has been the subject of extensive research,[29] including the development of dynamical mechanisms to explain it.[30] In my opinion, the dynamic systems models fall well short, partially for the reason that A-not-B cannot be isolated from the whole developmental complex – here being (only minimally) described – of which it is a part. We will touch on this debate later in this chapter..

Stage 5 (12-18 months)

In this stage:

> Time definitely transcends the *duration* inherent in personal activity, to be applied to *things* themselves and to form the continuous systematic link which unites the events of the external world to one another.[31]

There is now systematic search for the vanished object, taking into account multiple displacements. An object hidden in A, found in A, hidden now in B, is no longer looked for in A (the former source of practical, action-issued success), but directly in B (though only for visible displacements). For the first time, the child seems capable of elaborating an "objective series."

Causality too is becoming "objectified." Such causality, on permanent objects, in an ordered space, entails the order of events in time. Jacqueline is watching a toy comprised of a revolving ball with chickens. The slightest movement of the ball puts the chickens in a pecking motion.

> Jacqueline, after examining for a moment the toy which I put into action by displacing it gently, first touches the ball and notes the concomitant movement of the chickens. She then systematically moves the ball as she watches the chickens. Thus convinced of the existence of a relationship which she does not understand in detail, she pushes the ball very delicately with her right index finger each time the swinging stops completely... She definitely conceives the activity of

the ball as causing that of the chickens... Moreover the ball is not, to her, a mere extension of her manual action.[32]

The self has now become an object among other objects, just one source of force among other forces:

> Jacqueline, instead of pushing the object, or even giving it a shake by a simple touch, makes every effort to put it [a toy] down as rapidly as possible and let go of it immediately, as though her intervention would impede the toy's spontaneous movements instead of aiding them! After several fruitless attempts she changes method... finally she places it on a sloping cushion and lets it roll.[33]

Or:

> Jacqueline places a red ball on the floor and waits for it to roll. Only after five or six attempts does she push it slightly. The ball, like the plush toy, has therefore become an autonomous center of forces, causality thus being detached from the action of pushing to be transferred onto the object itself.[34]

Objects are seen in causal relation to other objects:

> Jacqueline touches with her stick a plush cat placed on the floor, but does not know how to pull it to her. The spatial and optical contact between the object and the stick seem to her sufficient to displace the object. Causality is therefore spatialized but without yet making allowance for the mechanical and physical laws that experience will reveal (need for pressure of the stick in certain directions, etc., resistance of the moving object, etc.). Finally (two months later) she uses the stick correctly.[35]

The sticks, the strings used to make objects move, etc., are no longer only symbols of personal activity, but objects inserted into the web of events, therefore into conditions of time and place. Laurent, trying to reach an object, revolves a box serving as its support. The concepts "before/after" are no longer limited to her acts, but are applied to the phenomena – to their displacements, perceived and remembered.

Finally, the symbolic is itself emerging, where the symbol is at the level of action. Piaget is playing with his 16 month old daughter Lucienne, and has hidden an attractive watch chain inside a matchbox, reducing the opening to a very small slit. Lucienne tries to open it with two "schemas" or plans for action she already possesses, turning the box over to empty it and then attempting to slide her finger in the slit and extract the coveted item. Both fail.

> She looks at the slit with great attention; then, several times in succession she opens and shuts her mouth, at first slightly, and then wider and wider...But due to the inability to think out the situation in words or clear visual images, she uses a simple motor indication as "signifier" or symbol...Soon after this phase of plastic reflection, Lucienne unhesitatingly puts her finger into the slit... pulls to enlarge the opening.[36]

Stage 6 (19+ months)

The child can now handle even invisible displacements. The elaboration of the temporal field requires the development of images, i.e., representations. This is why the earlier series are so short! These operations are nothing other than evocative memory.

> … such representative series relating to external events encompass at the outset the memory of personal activity, no longer the purely practical memory of the primitive series, but an evocation properly so called, *making it possible to locate in time the actions of the self amidst the other events.*[37]

Infantile Amnesia and the COST of Explicit Memory

If we sum up what is being said about the development of explicit memory, it might be said simply: there is no full explicit memory without at least some COST. Here COST stands for Causality, Object, Space, and Time. Together these concepts form an interrelated, supporting group, and together they grow from inter-coordination of actions. As Piaget describes it from the perspective of the development of one of these, namely from the concept of the *object*, from a mere extension of the child's activity, the object is gradually dissociated from activity. Resistance initiates this dissociation, e.g., obstacles or complications of the field of action as in the appearance of a screen obscuring the favorite toy.[38] Action gradually becomes a factor among other factors, and the child comes to treat his own movements on a par with those of other bodies.

> To the extent that *things* are detached from *actions* and that action is placed among the totality of the series of surrounding events, the subject has the power to construct a system of relations to understand these series and to understand himself in relation to them...To organize such series is to form simultaneously a spatio-temporal network and a system consisting of substances and of relations of cause and effect...Hence the construction of the object is inseparable from that of space, time and causality.[39]

The emergence of COST, Piaget argues, is the event that supports true explicit memory. This occurs gradually, emerging in Piaget's sixth stage, at 18-24 months.

The current literature on infantile amnesia, from what I can see, is unaware of this or unimpressed. Howe. in an excellent book reviewing the subject, contains *one* small reference to Piaget. Infantile "amnesia" is the curious phenomenon wherein adults have little ability to recall experiences that occurred before the age of two or three years.[40] Howe and Courage rejected explanations that relied on retrieval failures (e.g., repression, mismatches between initial encoding and later retrieval contexts) or storage failures (perceptual or neurological immaturity, inadequate "encoding").[41] To account for this discontinuity, and the sudden growth of memories past the age of two, they evoke the emergence of the "cognitive self" around this age. Taking a page from connectionist theory, they argue that once the self develops its "features" (as though the self is a "vector" of features), these features can be incorporated into the memory "trace" along with features of the (external) event in which the child is participating. As more features of the self are accumulated, the more the probability of sampling a set of these features and including them in the memory "trace."

Howe and Courage are perhaps not so committed to the "feature" theory as they are to the general proposition that autobiographical memories can be accounted for by general properties of contemporary memory models, where the self takes its place "as a system of knowledge that organizes memories like any other knowledge structure."[42] The "features" of this self are not at all articulated, but noted are the interpersonal self, the ecological self (fundamentally the infant's response to Gibson's invariants), and the conceptual self. The conceptual self "enables infants to take themselves as *objects* of thought."[43] Here parent-child interactions are discussed, fostering the child's awareness of himself as an object of attention. Piaget's perceptive theory of causality, object, space and time, and the dynamic developmental trajectory implied, which truly provides an analysis of the development necessary to support this "self as an object of thought," i.e., the very meaning of this phrase, is unmentioned.

The Birth of the Symbolic

Let us take perspective. The brain is initially presented an undifferentiated external field (environment). The field is an extensity (not abstract or constructed space, i.e., not a continuum of "positions"), a non-differentiable flow or duration (not abstract time, i.e., an abstract series of "instants"), qualitative (not quantity), a subjective event field (without external "causes"). From this the brain must carve its invariance laws – its "object language." Invariants are isolated by transformations upon this field, and the transformations are naturally effected through actions. It is actions that drive the developmental dynamics, and this dynamics drives towards a base set of constructs. The base set of fundamental constructs of object, causality, (classical) space and time in which the self takes it place as an object among others, is foundational to the entire structure of thought, which is to say, this set lies at the core of *representation*. Explicit memory, in its developed form, is at its heart a problem of representation.

Simultaneously, then, this dynamical trajectory is driving towards liberation from perception, a going beyond the present as Piaget insists, towards *representation by an image*, emerging only at the sixth stage.

> That is why the temporal series just described are revealed as so short and so dependent on the constructions characteristic of object, space, and causality; it is why, *for lack of representations properly so called*, the time developed by the series necessarily remained linked with present percep-tions, with practical memories derived from recent action, and anticipations in accord with action in progress.[44]

The "objective series," where the permanence and displacements of objects are gradually embodied in practical action, are now extended as the representative series. It is the same operations, now performed on the mental, the representative level. To Piaget, this is nothing other than *evocative* memory, but equally, this evocative memory is not a special faculty, but only mental or "reproductive assimilation" (i.e., a relation of object-images to actions), to the extent that it constructs mentally, not in the physical world, a more extensive past. And indeed, this reproductive ability had to be present from the beginning; it is the fundamental basis of explicit memory; it is the ability of the brain to redintegrate a past experience. *There is no necessary implication here at all that the events of an infant's or young child's past are lost, or never stored.* The resultant of this dynamical development towards COST that Piaget is trying to describe is a *representative* form, the ability to treat these events as *symbols* within a localized past.

> Jacqueline (19 months) picks up a blade of grass which she puts in a pail as if it were one of the grasshoppers a little cousin brought her a few days before. She says "Totelle [sauterelle, or grasshopper] totelle, jump, boy [her cousin]." In other words, perception of an object which *reminds her symbolically* of a grasshopper enables her to evoke past events and reconstruct them in sequence.[45]

The developed explicit memory, the symbolic function and COST are all inter-related, mutually supportive. The infant brain can create neural patterns redintegrating past events until the cows come home, but until these past events can become symbolic, until they take their place within a conceptual past, they are little more than present phantoms.

The Simultaneity of the Symbolic State – Cassirer

I wish to underline the critical aspect of this symbolic representation, namely the "articulated simultaneity" noted in my introductory comments. It is not only the events of the past that become symbolic. For Cassirer, it is the events of perception as well. The pathologies, he thought, indicate that, "the contents of certain sensory spheres seem somehow to lose their power of functioning as pure means of representation..."[46] Some aphasics cannot make a simple sketch of their room, marking in it the positions of objects. Many patients can orient themselves on a sketch if the basic schema is already laid down, e.g., the doctor prepares the sketch and indicates by an X where the patient is. But the truly difficult operation is the spontaneous choice of a plane as well as a center of coordinates. Thus, one of Head's (1926) patients would express his problem as the "starting point, but once it was given him everything was much easier."[47]

The same principle operates in the aphasic's dealing with number and time. One patient could recite the days of the week or the months of the year, but given an arbitrary day or month, could not state what came before or after. Though he could recite the numbers in order, he could not count a quantity. Given a set of things to count, he could not progress in order, but frequently went back again. If he had arrived, for example, at "six," he had no comprehension that he had a designation for the quantity thus far achieved, i.e., a cardinal number. When asked which of two numbers are larger, say 12 or 25, many aphasics can do so only by counting through the whole series, determining that in this process the word 25 came after the word 12.

As Cassirer notes, "where quantity no longer stands before us as a sharply articulated multiplicity, it cannot be strictly apprehended as a unity, as a whole built up of parts."[48]. But to achieve this, exactly as in the seriated set of flows of Piaget, every number must carry a *dual* role. Thus to find the sum of 7 + 5, or the difference 7 - 5, the decisive factor is that the number 7, while retaining its position in the first series of 7, now is taken in a new meaning, becoming the starting point of a new series where it assumes the role of zero (Figure 5.3). Again, as in the representation of space, we have a free positing of a center of coordinates. *"The fundamental unities must be kept fixated, but precisely in this fixation be kept mobile, so that it remains possible to change from one to the other."* [49] The number 7 must maintain its meaning as 7, yet *simultaneously* assume the meaning of zero. This is a pure problem of representation in time. More precisely, as I will discuss below, it is a problem of representation in an *extended* time supporting true simultaneity.

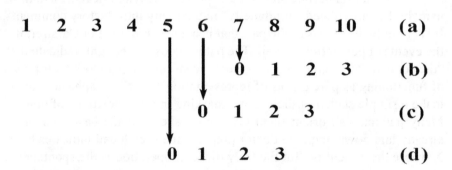

Figure 5.3. The problems: 7 + 3 = 10, 6 + 3 = 9, 5 + 3 = 8. The number 7 functions simultaneously as zero in (b), 6 functions as zero in (c), and 5 as zero in (d). (After Cassirer, 1929/1957)

This extends to the sphere of action, in the apraxias. One patient (Gelb and Goldstein, 1918) could knock on the door if the door was within reach, but the movement, though begun, was halted at once if he was asked to move one step away from the door. He could hammer a nail if, hammer in hand, he stood near the wall, but if the nail was taken away and he was asked to merely indicate the act, he was frozen. He could blow away a scrap of paper on the table, but if there was no paper, he could not blow. This is not the loss of memory images, as was once widely held. He just blew the paper, how could the image have been lost? It is not a failure to create a sensuous "optical space" as Gelb and Goldstein thought. He is staring at the door, and still cannot act. It is the inability to create an abstract, free space for these movements.

> For this latter is the product of the "productive imagi-
> nation": it demands an ability *to interchange present and non-
> present*, the real and the possible. A normal individual can
> perform the movement of hammering a nail just as well into a
> merely imagined wall, because in free activity he can vary the
> elements sensuously given; by thought he can exchange the
> here and now with something else that is not present... [this]
> requires a schematic space.[50]

Analogy - The Symbolic Beneath

This extends to analogy. Thus the psychic blindness patient of Gelb and Goldstein was utterly unable to comprehend linguistic analogy or metaphor. He made no use of either in his speech, in fact, rejected them entirely. He dealt only in realities. Asked by Cassirer, on a bright, sunny day, to repeat, "It is a bad, rainy weather day," he was unable to do so. Again, analogy requires precisely the same achievement of representation. To say, "The spoon is a catapult," (after using it to launch a pea) the spoon must be taken simultaneously in two different modes. One must place oneself simultaneously now in one, now in another meaning, yet maintain a vision of the whole. It is this "articulation of one and the same element of experience with different, equally possible relations, and *simultaneous* orientation in and by these relations, [that] is a basic operation essential to thinking in analogies as well as intelligent operation with numbers..."[51] While we have seen the critique of connectionist and symbolic programming approaches to analogy as giving away the problem, this simultaneous articulation represents yet another dimension that must be supported.

It is this simultaneous articulation that supports little Jacqueline and her "grasshopper." Again, as Cassirer argued, there is an interchange of present and non-present, i.e., of present and past. The little piece of grass can now be a symbol; it can be simultaneously both a piece of grass – a *perceptual image* – and a "grasshopper" which once she saw hopping around. But now we find ourselves inevitably relating this to the problem of Weiskrantz and his "product" (present x past event). When H.M. looks at the mirror tracing apparatus, should it not be simultaneously both the present apparatus and the past apparatus upon which he once worked? Sitting on the porch, the wind chimes instantly become a "symbol," simultaneously both of themselves and the memory of buying other chimes for my wife for an anniversary. All such surrounding objects can become *symbolic* of the past. But now we see this apparently simple ability through the underlying complexity of the dynamic that must support it.

The physical organism spends several years and a great deal of effort following this "law of evolution" or developmental trajectory to produce this dynamical possibility. In the sphere of explicit memory, and in the spheres Cassirer discussed – sketching, analogy, numbers, time, voluntary actions – an essential feature of the underlying dynamic in each is the articulated simultaneity supporting the symbolic nature of these functions. This can apparently be disrupted in each. In the case of amnesia, I would argue, damage to the neural circuitry underlying the concrete dynamics required for explicit recall is effectively disrupting the ability to sustain the articulated simultaneity in time necessary for the present event to be simultaneously in a symbolic relation to the past.

In one of the cases above, Cassirer discussed ideomotor apraxia, often defined as "inability to carry out a motor command, e.g., act as if you are brushing your teeth." It is a phenomenon for which lesions to the a supposed information channel in the brain termed the "dorsal stream" (or the "how" system) are currently implicated, or perhaps the ventro-dorsal as we have seen Gallese argue.[52] Gallese, in his review, argues that different and parallel parieto-premotor networks which receive visual information processed within one part of the dorsal stream create internal representations of actions, to include action preparation, action understanding, space and action conscious awareness. But again, the simple notion of an "information stream" (or its disruption) is insufficient to explain the specific problem Cassirer is discussing in relation to action, or for that matter, in the problems relating to sketching, analogy, number and time which all appear to share the same cause. We are asking how "the unities can be fixated, yet simultaneously be kept mobile," or how one and the same element can oscillate between one meaning and another, while comprising a whole. This bespeaks of a dynamic, in the very concrete sense I have indicated, which is intrinsically participating in the concrete, indivisible or non-differentiable motion of the matter-field in time.

Failure to Net Piaget

The connectionist modelers have of course attempted to weigh in (or weight in) on Piaget's tasks. Rogers and McClelland, in support of their connectionist vision of the development of cognition, note that several connectionist models have been developed which can perform developmental learning tasks.[25] One such is the balance scale problem of Piaget. Here we have a small apparatus, like a small teeter totter, upon which the child can hang weights on each side to balance the "teeter totter" arm. The children gradually (again, in stages, over years) learn the principle of torque, i.e., the rule for balancing two differing weights (say a five gram weight and a ten gram weight) on each side, allowing compensation by varying the distances from the center of the scale. For example a five gram weight on the right, and two feet from the center, will balance a ten gram weight on the left, only one foot from the center (length x weight = length x weight, or 5 lbs x 2 ft = 10 lbs x 1 ft). Yet Quinlan et al., in a detailed analysis, have shown that in balance scale learning simulations, connectionist networks *never* in fact learn the principle of torque, nor do their internal weight representations ever approximate intermediate rules that correspond to the human phases of learning.[53] Here the mere *approximation* of connectionism to human developmental learning is on display.

There is a significance to this. Again it is that connectionist models are insensitive to the transformations and invariants defining events. Balancing a scale is an event. The full semantics of the principle of torque exists across a set of such events with varying weights and distances; there is again the perception of an invariance law (length x weight = length x weight) over these balancing transformations. It would be a quite feasible exercise to show that this will be true for nearly all Piagetian tasks. We shall see this forcefully in the tunnel-bead experiment of Piaget in Chapter VI, where again, as dynamic, self-organizing systems, the children require several years to master the task.

After seeing the requirements for mastering the coordination of flows discussed above, with the intrinsic reliance on the explicit/symbolic (or COST), the reader is now in position to appreciate the actual magnitude of the task that would truly face the connectionist networks in trying to simulate this development. These Piagetian tasks require explicit memory and the symbolic function. The connectionist network is approaching these tasks in a pure syntactic mode as a device (network) whose operations function logically in an abstract time. Without the benefit of a dynamics that is integrally part of the non-differentiable flow of time, such a network has no hope of faithfully modeling these tasks.

Failure to Mass-Spring Piaget

Having arrived at this point in the advent of the symbol, let us return briefly to the A-not-B error. Thelen et al. attempt to treat this by modeling the decision as a dynamic field which evolves continuously under the influence of the specifications of the task environment, the specific cue to reach A or B (which must be remembered), and after the first reach, the memory dynamics which bias the field (almost as though biasing the release of a mass-spring) on a subsequent reach.[54] The field represents the relative activation states of the parameters appropriate to planning and executing a reach in a specific direction to the right (A) or left (B). But consider the reflections of the authors in trying to account for the reasons for change of, and the origins of, the critical parameter (h, or cooperativity) values in their model that determine a reach to A or to B:

> They learn to shape their hands in anticipation of objects to be reached and then to differentiate the fingers to pick up small items...They start to incorporate manual actions with locomotion such as crawling and walking. And they begin to have highly differentiated manual activities with objects of different properties, such as squeezing soft toys and banging noisy ones. It is a time of *active exploration of the properties of objects by acting on them* and of active exploration of space by moving through it.[55]

This is exactly what we viewed Jacqueline, Lucienne and Laurent doing, but the above description simply strips out the embedding in the larger dynamic trajectory Piaget is trying systematically to describe. It is, yes, but a weak "redescription" of Piaget. The simple activities Thelen et al. note, when viewed as we have above from a larger perspective, are part of the emergence of causality, of sequence in time, of the self as object among other objects, of the body as a force among other forces, i.e., an emerging complex of base concepts.

Despite this weakness, Thelen et al. proposed that this general dynamical model will ultimately apply to *all* Piagetian tasks. This would include the stick seriation task and the ordering of two liquid flows discussed above, and many others equally and more complex. This is a severe undervaluing of the problem of representation, i.e., of explicit, conscious thought. If the ordering of two liquid flows example isn't already enough, when we view the Tunnel-Bead task in Chapter VI, we shall see how vastly inadequate is the attempt to reduce Piaget and his children to mass-springs.

Recognizing the Explicit

I must make a final clarification here, one of many that could be made, on a confusion that plagues the house of psychology. Explicit memory is clearly considered a more advanced form of memory. Symmetrically, there has been the argument that the implicit "system" is the more primitive – present early in infancy – while the explicit "system" develops gradually, gaining critical mass, as we have seen, around two years. If infants manifest only primitive, implicit memory, a memory by definition "unconscious," then this has even been interpreted by some to mean that infants are not yet *conscious* until this development of the explicit system is complete. This is absurd. As I noted in Chapter II, frogs and chipmunks are conscious. Infants are conscious. Perception *is* consciousness. This latter – that perception *is* consciousness – unbelievably, is not understood, hence the fixation on explicit memory as the key ingredient.[31] Infants certainly have perception. They don't have explicit memory, but they do have a basic form of memory.

Rovee-Collier and associates (developmental theorists) in their extended examination of the entire implicit-explicit distinction in infancy, feel they are able to show that infants display explicit memory way before the completed development of COST.[56] (I think this may have been a reaction to the notion that infants are not conscious because they don't have explicit memory. Therefore, let us show that the explicit exists very early, hence consciousness exists.) These theorists need to have given a little more weight to Piaget. Throughout *The Construction of Reality in the Child*, he makes it clear that a basic form of memory is present; it is just not the developed memory relying on COST which allows for localization of events in time. Thus when he speaks of the form of memory manifesting in the first few stages, he notes that "the only form of memory evidenced... is the memory of recognition in contradistinction to the memory of localization or evocation."[33] Of this recognition, he was not willing to grant it any mature status, noting "...

it is not proved that recognition transcends a global sensation of the familiar which does not entail any clear differentiation between past and present but only the qualitative extension of the past into the present."[34]

Rovee-Collier et al., I think it can be said, base much of their argument for the existence of the (very early) explicit in infants on this very form of recognition. For example, an infant is shown a mobile hanging over his crib to which his foot is tied such that he can make the mobile move. At a later time, perhaps a few days, the mobile is shown again, and the infant's memory is judged by his reaction. If he again moves his foot to move the mobile, this is considered a *recognition* of the past situation. Piaget would allow this, but with the qualification already noted above, i.e., this is not explicit memory.

But the status of this *recognition* and its role in memory has been utterly obscured to current theorists by the computer model of mind and/ or the information theoretic framework. This is because there is a form of recognition that can be more than just an implicit (unconscious) memory and less than the explicit. It is neither, but is has a status. It can be indeed a *feeling* of familiarity due to the presence of an organized motor accompaniment that has been created and now marks a situation, e.g., the everyday walk down my driveway to the barn, or walking into my office. Such a feeling of course implies a being that exists over a continuous time.[57]

Explicit Final Note

We have viewed the dynamic trajectory that takes the human to COST, to the explicit, and to the symbolic with the articulated simultaneity of *present x past* required and underlying all of this. This is a trajectory that is obviously embracing a dynamically developing/changing physical system, i.e., the body and brain, that is requiring two years just to get to this critical ability, and will take yet more years to get to the point where it can coordinate two flows of water or predict the result of N turns of the tunnel with its hidden beads. Nature seems to think that this form of gradual development of the system's dynamic capability – this trajectory – is required. This is the question: Why would those who plan to develop their super-intelligent robots – human equivalent and beyond — think they can avoid replicating such a trajectory? And what is their current understanding of its nature and how to replicate it?

Chapter V: End Notes and References

1. Scoville, W. B., & Milner, B. (1957). Loss of recent memory after bi-lateral hippocampal lesions. *Journal of Neurology, Neurosurgery and Psychiatry, 20*, 11-21.
2. Gray, J. A. (1995). The contents of consciousness: A neuropsychological conjecture. *Behavioral and Brain Sciences, 18*, 659-722.
3. Weiskrantz, L. (1997). *Consciousness Lost and Found.* New York: Oxford.
4. Winocur, G., and Weiskrantz, L. (1976). An investigation of paired-associate learning in amnesiac patients. *Neuropsychologia, 14*, 97-110.
5. Knowlton, B.J., Ramus, S.J., & Squire, L.R. (1992). Intact artificial grammar learning in amnesias: Dissociation of abstract knowledge and memory for specific instances. *Psychological Science, 3*, 172-179.
6. Squire, L. R., & Knowlton, B. (1995). Leaning about categories in the absence of memory. *Proceedings of the National Academy of Sciences*, USA, 92, 12470-12474.
7. Wood, F., Ebert, V., & Kinsbourne, M. (1982). The episodic-semantic memory distinction in memory and amnesia: Clinical and experimental observations. In L. Cermak (ed.), *Human Memory and Amnesia*, Hillsdale, NJ: Erlbaum.
8. Weiskrantz, L. (1997). *Consciousness Lost and Found.* New York: Oxford.
9. Van der Linden, M, & Coyette, F. (1995). Acquisition of word processing knowledge in an amnesic patient: implications for theory and rehabilitation. In R. Campbell & M. M. A. Conway (Eds.), *Broken Memories*. Oxford, UK: Blackwell.
10. Schacter, D. L. (1987). Implicit memory: history and current status. *Journal of Experimental Psycholgoy: Learning, Memory and Cognition, 13*, 501-518.
    Graf, P. & Schacter, D. L. (1985). Implicit and explicit memory for new associations in normal subjects and amnesic patients. *Journal of Experimental Psychology: Learning, Memory, and Cognition. 11*, 501-518.
11. Light, L., Kennison, R. (1996). Guessing strategies in perceptual identification: Reply to Mckoon and Ratliff. *Consciousness and Cognition, 5*, 512-524.
    McKoon, G., & Ratliff, R. (1996). Separating implicit from explicit retrieval processes in perceptual identificagtion. *Consciousness and Cognition, 5*, 500-511.
    Bower, G. (1996). Reactivating a reactivation theory of implicit memory. *Consciousness and Cognition, 5*, 22-72.
12. Dienes, Z, & Perner, J. (1999) A theory of implicit and explicit knowledge. *Behavioral and Brain Sciences*, 22 (5): 735-808.
13. See for example:
    Kihlstrom, J., Dorfman, J., & Park, L. (2007). Implicit and explicit learning and memory. In M. Velmans and S. Schneider (Eds.). *A Companion to Consciousness*, Blackwell, 539-535.
14. Pylyshyn, Z. (2002). Mental imagery: In search of a theory. *Behavioral and Brain Sciences, 25*, 157-238.
15. Block, N. (1995). On a confusion about the function of consciousness. *Behavioral and Brain Sciences, 18*, 227-247.
16. Rakison, D. (2007). Is consciousness in its infancy in infancy? *Journal of Consciousness Studies, 14*, 66-89.
17. Ibid.

18. Piaget, J. (1968). *On the Development of Memory and Identity.* Clark University Press.
19. Piaget, J. (1927/1969). *The Child's Conception of Time.* New York: Basic Books.
20. Gopnik, A. (1996). The post-Piaget era. *Psychological Science.* 7(4), 221-225.
21. Lourenco, O., & Machado, A. (1996). In defense of Piaget's theory: A reply to 10 common criticisms. *Psychological Review, 103* (1), 144-164.
22. Piaget, J. (1954). *The Construction of Reality in the Child.* New York: Ballentine, p. 381.
23. Brainerd, C. J. (1978). The stage acquisition in cognitive developmental theory. *Behavioral Brain Sciences,* 2, 173-213.
24. Van deer Maas, H.L.J, & Molenaar, P. C. M. (1992). Stagewise cognitive development: an application of catastrophe theory. *Psychological Review,* 99, 395-417.
    Raijmakers, M. E. J., van Der Maas, H. L. J., & Molenaar, P.C.M. (199). On the validity of simulating stagewise development by means of PDP networks: Application of catastrophe analysis and an experimental test of rule-like network performance. *Cognitive Science,* 20, 101-136.
    Molenaar, P., & Raijakers, M. (2000). A causal interpretation of Piaget's theory of cognitive development: Reflections on the relationship between epigenesis and non-linear dynamics. *New Ideas in Psychology,* 18, 41-55.
25. Piaget, J. (1954). *The Construction of Reality in the Child.* New York: Ballentine,p. 393, emphasis added.
26. Piaget, J. (1954), op cit., p. 369.
27. Piaget, J. (1954), op. cit, p. 375.
28. Piaget, J. (1954), op cit., p. 377.
29. Markovitch, S. & Zelaso, P. (1999). The A-not-B error: Results from a logistic meta-analysis. *Child Development, 70,* 1297-1313.
    Munakata, Y. (1998). Infant preserverative and implications for object permanence theories: A PDP model of the A-not-B task. *Developmental Science, 1,* 161-184.
30. Thelen, E., Schoner, G., Scheler, C., & Smith, L. (2001). The dynamics of embodiment: A field theory of infant preserverative reaching. *Behavioral and Brain Sciences, 24,* 1-86.
31. Piaget, J. (1954), op cit., p. 385.
32. Piaget, J. (1954), op cit., p. 310.
33. Piaget, J. (1954), op cit., p. 309.
34. Piaget, J. (1954), op cit., p. 309.
35. Piaget, J. (1954), op cit., p. 321.
36. Piaget, J. (1952). *The Origins of Intelligence in Children.* New York: International universities press.
37. Piaget, J. (1954), op cit., p. 394.
38. Piaget, J. (1954), op cit., p. 321.
39. Piaget, J. (1954), op cit., p. 103.
40. Howe, M. (2001). *The Fate of Early Memories.* Washington, D.C.: The American Psychological Association.
41. Howe, M., & Courage, M. (1993). The emergence and early development of autobiographical memory. *Psychological Review,* 104 (3), 499-523.
42. Howe, M., & Courage, M. (1993), op. cit., p. 513.
43. Howe, M., & Courage, M. (1993), op. cit., p. 507.
44. Piaget, J. (1954), op cit., p. 391, emphasis added.

45. Piaget, J. (1952), op cit., p. 391, emphasis added.
46. Cassirer, E. (1929/1957). *The Philosophy of Symbolic Forms, Vol. 3: The Phenomenology of Knowledge.* New Haven: Yale University Press, p.236.
47. Head, H. (1926). *Aphasia and Kindred Disorders of Speech (Vols. I and II).* Cambridge: Cambridge University Press.
48. Cassirer, E. (1929/1957), op. cit., p. 250.
49. Cassirer, E. (1929/1957), op. cit., p. 230.
50. Cassirer, E. (1929/1957, op. cit., p. 271, emphasis added.
51. Cassirer, E. (1929/1957), op. cit., p. 257.
52. Gallese, V. (2007, April). The "conscious" dorsal stream: embodied simulation and its role in space and action conscious awareness. *Psyche,* 13 (1), 1-20.
53. Quinlan, P., van der Maas, H., Jansen, B., Booij, O., & Rendell, M., Re-thinking stages of cognitive development: An appraisal of connectionist models of the balance scale task. *Cognition,* 103, 413-459.
54. Thelen, E., Schoner, G., Scheler, C., & Smith, L. (2001). The dynamics of embodiment: A field theory of infant preseverative reaching. *Behavioral and Brain Sciences, 24,* 1-86.
55. Ibid., p. 31, emphasis added.
56. Rovee-Collier, C., Hayne, H., Colombo, M. (2000). *The Development of Implicit and Explicit Memory.* Amsterdam: John Benjamins.
57. I have discussed the problem of recognition further in:
Robbins, S. E. (2012). *Time and Memory: A primer on the Scientific Mysticism of Consciousness.* Atlanta: CreateSpace.

CHAPTER VI

The Broadly Computational Transformations of Thought

The psychical entities which seem to serve as elements in
thought are certain signs and more or less clear images which
can "voluntarily" be reproduced and examined... The above
mentioned elements are in my case, of visual and muscular type.

— Einstein: Letter to Jacques Hadamard[1]

Pure memory, though independent in theory, manifests itself as a
rule only in the colored and living image which reveals it.

— Bergson, *Matter and Memory*

Return of the Mousetrap

I would like us to return now to that little problem of analogical design – the mousetrap. In it, we see not only the problem of analogy and explicit memory, but also a fundamental feature of conscious thought – transformations within an indivisible flow of time. Our mousetrap, I will show, while seemingly innocent, has actually trapped AI in a deep controversy, yet with barely anyone's awareness that it has done so.[2]

Michael Behe, an academic biologist, began the controversy when he challenged the possibility of the algorithmic approach to design espoused by evolution theorists (*Darwin's Black Box*).[3] Though Behe dealt heavily in the biochemical realm, he placed the problem initially in the intuitive context of a mousetrap. The (standard) mousetrap consists of several parts (Figure 6.1). As a functioning whole, he argued, the trap is "irreducibly complex." For the device to work as designed, all the parts must be present and organized correctly, else it does not function.

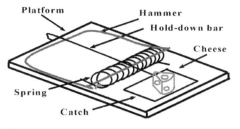

Figure 6.1. Mousetrap, M1A5, standard military issue.

The urge is to break the problem of instantiating this design into simpler components – evolving the separate, smaller parts. Natural selection buys nothing here, Behe argued. Natural selection picks some feature or form or component to continue because it happens to have been proven useful for survival. Evolving a single part (component), which by itself has no survival value, is impossible by definition – impossible, that is, by the definition of the role and function of natural selection. But even if by chance the parts evolved simultaneously, there remains the enormous problem of organization of the parts. How does this happen randomly? Each part must be oriented precisely spatially, fitted with the rest, fastened down in place, etc. There are enormous "degrees of freedom" here – ways the parts can rotate, translate, fit together and move around in space – which drive the odds against randomness to enormous proportions.

The evolutionists quickly countered. An argument, often cited as though it were a definitive critique, was provided by McDonald to demonstrate how the mousetrap could have simpler instantiations.[4] His caveat is that this is not an analogy for evolution per se, but the argument *is* taken as a critique of

Behe.[5] Working backwards, McDonald gradually simplified the trap, producing four "predecessor" traps of decreasing complexity. Behe argued, however, it is not that simpler mousetraps (still irreducibly complex) do not exist. The question is progression – the actual mechanism of movement from version A to B to C.[6] If McDonald *is* taken as a defense of evolution, Behe easily produces a strong counter argument.[7] Starting with McDonald's first and least complex trap (Figure 6.2, left) in the "sort of evolving" series, he examined the steps needed for McDonald to arrive at the second trap (Figure 6.2, right). The first (or single piece) trap has one arm, under tension, propped up on the other arm. When jiggled, the arm is released and comes down, pinning the mouse's paw. It is a functional trap.

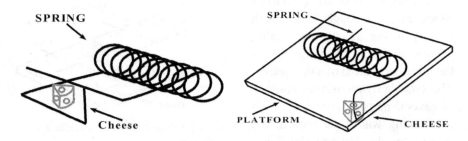

Figure 6.2. Mousetraps #1 (left) and #2 (right).

The second trap has a spring and a platform. One of the extended arms stands under tension at the very edge of the platform. If jiggled, it comes down, hopefully pinning some appendage of the mouse. To arrive at the second, functional trap, the following appears needed:

1) Bend the arm that has one bend through 90 degrees so the end is perpendicular to the axis of the spring and points toward the platform.
2) Bend the other arm through 180 degrees so the first segment is pointing opposite to its original direction.
3) Shorten one arm so its length is less than the distance from the top of the platform to the floor.
4) Introduce the platform with staples. These have an extremely narrow tolerance in their positioning, for the spring arm must be on the precise edge of the platform, else the trap won't function.

All of this must be accomplished before the second trap will function – an intermediate but non-functional (useless) stage cannot be "selected." This complicated transition is a sequence of steps that must occur coherently.

With each step required, we decrease the probability of random occurrence exponentially. The probability (or improbability) is clearly a function of the number of transition "steps" identified. The "four" steps in the mousetrap transition above is an arbitrary number, and indeed could be decomposed to many further sub-steps when dealing with the level of random mutations.

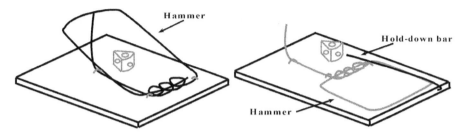

Figure 6.3. Traps Five (left) and Six (right) from the second series. Trap Six now has a hold-down bar hooked into the platform and lodged (lightly) under the hammer arm.

Each of the subsequent transitions (trap 2 -> trap 3, 3->4, 4->5) proved subject to the same argument. McDonald then produced a more refined series of traps.[8] He argued that the point was made that a complicated device can be built up by adding or modifying one part at a time, each time improving the efficiency of the device. Yet there are still problematic transformations between many of his steps.[9] For example, in the second series, the transition between a simpler spring trap (Figure 6.3, Trap Five) and one now employing a hold-down bar (Figure 6.3, Trap Six) is a visual statement of the difficulty of the problem. Even if the simpler trap were to become a biologically based analog – a largish "mouse-catcher beetle" – sprouting six legs and a digestive system for the mice it catches, the environmental events and/or mutations which take it to the next step (as in Trap Six) would be a challenge to define.

But the most apparently decisive evolutionary argument is that indeed biological "parts" exist that in themselves are independently functional. In essence, then, evolution has available to it pools of independently functional components from which to select, and from which to build various larger functioning wholes. Kevin Miller applies this logic to the mousetrap. Each component can be conceived to be an independently functional part.[10] For example, the hold-down bar can serve as a "toothpick," the platform as "kindling," three of the components can work together as a "tie clip" (platform, spring and hammer), and so on. The implication of this argument is disturbing, for it indicates that the grasp of the problem is deeply insufficient. Either the evolutionists, at this point, have simply become very weak AI theorists, or they know something the AI folks don't know. The fact is, this is where the evolutionists have blundered into the problem we have already met in Chapter III, that greatest of unsolved, if not abandoned, problems of AI – *common sense knowledge*.

Transformations

McDonald, as we saw, performed two "bending" transformations on the wire of mousetrap #1 to obtain mousetrap #2. This form of dynamic transformation in thought heavily impressed the Gestalt psychologist, Max Wertheimer (*Productive Thinking*, 1945).[11] He had observed children in a classroom being taught, via drawings of a parallelogram on the blackboard, the traditional, algorithmic method of dropping a perpendicular to find the area, a method which in effect turns the figure into a rectangle for easy computation of the area (length × height). Yet, when Wertheimer himself went to the board and drew a slightly rotated version of the parallelogram figure, he was shocked to see that the children failed to extend the method. They no longer knew what to do, exclaiming, "We haven't had that yet!" But outside the algorithmic-oriented classroom, Wertheimer observed a five year-old who looked at a cardboard cutout of a parallelogram, then asked for a scissors so she could cut the (triangular) end off and move it to the other side to make a rectangle (to now compute the area easily). This was bettered by the dynamic transformation exhibited by another five year-old child who formed the cardboard parallelogram into a cylinder, then asked for a scissors to cut it in half, announcing it would now make a rectangle.

It is this dynamic "folding" transformation among others that physicist and mathematician Roger Penrose (*Shadows of the Mind*) uses in examples of what he felt is "non-computational thought" – forms of thought that he felt could not be handled by the computer model of mind and its foundational concept of "computation."[12] The formal definition of "computation" was provided by Alan Turing and embodied in an abstract computing machine we have discussed earlier, consisting of a read-head and an infinite tape, now termed the *Turing Machine*. All current computers, including neural nets, are simply concrete versions of a Turing Machine, i.e., they are always doing computations that fit the definition of a Turing Machine. Obviously, if thought is truly "non-computational," it is then beyond the computer mode, for it is then beyond the computation of a Turing Machine. Thus the computer-as-mind theorists attacked Penrose mercilessly. None of his critics noticed that in his examples of non-computational thought, Penrose *had gravitated towards transformations and invariance*. That is, none of his critics grasped its significance – or perhaps wanted to.

Penrose considers a proof involving "hexagonal" numbers. A hexagonal number, such as 19, can be arranged in a little hexagon such as in Figure 6.4 (bottom, right). His proof is that successive sums of hexagonal numbers are *always* a cubical number (a number that can be arranged as a cube) and hence this is "a computation that does not stop." This is to say, I can add one hexagonal number to the next and always get a cubical number – for an infinity of such additions. In his proof, he initially *folds* a hexagonal structure into a three-sided cube (each with a side, a wall and a ceiling). He then has us imagine building up any cube by successively stacking (another transformation) these three-faced arrangements, giving each time an ever larger cube (Figure 6.4). This is a dynamic transformation over time, in fact multiple transformations with invariants across each. We can expand the hexagonal structures successively, from 1, to 7, to 19, etc., each time preserving the visual hexagonal invariant. Then, each is folded successively,

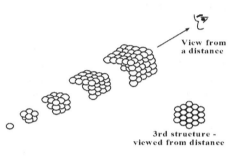

Figure 6.4. Successive cubes built from side, wall, and ceiling. Each side, wall, and ceiling structure make a hexagonal number (1, 7, 19, 37...)

each time preserving the three-faced structural invariant. Then imagine them successively stacking, one upon the other, each operation preserving the cubical invariance. Over this event, the features (or transformational invariance) of the transformation are defined.

As a simpler example, Penrose considered how we understand that $3 \times 5 = 5 \times 3$. Each side of the equation is different, and we can display this visually as:

3×5   (•••••) (•••••) (•••••)
5×3   (•••) (•••) (•••) (•••) (•••).

A *computational* procedure to ascertain the equality of 3x5 and 5x3 would now involve counting the elements in each group to see that we have 15 in each. But we can see this equality must be true by visualizing the array:

• • • • •
• • • • •
• • • • •

If we rotate this through a right angle in our mind's eye, we can see that nothing has changed – the new 5x3 array we see has the same number of elements as the 3x5 array pictured. We have invariance. Thus, as I noted, it is to the perception of invariance which Penrose gravitates as a natural exemplar of non-computational thought – thought which he felt requires *consciousness*. This indeed requires consciousness, we have seen, because these transformations must take place in a non-differentiable flow. These perceived invariants form his "obvious understandings" that become the building blocks for mathematical proofs. As we have seen of invariants, these obvious understandings, Penrose felt, are inexhaustible. From this he argued in effect, will arise the elements of an object language employed in a proof. But in this he was well preceded by the likes of Wertheimer (*Productive Thinking*, 1945), Arnheim (*Visual Thinking*, 1969), Bruner (*Beyond the Information Given*, 1973), Montessori (e.g., her mathematical program), Hanson (*Patterns of Discovery*, 1958), and if one looks closely, Piaget, and others.

That Darn Image

In the *symbolic manipulation* framework of thought, with its frame axioms, symbols and rule manipulation schemes, etc., an influential theorist in the cognitive science field, Zenon Pylyshyn, early in the game, initially denied any need for mental images, arguing that if images are simply constructed via the data elements and rules for manipulation, the image is simply redundant – all the knowledge is in the rules and data structures in the first place.[13]

> In other words, the image has lost all its picture-like qualities and has become a data-structure meeting all the requirements of the form of representation set forth in earlier sections. In fact, it can be put directly into one-to-one correspondence with a finite set of propositions... [My note: For "propositions," think frame axiom-like statements.] Similarly, "seeing the image" has been replaced by a set of common elementary and completely mechanical operations, such as testing the identity of two symbols.

Though he asserted that the experience of the image "is not to be questioned," one would ask why not? Clearly we have worked to the point where, with a great sigh of relief, we can throw the pesky things away. They are indeed difficult to account for or justify in a computer. Even if the machine were to generate one, would it then "look" at it? A useless effort surely, especially given that it can't obtain any knowledge from it – it generated it in the first place from its data structures. This is indeed a curious gloss on our earlier discussion of the problem of perception, for this makes it quite clear in the case of the *perceptual* image that cognitive science and the machine model truly do not need an image of the external world at all. The machine is quite happy being utterly blind. Thus, for Pylyshyn, what good could images do? He could conceive of no need for them. Yet, strangely, they exist, for apparently no reason, at least for the computer model of mind.

Unfortunately, even many Gibsonians follow in Pylyshyn's dilemma-strewn path. The clouded, abstract and vague understanding of direct perception and of the origin and nature of the image of the external world takes its toll as soon as the discussion moves to cognition and memory. On the subject of cognition, Chemero's rightful stance against representations inside the brain for perception is extended wrongfully against representations in thought. Even analogy making is made grist for an attempt to take this function down to the utterly non-representational.[14] But when one has a very fuzzy model of the image of the external world, as I noted in Chapter II, that is, no clear theory of the origin of the perceptual image, one will tend to deny the memory image, yes, right in league with the exponents of the computer metaphor – in fact one has not much of a theory of memory. Thus Chemero too struggles against a fundamental intuition, namely our obvious use of representations in thought – I can clearly imagine the construction of a new chicken coop. Some of this bleeds into contortions such as, "on the Turvey-Shaw-Mace view, either babies do not perceive their mothers (because information for direct perception of "mother" is unavailable) or they do not perceive them directly," and rather strange somersaults to resolve this. But surely I can see my mother as my mother because of memory, in fact, this is just a very bad neglect of the problem of explicit memory as well.

Another Gibson expositor, Louise Barret (*Beyond the Brain*), after noting that Gibson does not deny imagination, memory images, fantasy or dreaming, immediately takes us to the idea that this – his non-denial of images – doesn't really matter anyhow. Why? Shades of Pylyshyn – because we should, "…remember that mental representations are theoretical constructs that we use to try to better understand certain aspects of our own and other animals lives."[15] These "constructs" include memory images. Again, if you are vague as to what the perceptual image is, you will definitely be so about the memory image. This "mere theoretical construct" stance is taken to its ultimate when Barret approvingly discusses an experimental robotic mouse which, without any memory storage, learns to negotiate a T-maze correctly for reward, using its connectionist network and via a few cues in the environment such as a red wall to its right and a stick leaning in the corner at the T.[16] Here, in the robot, we have no storehouse of memories/experiences, and of course no need of memory images. Similarly, she approves Rowland's view that, when seeing a dog whimpering beside a road and being told the dog was nearly run over six months previously, we mistakenly attribute a memory experience to the dog when this notion should only be considered a convenient "construct" to make sense of his whimpering behavior – the dog too is just the robotic mouse. Thus, she argues, due to our fondness for the storage metaphor of memory, we aren't used to thinking about memory (or remembering) as mere theoretical props to explain what we and other animals do, i.e., the non-memory-experiencing robotic mouse is the true model.

This sounds sophisticated, but it flies in the face of our experience – we clearly experience the image/memory of, say, our wedding or a canoe trip, etc., but – shades of Dennett – we're supposed to deny this memory image of the wedding, declaring it as some form of illusion, and call it a mere theoretical construct to help us explain – what? – why, this experience of remembering with its images. In other words, while we are experiencing the image of the event, we are simultaneously supposed to be telling ourselves this is a mere construct and that we are not experiencing it. This contortion stems from the Gibsonians' failure to set Gibson (and his direct perception) within the metaphysic he was using implicitly and which Bergson was stating explicitly. Gibson, we saw, ridiculed the storehouse concept – that is, the idea of storing experience inside the brain. This does not mean that experiences cannot be retrieved. There is nothing here on cognition and memory, in either Barret or Chemero, that AI would find threatening to its view of mind.

Kosslyn and Koenig, two cognitive scientists and imagery theorists, while defending imagery's existence, are less logically consistent while nevertheless ending at what is essentially the same "no-need-for-them" concept:

> We use imagery to access stored information about an object by generating an image and then inspecting the imaged object for the sought information. This is accomplished by first looking up a description of the object in associative memory, and then using the code corresponding to the object to activate the appropriate visual memory of the object. This will produce a spatial pattern of activation in the visual buffer, which is the image proper.[17]

Questions on this passage that immediately come to mind are: (1) What is in the image that is not already in the "description of the object in associative memory?" If all the information is there to generate the object, what more information is there in the image? (2) What access method is the brain using such that a "code" for retrieval (of the visual memory) is effective? How are the visual memories "keyed" and how/when is the key assigned? I can understand a context sensitive memory, as in the redintegration principle, where an aspect of the object can retrieve the memory, but Kossyln and Koenig appear to have some other programming technique in mind, and once explicated, I think would be extremely questionable. (3) The spatial pattern of activation in the visual buffer *is the image proper*? The visual buffer here is literally a screen on which a picture/pattern can be displayed, connected either to a camera (the eyes) or a tape recorder (memory). But this is typical current theoretical sleight of hand. This picture/pattern is again a pattern of *neural activity*. How can it be a pattern of neural activity *and* the phenomenal experience of the image as well? If it is a neural activity pattern what is the experience of the image? And who sees it? The visual buffer is only a handy theater screen for viewing by the theoretician's friend – the homuncular eye.

Kosslyn and Koenig would argue that the homunculus regress indicated above is "easily" avoided. The "mind's eye" is simply a set of "tests" after the computer analogy. A matrix of values defining line patterns can undergo certain tests to see for example if two lines meet at a point or diverge. These tests, they say, constitute "seeing" the image. But this is simply the coding problem revisited. A set of values in a matrix can "stand for" anything. Three dots (...) in a cell of the matrix, as I have pointed out, can stand for the letter S, the number 3, a cloudy day, or the three blind mice. Something must again understand the "image" to use the code (or an encoding) just as something needs to understand the external world to know what a (perceptual) code would "stand for." Tests can be run on the code at great length, but running tests does not solve this problem. The test processes no more know what the image (or the external world in the case of perception) looks like than does the homunculus, for which "tests" are a subtle substitution.

Thirty years later, then, while not denying their existence, Pylyshyn again challenged the cognitive science field (that is, the choir) to explain why images are needed.[18] He particularly focused on Kosslyn with arguments similar to those I expressed above and in more depth. The challenge he issued is in the form of a "null hypothesis." Though now admitting that his abstract symbol manipulations are likely insufficient to account for the form our representations take when experienced as imagery, he asked any future theory to explain, why not? Formal language and symbolic calculi, he noted, at least meet the dual requirements of *compositionality* (abstracted elements or concepts) and *systematicity* (lawful manipulation of the elements) essential for reasoning. In contemplating certain "mental folding" experiments, where subjects were required to mentally fold paper into objects of certain forms, he noted that the subjects had, by necessity, to proceed sequentially through a series of folds to attain the result. Why? "Because," he argued, "*we know what happens when we make a fold.*" It has to do, he stated, with "how one's knowledge of the effects of folding is organized."

Aaron Sloman, in a seminal paper for an AI conference in 1971, already gave Pylyshyn his answer.[19] He contrasted the syntactic mode of representation (with its symbols and rules) with what he termed the *analogic* mode. In essence, this is the mode of images. In the analogic mode, there is the natural representation of *constraints* (read "laws"). Just as the cup in coffee stirring, the paper does not bulge and shrink while it is being folded. It does not disintegrate. The edges stay stable and move to overlap one another. One surface generally stays stationary. All these constraints are in fact invariance laws defined over these transformations, i.e., *events*. On the other hand, in syntactic systems, failures of reference are commonplace. The syntactically correct, "The paper screeched and burbled as it was folded," makes little semantic sense – it instantly violates an invariance across folding events. To Sloman, the greatest challenge faced by AI was achieving this (analogic) form of representation. The frame problem is simply a restatement of this problem of representational power.

We can recast Sloman's challenge: what type of "device" is required to support this form of representational power? But this is only to ask: what type of device can support perception? No visual imagery ever occurred without visual perception. The congenitally blind bear witness to this. The image is a function of, 1) perception and, 2) the memory of this perception. In turn, the image *is* the knowledge. It is no less the knowledge than the actual perceiving of an *event* of "folding" is simultaneously – knowledge.

All abstraction is defined over something concrete. There is no abstract transformation of "bending," for example; some *thing* is being bent, whether spoons, paper, or the law. The abstract "bending" is an invariance having no reality other than its definition over these concrete events. What is a "fold" other than an invariant defined over these transformations in concrete experience? We have seen folds made in sheets, folds made in paper, folds made in arms/elbows, folds made in sails, folds made by Roger Penrose in three-faced hexagonal structures to make partial cubes, and even folds made with poker hands. And we have made the folds with bodily action. *Something* is always being folded. There is no such thing as an abstract "folding." "Fold" is not simply an abstract symbol among other symbols. A folding is a dynamic transformation preserving an invariant and specified in our concrete, perceptual experience. As an invariant over experience, just as the piece of grass could become a symbol for Jacqueline's grasshopper, a linguistic sound – "bend," "fold" – can be employed as a symbol for this invariant.

It is the common misconception of the computer metaphor that the *abstract can exist without the concrete.* But we have seen in Piaget that the abstract is defined upon the concrete. In fact, it was the failure to realize this that supported the illusion for many years that Piaget was amenable to the information processing model. But an entirely different form of "device" is required for Piaget.[20]

Tunnels and Beads

AI understands "Artificial;" it has an extremely impoverished grasp of the meaning of "Intelligence." Particularly, AI fails to grasp the implications of the developmental "trajectory" or path required by the child to achieve the ability to perform cognitive operations. Piaget, as we saw, studied and described the developmental path existing across many fairly elementary tasks. One task I wish to discuss now is the Tunnel-Bead experiment.

This simple experiment tests children aged 3-7 (*The Child's Conception of Movement and Speed*). Three beads are strung on a wire which in turn can be fitted into a small cylindrical "tunnel" (Figure 6.5). The beads are of different colors, but we'll call them A, B, and C. The beads are run into the tunnel and the tunnel semi-rotated (180 degrees) from 1 to N times.

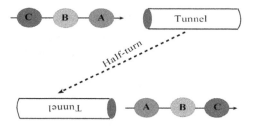

Figure 6.5. The Tunnel-Bead Experiment

A series of questions is asked, ranging from a simple, "What order will the beads come out?" after one semi-rotation (or half-turn), to the ultimate question on the order of the beads after any (n) number of half-turns. The child comes to a point of development where he can visualize the consequences of a 180^0 rotation which moves ABC to CBA and another 180^0 rotation which moves things back again to ABC, i.e., an invariance of order under a 360^0 rotation. When now asked in which order would the beads come out when the tunnel is semi-rotated 5 (or 4, or 6, or 7, etc) times, he evidences great difficulty. Some children appear to be exhausted after imagining three or possibly four semi-rotations, and they become lost when jumps are made from one number to another. As Piaget notes:

> ...But since the child, upon each half turn, endeavors to follow the inversion in every detail in his thoughts, he only gradually manages accurately to forecast the result of three, four, five half turns. Once this game of visualizing the objects in alternation is set in train, he finally discovers ...that upon each half-turn the order changes once more. Only the fact that up to this upper limit the subject continues to rely on visualizing intuitively and therefore needs to image one by one the half-turn, is proved because he is lost when a jump is made from one number of half-turns to any other.[21]

After this gradual perception of a higher order invariant (the "oscillation of order") defined over events of semi-rotations, there comes a point when the child can easily answer the ultimate question for the resultant order for any n-turns. Piaget's explanation, describing the "operational" character of thought, is foundational to his theory:

> Operations, one might say, are nothing other than articulated intuitions rendered adaptable and completely reversible since they are emptied of their visual content and survive as pure intention... In other words, *operations come into being in their pure state when there is sufficient schematization*. Thus, instead of demanding actual representation, each inversion will be conceived as a potential representation, like the outline for an experiment to be performed, but which is not useful to follow to the letter, even in the form of performing it mentally (emphasis added).[22]

Thus, according to Piaget, operations, freed of their imaginable content, become infinitely *compositional*. This becomes the basis for forecasting the result of n-turns, and it takes the child to about the age of seven. The operations become the generalization of actions performed through mental experiment. But this is not simply abstract rules and symbols. It is not simple "rule learning." As we have seen, these "schematic" operations are built upon and do not exist without the dynamic figural transformations (images) over which invariance emerges. They are the result of a dynamical developmental trajectory required by the brain as a *self-organizing dynamic system*. This developmental path incorporates these figural transformations and requires on average *seven years*. This is the origin of the "compositional" capability of intelligence so respected, so demanded by Fodor and Pylyshyn, but so misunderstood by AI theory.

It is worth noting here that it was precisely this form of developmental trajectory, in this case over the first two years, that results in COST (Causality, Object, Space, Time) and the ability to support explicit memory. It is precisely these developmental trajectories, crucial to the self-organizing system that is the brain, that the robotics theorist seems to believe can be simply ignored, somehow manufacturing the results in one fell swoop in his robots.

Current cognitive science has persuaded itself that the computer model of mind can handle Piaget and his "abstract" operations. At this point, it should be clear that this is absurd. These operations are simply schematic transformations born of the concrete images of events – the exact thing neither AI nor computer modelers know how to account for. Beneath Piaget's operations there resides Bergson's "device."

Whether we deal with invariance over transformations, or change over transformations, we have entered the realm of time. Transformations are time-extended. Cubes are rotating. Tunnels are half-turning. Flies are buzzing by. Hexagons are "folding." As we have seen, this time-extension cannot be conceived simply as an abstract series of "instants." To support intelligence, to support cognition, we require a device that supports time-extended transformations and invariance. In other words, for cognition we require consciousness; we need a memory that spans the "instants." We need a conscious device.

The Broadly Computational Device

We return then to the "device" underlying design. In the mousetrap task, we are designing from existing materials. I do not say from "existing components" because none of the objects are yet true components, though they have an independent function (e.g., a pencil, a rubber band). The possible "components" are being inserted into the invariance structure of an event –

the drawing back and firing of a crossbow, the striking down of the axe. In the process, their requisite features emerge. This is the *analogy* defining the features.

This is a powerful transformation over a non-differentiable time. I have laid out the basis for a device with sufficient representational power to support it. As Penrose argued, it is not computational in the standard, abstract sense. This sense was laid out in the authoritative definition of *computation* given by Alan Turing, and as already noted, is embodied in the definitional paradigm of all existing computers – the abstract "Turing Machine" with its infinite tape and read head. As also noted, every standard computer today is a Turing Machine. The neural networks are Turing machines. This is to say that the computer is always doing a form of computation that a Turing Machine could do, where the Turing machine performs it not as efficiently, not as quickly, but just as accurately. Yet Turing specifically defined the form of computation that he would formalize in terms of *mechanical* operations. He was thinking of the ubiquitous types of computation then found everywhere – the calculations of a bank officer balancing the ledger or of a clerk computing a total cost of purchase. "Computation" consisted of the steps a human computer could carry out, a human acting mechanically *without intelligence, i.e., without semantics.* It was this form of computation that he would formalize in terms of the Turing machine. This captured the mechanical knowledge and calculations of the parallelogram-challenged children in Wertheimer's classroom. But Turing did not capture the form of computation of the five year-old who looked at a cardboard cutout of a parallelogram, then asked for a scissors so she could cut the (triangular) end off and move it to the other side to make a rectangle. Nor did it capture the dynamic transformation exhibited by a five year-old child who formed the cardboard parallelogram into a cylinder, then asked for a scissors to cut it in half, announcing it would now make a rectangle.

As we have viewed the form and nature of the understanding underlying that which we can term a *semantic* "computation," it is clear that the Turing concept of computation is purely derivative. By this I mean that computation, in the Turing sense, is a simply a residue, a spatialized husk of far more powerful operations of mind supporting representative thought, in turn based in the non-differentiable motion of the matter-field. The manipulation of discrete symbols in an abstract space cannot support this, nor will a dynamical device that cannot support perception. The dynamics of the device, which cognitive science has tended to view as simply supporting an abstract set of *computations*, in fact is oriented to a far more concrete purpose, as concrete as the generation of a field of force; the dynamical brain or robotic system must generate a very concrete waveform in concrete, non-differentiable time, a wave which supports a broader form of computation, broader than Turing's narrow definition, but consonant with a broader definition he did in fact leave fully open.[17] In a word, Turing computation is again a limiting case, fundamentally based in the "projection frame" of the ever underlying abstract space and abstract time in which we tend to think (and theorize), itself a derivative concept from perception and its "objects." As with physics, this frame is what must be peeled away.

AI and Evolution

There are many alliances between AI and evolution. This includes the notion of "genetic algorithms" that will be unleashed to randomly evolve robots, super intelligent evil machines, even create mousetraps. AI feeds off the supposed success of evolutionary theory in explaining the transformations of devices (organisms) from version to version. I have merely attempted in this work to show what would really be involved in building a simple mousetrap from components, or in transforming it from version A to version B to version C. If we are talking human thought, the construction and transformation of mousetraps requires an entirely different form of "device" than that envisioned by AI. If we are talking in terms of evolution, it requires the universe itself to be an entirely different form of "device" than that envisioned by AI, or similarly, by Seth Lloyd who envisions the universe as a vast quantum computer which, seeded by random chance with a few simple programs, enabled the bootstrapping of the whole complex production algorithm and machinery into existence, eventually creating all the birds, butterflies and brontosaurs of this universe.[23] But the quantum computer is still a Turing Machine. Symmetrically, the evolutionist, it can be argued, implicitly relies on the supposed success of AI in demonstrating that consciousness is an unneeded element in algorithms that will create and transform devices.

Thus Kevin Miller's proposal that evolution proceeds by reusing various components at hand – the spring for a paperclip, the platform for kindling, etc. – was in fact well preceded by Darwin. Michael Shermer (*Why Darwin Matters*) quotes Darwin's concept of "exaptation:"

On the same principle, if a man were to make a machine for some special purpose, but were to use old wheels, springs, and pulleys, only slightly altered, the whole machine, with all its parts, might be said to be specially contrived for that purpose. Thus throughout nature almost every part of each living being has probably served, *in a slightly modified condition*, for diverse purposes, and has acted in the living machinery of many ancient and distinct specific forms. (Darwin, quoted by Shermer, my emphasis).[24]

The old "slightly modified" trick, just like slightly modifying and bending the spring-arms of the mousetrap, or adding hold-down staples and platforms, or slightly modifying the pencil to be an arrow, or to be an axe handle, or to be a pungi stake, etc., etc. Though Darwin is clearly going to be no better off than Miller in coaching AI on the design of mousetraps, the premier expositor of evolution, Richard Dawkins (*The God Delusion*), while ridiculing Behe to the point of impugning his motives for publishing, approvingly references Miller's concept, arguing that a mechanism used by parasitic bacteria for pumping toxic substances through cell walls is similar enough to a component in the bacterial flagellum – the little whip-like motor that moves the bacteria around – that evolution must have simply "commandeered" this component. In lieu of "commandeer," Shermer confidently employs the term "co-opt," as in evolution "co-opts" features to use for another purpose. For "commandeer," Eugenie Scott (*Evolution vs. Creationism*) uses "borrowing and swapping."[25] Meanwhile, for "commandeer," Dennett (*Darwin's Dangerous Idea*) substitutes the term "generate and test," holding, with no explication, that evolution simply "generates" new devices such as flagellar motors (or mousetrap #5) to test them out.[26] Finally, Kevin Miller himself simply uses "mix and matching" saying, "…it is to be expected that the opportunism of evolutionary processes would mix and match proteins to produce new and novel functions."[27] None of these phrases hides well the fact that their proponents are actually referring to the algorithms or programs of evolution – sans any form of consciousness – that they believe carry these transforms out.

I submit that the actual power of the alliance between AI and evolutionary theory is very illusory, i.e., neither is actually helping the other, but rather, each is creating a mutual delusion. But if Dennett, Shermer, Miller or the evolutionary biologists know secretly how to program these things, if they have solved the problem of common sense knowledge, they should be teaching the folks in AI.

Chapter VI. End Notes and References

1. Ghiselin, A. (962). *The Creative Process.*
2. This chapter is a modified version of the following article:
    Robbins, S. E. (2012). Meditation on a mousetrap: On consciousness and cognition, evolution and time. *Journal of Mind and Behavior, 33,* 69-96.
3. Behe, M. (1996). *Darwin's black box: The biochemical challenge to evolution.* New York: The Free Press.
4. McDonald, J. (2000). A reducibly complex mousetrap. //http://udel.edu/~mcdonald. oldmousetrap.html
5. Miller, K. (2003). Answering the biochemical argument from design. In N. Manson (Ed.), *God and Design: The Teleological Argument and Modern Science.* London: Routledge., 292-307.
    Young, M., & Edis, T. (2004). *Why Intelligent Design Fails.* New Jersey: Rutgers University Press.
6. Behe, M. (2007). *The edge of evolution: The search for the limits of Darwinism.* New York: Free Press.
7. Behe, M. (2000a). A Mousetrap defended: Response to critics. http://www.arn.org/docs/ behe.mb_mousetrapdefended.htm
8. McDonald, J. (2002). A reducibly complex mousetrap. //http://udel.edu/~mcdonald. mousetrap.html
9. Because (for example) simpler mousetraps are shown to exist, irreducible complexity is critiqued as vague. The two traps of Figure 6.3 however clarify the issue. Trap Five is simpler than trap Six. But each trap is irreducibly complex; each fails to work as designed without all its components.
    In some cases, the trap is indeed a slightly simpler version of the same design, as trap Six of Figure 6.3 might be taken as a simpler version of a standard mousetrap which works without one of the standard trap's parts. But inevitably the simpler traps morph to different designs, no longer effecting quite the same function (e.g., trapping a paw vs. smashing the poor creature).
10. Miller, K. (2003). Answering the biochemical argument from design. In N. Manson (Ed.), *God and Design: The Teleological Argument and Modern Science.* London: Routledge., 292-307.
11. Wertheimer, M. (1945). *Productive Thinking.* New York: Harper and Row.
12. Penrose, R. (1994). *Shadows of the Mind.* Oxford: Oxford University Press.
13. Pylyshyn, Z. (1973). What the mind's eye tells the mind's brain: a critique of mental imagery. *Psychological Bulletin, 80,* 1-22.
14. Chemero, A. (2009). *Radical Embodied Cognitive Science.* Cambridge,MA: MIT Press, Chapter 9.
15. Barret, L. (2010). *Beyond the Brain: How Body and Environment Shape Animal and Human Minds.* Princeton University Press, p. 109.
16. Ibid., Chapter 11.
17. Kosslyn, S., & Koenig, O. (1992). *Wet Mind: The New Cognitive Neural Science.* New York: The Free Press, pp. 144-145.

18. Pylyshyn, Z. (2002). Mental imagery: in search of a theory. *Behavioral and Brain Sciences, 25*, 157-237.

19. Sloman, A. (1971). Interactions between philosophy and artificial intelligence: the role of intuition and non-logical reasoning in intelligence. *Second Int. conference on artificial intelligence.* London.

20. The first chapter of Piaget's *Insights and Illusions in Philosophy* (1971) can be consulted for some insight into the effect of Bergson on Piaget. This book however goes on to use Bergson virtually as a whipping boy for Piaget's contempt of the "reflective" approach of philosophy as opposed to the "scientific" approach founded in observable facts. Given Piaget's comments on some of the philosophers who appear to have been in his environment, he appears to have had cause. Bergson, however, ever the clear exponent of "tying philosophy to the fact," who spent five years studying the research on memory before writing *Matter and Memory*, would have strongly supported Piaget and his work. But Piaget devotes a chapter in this book to the foundering of philosophers upon the "rock" of relativity theory (and therefore on the "facts"), using Bergson's critique of the theory as the exemplar. But more precisely, Bergson's critique was of the theory's *interpretation* (originally by Langevin in 1911) in the context of the twin paradox, and this problem is far from settled. Piaget however makes it quite clear to me that he did not at all understand the issues in Bergson's relativity debate (see my *The Mists of Special Relativity* reference).
    What is ironic, however, is that when the 1971 book was written, Piaget was unaware of the information processing avalanche that was poised to rush over his own intellectual efforts. Indeed, after discrediting a number of his findings, the entire information processing *philosophy* would be shoveled over his observations. And if there will be a way to dig him out, it will, in my opinion, be through the fantastic (surely to Piaget) Bergsonian model of the brain as a modulated reconstructive wave within a holographic field, and the definition of the role of Piaget's developmental theory of *operations in this context.*

21. Piaget, J. (1946). *The Child's Conception of Movement and Speed.* New York: Ballentine, p. 30.

22. Ibid, p. 30.

23. Lloyd, S. (2006). *Programming the universe.* New York: Alfred A. Knopf.

24. Shermer, M. (2006). *Why Darwin Matters: The Case Against Intelligent Design.* Times Books, p. 68.

25. Scott, E. (2004). *Evolution vs. creationism.* Berkeley: University of California Press.

26. Dennett, D. (1996). *Darwin's dangerous idea: Evolution and the meanings of life.* Simon and Schuster.

27. Miller, Kevin (2004). The flagellum unspun: The collapse of irreducible complexity. In Michael Ruse and William Dembski (eds.) *Debating Design.*
    In the context of the "flagellar motor," a thead-like propellar that propels a small bacteria through the water, Miller noted that a system termed TTTS (Type Three Secretory System) found in other systems is a component. Miller feels that since the TTTS functions in other organisms, but is a very reduced version of the arguably irreducibly complex flagellar motor, this proves that "the contention that the flagellum must be fully assembled before any of its parts can be useful is obviously incorrect." But the point is, you just don't evolve a "useful part" in isolation. If the part is indeed a "part," it had to be part of

a useful whole in the first place, with all the simultaneity implied wherein the other useful parts in the whole fit and function together, usefully. This is then a bootstrap problem. Yes, once the part is created in the functioning whole, it can be used again, though as we have seen in the context of the mousetrap, this "using again" is clearly more complex and difficult than Miller understands. But the bootstrap problem is this: how did you get the original, now reusable, part?

CHAPTER VII

The Requirements for a Conscious "Device"

For many people the mind is the last refuge of mystery against the encroaching spread of science, and they don't like the idea of science engulfing the last bit of *terra incognita*.

— Raymond Kurzweil quoting Daniel Dennett quoting
Herbert Simon
The Age of Spiritual Machines

I have no sooner commenced to philosophize than I ask myself why I exist... When finally a Principle of creation has been put at the base of things, the same question springs up: How – why does this principle exist rather than nothing?

— Bergson, *Creative Evolution*

A Requirements List

Now let us review. There is a set of requirements that we have been developing. These are the requirements – a minimum set of requirements – that must be met if we are to create an intelligent "device" equivalent to a human in intelligence. Yes, they are high-level requirements. They imply a vast amount of physics and engineering to work through. Yes, engineering – the implementation of a real, concrete dynamics – not software. This dynamics must function integrally within the indivisible flow of time. The requirements look like this:

1) The total dynamics of the system must be proportionally related to the events of the matter-field such that a scale of time is defined upon this field.

2) The dynamics of the system must be structurally related to the events of the matter-field, i.e., reflective of the invariance laws defined over the time-extended events of the field.

3) The information resonant over the dynamical structure (or "states") must integrally include relation to, or feedback from, systems for the preparation of action (for from the vast information in the holographic field, the principle of selection is via relation to possible action by the body).

4) The global dynamics must support a reconstructive wave.

5) The operative dynamics of the system must be an integral part of the indivisible, non-differentiable motion of the matter-field in which it is embedded.

6) The operative dynamics of memory retrieval must rely on the invariance structure of events as the modulating mechanism of the device.

7) The operative dynamics must support an articulated simultaneity within the non-differentiable flow of time.

8) The operative dynamics must achieve a trajectory supporting COST and the symbolic function.

9) The operative dynamics must support abstraction as a function of invariance defined over concrete experience (or the figural mode).

And a Conclusion...

This is but a small portion of the requirements that we could write. I have neglected the nature of voluntary action as a topic, also the implications of perception as virtual action (as related to requirement 3), just for two dimensions – of many. But this is a start for the Singularists to munch upon and to assess the reality of their worry. Within their current, outmoded metaphysic, the Singularity will not be reached in the one hundred years projected by Chalmers, nor in one thousand years. Unfortunately, it is not difficult to wonder whether this situation might hold: the simplest simulation of the brain will be the brain itself. But perhaps we can start more simply – perhaps a chipmunk brain. Even this little brain is a modulated reconstructive wave passing through the dynamically transforming holographic field, likely imposing a different (chipmunk) scale of time. But we are not yet worried, I presume, over AI-chipmunks enslaving the human race.